Risk Assessment in Forensic Practice

Risk Assessment in Forensic Practice sets out a concise critical review of the way in which risk is assessed in current forensic practice. Setting the area in its historical context, this text outlines current practice in an accessible and clear format and discusses major critiques as well as the ways in which current practice might be developed to improve public protection.

Providing an account of the main issues involved in risk and probability and the ways that these have been applied in practice, the book describes current forensic practice in relation to the dominant algorithmic and checklist-based methods. Critiques of these arising from social-legal, risk analysis and experimental psychology perspectives are summarised, and questions of the accuracy, fairness and lack of analysis are considered, along with the main challenges associated with making group and individual predictions of events. The text rejects the idea that clinical assessments of risk are generally ineffective and stresses the role of environmental context, training and expertise in improving practice. Through the author's work in the field, this text also offers insight into the ways in which current practice might be improved and calls for greater analysis and methodological rigour.

Risk Assessment in Forensic Practice appeals to a wide range of forensic practitioners including psychologists, psychiatrists, social workers, mental health nurses and lawyers. The text is also relevant to those involved in management and decision-making across forensic settings.

David Crighton is a Consultant Psychologist and Visiting Professor of Forensic Psychology at Durham University, UK. He was previously Acting Chief/Deputy Chief Psychologist at the Ministry of Justice, UK.

"*Risk Assessment in Forensic Practice* is an astonishing accomplishment. David Crighton provides a trenchant and sweeping analysis of cutting-edge research on the prediction and management of violent behavior. Historically grounded and written in clear, jargon-free prose, this work is sure to have an immense and long-lasting impact on the field."

—**John Monahan, PhD**
John S. Shannon Distinguished Professor of Law,
Professor of Psychology, University of Virginia, USA

"David Crighton has done the field a great service in writing this book. He provides an analysis of contemporary forensic practice that is both thoughtful and balanced and which invites the reader to engage with foundational knowledge about the history, meaning, and nature of risk. David then, rather gently it should be said, draws our attention to the problems that will inevitably surface if we continue to simply follow convention, before offering some concrete suggestions for strengthening and advancing practice. Whilst this is both an easy and engaging read, David challenges us all to do much better. Please take the time to read this important contribution!"

—**Professor Andrew Day**
School of Social and Political Sciences, University of Melbourne, Australia

"This book is an articulate and authoritative examination of risk assessment in forensic practice. An in-depth exploration of both current and historic issues in theory and practice that will be a catalyst for much needed discussion and reform. An invaluable and accessible resource for forensic psychologists and other scholars, front-line practitioners and policy makers."

—**Dr Roxanne Khan**
Director of Honour Abuse Research Matrix (HARM),
University of Central Lancashire, UK

"Based on the fundamental but often ignored distinction between risk and uncertainty, this comprehensive and easy-to-read book provides an excellent introduction to risk assessment, its tools, and its future. It is essential for forensic practice, but also for a better understanding of human judgment, the nature of probability, and the nature of rationality."

—**Gerd Gigerenzer**
Max Planck Institute for Human Development, Berlin

New Frontiers in Forensic Psychology

Series Editors

Graham Towl is Professor of Forensic Psychology at Durham University and was formerly Chief Psychologist at the Ministry of Justice, UK. He is the recipient of the British Psychological Society Award for Distinguished Contributions to Professional Practice and forensic academic knowledge.

Tammi Walker is Professor of Forensic Psychology and Principal of St Cuthbert's Society Durham University. She is a Chartered Psychologist and Fellow of the British Psychological Society. Her research interests are gendered interventions for managing self-harm and suicide in prisons, mental health, physical health and addressing sexual violence in universities.

New Frontiers in Forensic Psychology is a new series of forensic psychology books, which brings together the most contemporary research in core and emerging topics in the field, providing a comprehensive review of new areas of investigation in forensic psychology, and new perspectives on existing topics of enquiry. The series includes original volumes in which the authors are encouraged to explore unchartered territory, make cross-disciplinary evaluations, and where possible break new ground. The series is an essential resource for senior undergraduates, postgraduates, researchers and practitioners across forensic psychology, criminology and social policy.

Child to Parent Aggression and Violence
A Guidebook for Parents and Practitioners
Hue San Kuay and Graham Towl

New Perspectives on Arson and Firesetting
The Human-Fire Use Relationship
Faye K. Horsley

Risk Assessment in Forensic Practice
David Crighton

For a complete list of all books in this series, please visit the series page at: https://www.routledge.com/New-Frontiers-in-Forensic-Psychology/book-series/NFFP

Risk Assessment in Forensic Practice

DAVID CRIGHTON

Routledge
Taylor & Francis Group
LONDON AND NEW YORK

Cover image: Getty Images

First published 2023
by Routledge
4 Park Square, Milton Park, Abingdon, Oxon OX14 4RN

and by Routledge
605 Third Avenue, New York, NY 10158

Routledge is an imprint of the Taylor & Francis Group, an informa business

© 2023 David Crighton

The right of David Crighton to be identified as author of this work has been asserted in accordance with sections 77 and 78 of the Copyright, Designs and Patents Act 1988.

All rights reserved. No part of this book may be reprinted or reproduced or utilised in any form or by any electronic, mechanical, or other means, now known or hereafter invented, including photocopying and recording, or in any information storage or retrieval system, without permission in writing from the publishers.

Trademark notice: Product or corporate names may be trademarks or registered trademarks, and are used only for identification and explanation without intent to infringe.

British Library Cataloguing-in-Publication Data
A catalogue record for this book is available from the British Library

Library of Congress Cataloging-in-Publication Data
Names: Crighton, David A., 1964- author.
Title: Risk assessment in forensic practice / by David Crighton.
Description: Abingdon, Oxon; New York, NY: Routledge, 2022. | Series: New frontiers in forensic psychology | Includes bibliographical references and index. |
Identifiers: LCCN 2021060885 (print) | LCCN 2021060886 (ebook) | ISBN 9780367622671 (hardback) | ISBN 9780367622534 (paperback) | ISBN 9781003108665 (ebook)
Subjects: LCSH: Forensic psychology. | Forensic sociology. | Risk assessment.
Classification: LCC RA1148 .C737 2022 (print) | LCC RA1148 (ebook) | DDC 614/.15—dc23/eng/20220121
LC record available at https://lccn.loc.gov/2021060885
LC ebook record available at https://lccn.loc.gov/2021060886

ISBN: 978-0-367-62267-1 (hbk)
ISBN: 978-0-367-62253-4 (pbk)
ISBN: 978-1-003-10866-5 (ebk)

DOI: 10.4324/9781003108665

Typeset in Avenir and Dante
by codeMantra

Contents

Series Foreword   *xi*
Acknowledgements   *xiii*
Disclosure   *xiii*

Introduction   1

1   Key Issues in Risk   4

    Risk and Uncertainty   *4*
    Probability   *8*
    Measuring Probability   *9*
    The Principle of Indifference   *11*
    Types of Probability   *12*
       Relative Frequency Probability   12
       Knowledge-Based Probability   13
       Problems with Knowledge-Based Probability   16
    Applying Probability   *16*
    Descriptive and Inferential Statistics   *16*
    Conclusion   *17*

2   The Language of Risk   19

    Risk Assessment   *22*
    Risk Treatment   *23*
       Dose Response   24
    Risk Management   *25*

Cautionary and Precautionary Principles 26
Robustness and Resilience 27
Risk and Protective Factors 27
Conclusion 30

3   Current Practice in Risk: Actuarial and Algorithmic Approaches   31

Use of Actuarial and Algorithmic Approaches in Practice 34
   Policing 34
   Sentencing and Conditional Release 35
   Risk Treatment 37
The Case for Using Actuarial and Algorithmic RAIs 40
Conclusion 42

4   Current Practice in Risk: Structured Clinical Judgement Approaches   43

Use in Practice 47
   Policing 47
   Sentencing and Conditional Release 51
   Risk Treatment 52
The Case for Using Checklist RAIs 54
Conclusion 55

5   Critiques of Current Practice: Socio-Legal Perspectives   56

Fairness 58
Accuracy 67
   Individual and Group-Based Predictions 70
Impact 77
Conclusion 78

6   Critiques of Current Practice: Risk Analysis Perspectives   80

Risk Management 85
Risk Analysis 87
Measuring Risk 88
   Simplified Qualitative Analysis 90
   Standard Qualitative and/or Quantitative Analysis 90
   Model-Based and Primarily Quantitative Methods 92
Treating Risk as an Expected Value 93
Criticisms of Using Relative Frequency Probability 95
Criticisms of Using Knowledge-Based Probability 97

Syntactic Criterion 99
  Pragmatic Criteria 99
  Calibration 99
Treating Risk as a Product of History 100
Standardisation and Consensus 103
Using Models 104
Conclusion 104

7 Critiques of Current Practice: Psychological Perspectives　　106

Unbounded Rationality 108
Optimisation Under Constraints 108
Cognitive Illusions 109
Ecological Rationality 110
  Biases Associated with Cognitive Illusions 110
Representativeness 110
Availability 111
Anchoring and Adjustment 111
Affect 112
  Heuristics and Judgement 112
  Critiques of Cognitive Illusions Research 115
  Some Problems while Using Content-Blind Norms 118
  Studies of Heuristics 123
  Are Cognitive Illusions and Ecological Rationality
    Essentially Similar? 124
The Adaptive Toolbox 125
Conclusion 128

8 Dealing with Risk Better: Analysis and Treatment of Risks　　129

The Scale of the Problem 130
Analysing Risks 132
Barriers to Change 134
Doing Better 138
Risk Analysis: Planning 139
Risk Analysis: Methods 140
  Cause and Effect Analysis (CEA) or Ishikawa
    Diagrams 143
  Structured What If Technique (SWIFT) 143
  Fault Tree Analysis (FTA) 144
  Event Tree Analyses (ETA) 144

Bayesian Networks   145
Risk Analysis: Probabilistic Assessment   146
Risk Evaluation   148
Risk Treatment   149
Risk Management   151
Conclusion   152

9   Dealing with Risk Better: Probabilistic Risk Assessment   153

Changing Practice   156
How to Develop More Accurate Assessments   158
   The MacArthur Study   159
Conclusion   163

10   Dealing with Risk Better: Changing the Environment   165

Getting Rid of the 'Cargo Cult' Science   167
Changing Environments to Make Better Decisions   169
The Attractions of Simplicity   176
Conclusion   177

References   181
Index   197

Series Foreword

We very much welcome this new book to our *New Directions in Forensic Practice* series. The series aims to include authors introducing either new areas of forensic practice, or a new or different take on some existing areas of forensic practice. This book falls into the latter category with a widespread literature on risk assessment available. Indeed, this is an area where many practitioner psychologists working in forensic settings spend much of our time on. This book ranks amongst the very best that we have read on risk assessment. The work describes current risk assessment practice raising a number of trenchant criticisms, whilst also moving on to suggest more effective approaches.

Despite the secrecy surrounding the evaluation of, for example, programmes in prisons – as illustrated by the prison service Sex Offender Treatment Programme debacle when the evaluation data was sat on for five years (Towl and Podmore, 2019), they have grown in number over recent years. And this growth has been seemingly in spite of the evidence of no, or little, efficacy – most recently with reference to the violent offender programme – 'Resolve' (Robinson, Sorbie, Huber et al., 2021). To be fair at least this set of disappointing results were published. Linked to the programmes industry are risk assessment 'products' usually checklist based, and again as detailed in this book are of often questionable utility, despite the, at times, rather grandiose claims made by those selling such products. David Crighton persuasively argues for better training to further improve clinical decision-making whilst also ensuring a sound statistical understanding of actuarial data that may potentially be used to inform clinical decision-making most effectively. And this perhaps reflects a broader need within forensic practice to move away from unduly manualised approaches that have traditionally served to 'dumb down' the role of psychologists and instead to draw upon the evidence base to best inform one-to-one high-quality clinical work with those in state custody.

In this book, the author gives his perspective on how to address the difficult challenge of undertaking evidence informed risk assessments, providing a route forward that stresses the role of good quality evidence and training in taking the ways in which risk is dealt with forward in constructive and new directions.

Graham Towl and Tammi Walker
Series Editors
Durham University, UK

Acknowledgements

I would like to thank the series editors for commissioning this work on risk and the editorial team at Routledge for their support throughout. I am also indebted to two of the peer reviewers of the original proposal, for their thoughtful comments and very constructive suggestions for improvements. A great many friends and colleagues have also informed my thinking about risk, as the result of discussions over many years. I am immensely grateful to all of them.

Disclosure

David Crighton, as part of his routine practice uses a variety of risk assessments. He previously contributed to the development of the Cambridge Risk Assessment (CAMRA) framework (Towl and Crighton, 1996, 1997) a public domain clinical framework for the assessment of risk and uncertainty in forensic practice.

Introduction

The aim in writing this book is to look critically at the area of risk assessment in current forensic practice and in doing so address the needs of a range of practitioners. Doing this is a recognition of the reality that many of the issues around risk assessment cut across professional boundaries. Whether risks are seen in the context of corrections, policing, health, or social care, the challenges are similar. Adopting multi-disciplinary perspectives therefore seems both helpful and appropriate.

In recent years, forensic practice can be legitimately criticised for having become increasingly detached from the diverse academic evidence based on risk. What follows is hopefully a small step towards reversing this damaging trend. For forensic practitioners, this may involve uncomfortable questions, fundamental to any critical review. This requires consideration of some of the poorly considered ideas that have developed and persist in practice, leading in turn to unevidenced, inappropriate or poor solutions being advocated. In addressing the area of risk, a balance also needs to be struck between coverage, academic rigour and producing something of use to practitioners. This has provided a focus for decisions about what to cover and just as importantly, what to exclude. A guide used here has been to concentrate on those areas likely to be of most concern and greatest interest to practitioners, with the hope of providing a bridge into some of the most influential academic and applied research, without disappearing down too many academic rabbit holes.

In this spirit, it seemed helpful not to overload the text with academic references and footnotes. To do so seemed ill-suited to a book addressing practice issues. Similarly, publications in the area of risk necessarily involve statistical, mathematical and logical concepts. Many of those with interests in risk use formal representations as a means of clarifying and expressing ideas more elegantly but this is not an approach that works for all. It tends to be more warmly received by some disciplines than others. It has been avoided almost entirely here, opening up the criticism of oversimplifying ideas that might only be fully expressed in such terms. This seemed to be a price worth paying for a more widely useful and accessible text.

A striking aspect of current forensic practice is its lack of historical context. Even to non-historians, much of the current literature lacks such perspective, and this seems a likely contributing factor in many of the critiques of current practice. The development of idiosyncratic terminology as well as the persistence of outdated ideas about risk seem to directly flow from this. This brings to mind the often-quoted observation that "Those who cannot remember the past are condemned to repeat it" (Santayana, 1905). Forensic practice is, of course, not unique in this, although it does appear to be one of the more serious offenders. The tendency can be seen to have been unhelpful in several ways. Most critically perhaps it has made the exchange of ideas across disciplines, always a potentially fraught endeavour, more complex than it needs to be. In an effort to address this, some historical context has been woven into the discussion.

The points raised so far hint at something important about the area of risk, namely that it is, in scientific terms, a 'hard' problem or even a 'wicked' one (Fischbacher-Smith, 2016). It involves many complex challenges, and this explains the need for cross-disciplinary efforts to understand and, in turn, deal with it. It is an area where everyone reaches the limit of their competence at some point. This makes failures, evident in forensic practice, to take on research and learning from other areas all the more concerning.

There are a wide range of valid criticisms of current forensic practice in the area of risk and attempting to form all of these into a coherent discussion of practice seemed unwieldy and potentially confusing. As a result, the attempt to answer the question of what is wrong with current practice has been broken down into parts. Even then, the critiques often come from different perspectives that overlap in some areas but diverge and disagree in others. To try to deal with this and to produce a clearer and more coherent picture of the criticisms raised, these have been divided into broad areas, with each addressed in turn. These divisions, of necessity, have involved the drawing of arbitrary lines. There were, of course, many ways in which this could have been done, and the divisions used here are intended purely as an aid to discussion. Three broadly defined areas of critique have been used:

1 Socio-legal critiques
2 Risk analysis critiques
3 Psychological critiques

These have been used to summarise and explain the main concerns about current approaches to risk assessment in forensic practice, leading on to addressing the question of how things might be done better in practice. Any attempt at answering this kind of question will, necessarily, be more speculative than many of the criticisms of practice. In a text aimed at practitioners though, trying to answer this practical question seems essential. An understanding of the detailed critiques of current practice is important, indeed arguably central to good practice. They do not though absolve practitioners of the need to deal with a wide range of risks on a day-to-day basis.

The changes to practice advocated here suggest major departures from and changes to current forensic practice and has been illustrated by looking at some of the complex challenges that present themselves. The changes outlined will not appeal to all. Some will undoubtedly be controversial and contested by some and this is a good thing. Science, broadly defined as the application of critical common sense, rests on a process of testing disagreements. It does not rest on appeals to authority. Many of the ideas for change are therefore put forward with the aim of encouraging the use of this scientific thinking and method. If this publication encourages thought, debate and testing of better approaches to risk in forensic practice, then it will have succeeded in its main aim.

Key Issues in Risk 1

Risk assessment is built on a number of fundamental concepts and an adequate understanding of the subject requires consideration of these foundations as well as the assumptions that they rest on. The neglect of this is one major criticism of current forensic practice and was briefly touched on in the introductory comments. A full historical analysis of this is not attempted here, rather the aim is to give a brief outline of relevant areas and issues. Without this, it is difficult, some would suggest impossible, to adequately grasp scientific concepts such as risk assessment.

Risk and Uncertainty

As a starting point, it is worth being explicit that there is no universally agreed definition of risk, a fact that has led to a range of alternative and at times conflicting definitions. In modern use though, a relatively early and highly influential attempt to define risk was that of Knight (1921). An economist by training, Knight sought to address the linked areas of risk and profit, although his paper ranged well beyond this narrow focus. The area of risk was addressed in broad terms in an extended review that went on to strongly influence much of later thinking on the subject. This effect remains evident today.

Knight started his exploration of risk by grounding it firmly as an area of scientific exploration. He defined science as the effort to understand better and so more effectively predict the future, leading, in turn, to more intelligent conduct. In this respect, Knight's thinking appears to have been strongly influenced by the ideas of Descartes (1644) and his view that people perceive the world before reacting to it, based on their inferences rather than perceptions. In his review Knight (1921) argued, in line with this, that human action was intended to produce change in the future state of the world based on inferences. Such inferences were seen to be largely based on prior experience of similar situations and informed the decision whether or not to act. He noted that both perceptions and inferences would be imperfect. In turn, this would compound a less than perfect knowledge of the consequences of such actions and the inability to carry out actions perfectly, as planned or intended. This formed part of what may be seen as Knight's largely deterministic view of risk based on a number of fundamental propositions.

As a starting point, Knight proposed that the world consists of a practically infinite number of objects. In addition, he noted that human intelligence is limited and so needs to find ways to deal with this formidable task. In dealing with this problem, he assumed that the number of properties that people can distinguish and the range of behaviour available to them, are limited. He also argued that the properties of things in the world remain fairly constant with any changes in properties also tending towards constancy. Where we are unable to ascertain the properties of something, he argued that these tended to be associated with other determinable properties that are generally consistent with them in some ways. Based on these ideas, Knight suggested that quantitative aspects of properties and our ability to deal with this was fundamental, with the properties of many things differing in degree but not in kind. Put at its simplest, the argument was that many significant, often quantifiable, properties were common to large groups of things.

More generally, Knight suggested that, whilst the universe might not be ultimately knowable to us, the extent of 'knowability' was likely to extend far beyond our actual powers. As a result, he suggested that for many areas within the social sciences, this would have practical implications. He argued that a dependence on correlational research and probabilistic judgements was likely to be central to such areas of study. For Knight, this would provide a means of allowing an intelligent ordering of things, on the basis of observed contingencies that would not otherwise be possible. Probability was as a result seen as central to an understanding of both risk and decisions made under conditions of uncertainty and he described two fundamentally distinct ways of determining probability and a third indeterminate form. The first of these concerned *a priori* probability, referring to events where the likelihood and distribution could be logically determined. This involved some of the examples of probability commonly seen in introductory textbooks on statistics, such as rolling of dice, picking cards or spinning roulette wheels and so on. Here the likelihood of events is described as being known in advance or *a priori*. For example, when throwing a fair die, the chance of any number coming up will be equal. The chance of throwing a six using a fair six-sided die will be one in six and this probability can be determined in advance. Such events are also seen as independent of each other, so throwing a six on one trial does not affect the result of future throws. The second form of probability identified by Knight involved the relative frequency notion of probability, sometime called objective or frequentist probability. Here he argued that the likelihood of outcomes is not known *a priori* but that it can be empirically estimated, based on the sampling of a similar group or population of observations. This can be illustrated using a simple example of people's height. The probability of a woman in the UK population being between 70 and 72 inches (approximately 178–183 centimetres) tall is not known beforehand, in a comparable way to that in examples such as throwing dice or selecting playing cards. It can though be estimated based on observations of a relevant population: say taking a sample of 1,000 women at random from the UK population. From this, a distribution of heights can be drawn and the proportion of women in the 70–72-inch range can be calculated. If we know the *a priori* probabilities, Knight suggested that there is no need for such empirical estimation based on relative frequencies. It is known in advance that the probability of rolling a six for a six-sided die is one divided by six. Such conditions are though unusual. Examples like this, common in textbooks, represent a small group of what turn out to be atypical examples. It is rare in the real world to know a probability in advance in this way.

For Knight, the difference between these two approaches to probability largely depended on the accuracy of the classification of instances that were grouped together. For actuaries he suggested, the aim was to develop ever more precise sub-groups with greater levels of homogeneity. This would yield more precise measures closer to the 'true' values. He did though argue that in practice, these were unlikely to attain the level of the 'true' probability, with this remaining essentially unknowable but potentially open to closer and closer approximations. The third form of probability he described as estimates. These he felt were based on human judgement and Knight is generally very critical of this idea of probability. Here, Knight appears to conclude that this is not, in fact, a form of probability in the true sense at all, seeming to adopt a strong position of seeing these estimates as forms of classifications without a valid basis.

Perhaps the most enduringly influential aspect of Knight's work in this area was the distinction he drew between risk and uncertainty. Risk being defined as a measurable quality of the likelihood of something happening: with this being measurable in terms of either an *a priori* probability or a relative frequency estimate of probability. In contrast, he saw uncertainty as the unmeasurable or random part of likelihood. He rejected the then common distinction prevalent in economics that defined risk in terms of potential losses and uncertainty in terms of potential gains, arguing that this was ambiguous and deeply unhelpful.

Hence for Knight, risk was defined primarily as the outcome in a group of cases that is known, either *a priori* or as a result of empirical sampling. For unique situations, he argued that it was still possible to calculate risk, in the form of a probability, based on a sample of trials. Any fluctuations here would be likely to cancel each other out and the determinate factors would show a level of stability. Any random or accidental effects would be liable to reduce as the number of observations increased, in line with the 'principle of indifference' originally developed by Bernoulli (1954). Uncertainty was distinct from this he suggested, in that here there was no way to calculate or estimate probability empirically.

As an economist addressing the economic subject of profit, Knight looked to the area of insurance as illustrative here. In theory, insurance involves the grouping of equally probable events, with the proportions being determined empirically, the central challenges here being the degree to which cases can be formed into groups and how homogeneous these groups are. A simple example here would be the calculation of car insurance premiums based on characteristics such as sex, age, previous history of accidents, and recorded motoring offences. Knight suggested that such principles had a wider application in the area of risk, even in the event of an almost complete lack of scientific understanding of the area concerned. Even the most atypical situations he noted were insurable, using conservative criteria and judgement to form groups, with partial validity, to improve estimates of risk. Knight went on to consider the complex issues that arose from this distinction between risk and uncertainty, as they applied to social issues. He recognised the flux of human societies and that this was associated with a significant degree of uncertainty. Such uncertainty for Knight reflected a genuine indeterminacy, change and discontinuity. He saw the resolution to this in terms of grouping and the application of probabilistic reasoning to these derived groups. Recognising that this was not always feasible, he accepted that people would often fall back on intuitive judgements, although he was critical of these as having wide margins of error. In his review, Knight recognised the already established distinction between 'static' and 'dynamic' risk, a simple dichotomy still evident within much of forensic practice. However, he was rather critical of this simple treatment, suggesting that there was in fact a continuum here of progressive change. He went on to suggest that it was not possible to draw sharp and significant distinctions between progressive change and fluctuations within groups.

Based on his distinction between risk and uncertainty, Knight proposed that uncertainty could be reduced by converting it where possible into risk, described in terms of probability. He put forward a number of ideas about how this might be achieved, whilst accepting that an irreducible level of uncertainty may remain. Fundamentally, he suggested that this could be achieved by scientific study, with the data accumulated in this way, serving to reduce the extent of uncertainty. The pooling of uncertainty would serve, through large-scale groupings, to elicit determinative factors. In this respect, his thinking prefigured the current age of 'big data' (Marx, 2013). He also identified other means of reducing uncertainty, including increased levels of control or alternatively by slowing the rate of change or progress. All of these involved significant costs, and Knight appears to favour the former rather than the latter solutions. For him though, at a fundamental level, intelligent conduct as he termed it, involved concerted efforts to translate uncertainty into probabilistic risk estimates.

Knight's work has had long-term influences on the area of risk and risk assessment. It has also been extensively criticised over the past century on both fundamental and pragmatic grounds. Most significantly perhaps, his distinction between risk and uncertainty has been strongly challenged, with the view that this is not the main distinction of interest being put forward. Rather it has been suggested, the most important distinction is between problems or situations where it is possible to make accurate predictions and those where it is not (Aven, 2010). Here it has been noted that by describing situations where *a priori* or frequentist probability cannot be calculated as uncertainty, most questions of interest are removed from the area of risk altogether. At the very least, it relocates them to a new area of uncertainty assessment. For most problems, most of the time, the kind of objective empirical distributions favoured by Knight will not be available. It is also unlikely that these will be obtainable any time soon, if ever. In addition, Knight's reliance on a relative frequency view of probability has been noted and criticised. This of course is not the only concept of probability but adopting the main alternative, knowledge-based definitions of probability, would some have argued leave Knight's definition of risk empty of meaning (Aven, 2010). With knowledge-based approaches to probability, there simply would not be the kind of objective probabilities suggested by Knight. More generally, it can be suggested that the description of risk and the terminology proposed by Knight (1921) violates our intuitive understanding of risk, as being related to situations of uncertainty and lack of predictability.

Probability

A basic understanding of probability is fundamental to risk in general and to risk assessment, in particular. The area is though often subject to misunderstanding, errors and opaque presentation. It is therefore worth spending some time on some of the basic principles as these inform questions of risk. As a starting point, here it has, broadly speaking, been argued that knowledge can usefully be divided into directly obtained knowledge and knowledge obtained by argument (Keynes, 1921). In reviewing the area of probability, Keynes noted that probability is itself an inference, referring to the degree of belief it is rational to hold given certain conditions. Put more simply, he suggested probability was about the logical connection between evidence and conclusions. In turn, the weight attaching to such conclusions rested on the grounds for the evidence used to reach them. In this respect, it can be seen that Keynes view of probability diverged from that suggested by Knight. Algebraic approaches to probability, Keynes suggested, formalise this process of logical connection. However, they do not change the fundamental relational nature of probability. Hence for Keynes, probability always needed to be seen in relation to a broader context, which he illustrated using the analogy of distance. Nowhere can be said to be inherently far away in the absence of a reference point, it can only be far away from somewhere. Similarly, Keynes argued that nothing can be inherently probable; it can only be probable in relation to something else. This relational nature of probability carried with it a number of implications. Taking a simple example used to illustrate this, the fact that a is related to b may imply that it is rational to believe that b is true. We cannot though conclude anything about b in the absence of reference to a. This in turn places limits on what findings of this kind mean, for example, that it is not true to say that a and c together make b probable. This view fits with Bernoulli (1954) who stressed that probability described a lower level of rational belief than certainty. It was Laplace (1820: 1951) though who seems to have seen most clearly how the theory of probability could be applied to real-world issues. Before this, the area had been largely concerned with questions about dice and cards but largely due to Laplace, probability went on to be applied extensively across mathematics, science and engineering. However, the meaning of 'probability' remained controversial and contested. The essential question here has been whether probability involved measurement of some form of physical reality or it reflected a degree of belief about the physical world.

Measuring Probability

Measurements of probability can be seen as a way of comparing the weight that may be rationally attached to specific arguments. For example, an event with a probability of 0.05 or 1 in 20 is seen to be less likely than one with a probability of 0.95 (19 in 20). More contentiously, it has been suggested that numerical weights of this kind could be attached to any event and that numerical comparisons could be made of these probabilities. An example of this kind of view is provided by the work of the philosopher Jeremy Bentham (1748–1832). Bentham argued for the application of numerical probability to the area of judicial decision-making, amongst others. His work Rationale of Judicial Evidence

(Bentham, 1827) sets his ideas out in detail and suggested the application of probabilistic thinking to legal decision-making and sentencing. The school of utilitarian thinking that he founded went on to be highly influential for much of the 19th century in Britain, Ireland and beyond, with profound impacts on social policy still evident in areas such as corrections, education and welfare policy. Many of the claims made for the approach though appear to be poorly founded. It is though worth noting that Bentham and later utilitarian thinkers were advocating these ideas as a means of addressing the flagrant and brutal abuses that had grown increasingly prevalent across the British courts under what, with good reason, came to be known as the 'bloody code'. The utilitarian idea of using probability as the basis for judicial decision-making was though, even at its height in the 19th century, seen by most as a step too far.

Efforts to measure probability have often used references to real-world examples to illustrate the scope for accurately measuring and comparing the probabilities of events. Here, insurance has again been used, possibly because it is seen as allowing the calculation of often very precise numerical probability estimates of risk. These are often for group-based information that seeks to estimate population values, although this is not invariably the case with insurance also involving single events. A typical example of calculation of values for insurance might involve the level of risk of a claim from a 17 year old driving a specific make of car for 5,000 miles in a year. Such estimates need to work, in the sense that the premiums paid need to exceed any claims, with any insurer who fails in this respect being likely to go out of business. The idea that this paradigm provides convincing evidence for the ability to accurately measure probability, in the way claimed has though been challenged. The idea that these probability estimates need to be accurate reflections of the likelihood of outcomes has in practice been dismissed as incorrect (Keynes, 1921). In relation to insurance, Keynes noted that in fact all that is required is that the premiums exceed the probable risk, not that the probability of the risk is accurately measured. He went on to note that it is unlikely that the process for estimating this follows the formal logic of probability, or that two equally competent insurance brokers would reach similar values. This also suggests that for the insurance of unclear risks, similar principles to those used in gambling may apply. This would mirror that of a bookmaker taking bets on a sporting event. All that is needed for the bookmaker to make a profit is that the spread of bets is covered for all the possibilities (Keynes, 1921). The use of the calculation of insurance premiums, so often used to illustrate the calculation of probability, can therefore be seen to undermine rather than support ideas that accurate probabilities are calculable for all or even most events.

Practically, it is not always clear that it is possible to rank the likelihood of events or outcomes numerically, or that even where this can be done that these rankings would be comparable. This clearly contradicts Bentham's view that legal evidence could be treated in such an actuarial manner. Legal decision-making though is very clearly concerned with questions of probability. Courts are required to address questions about probability and evaluate a range of probabilistic information, such as how likely it is that a witness is accurate or truthful. Whether such questions can ever be quantified numerically though is far from clear. Concepts such as 'beyond reasonable doubt' or even on the 'balance of probabilities' are typically not numerically specified and most legal systems have been resistant to the idea of trying to do so. There have been some changes in this respect, particularly in some U.S. states, where there has been a greater willingness to try to attribute numerical values to evidence, these remain the exception to the rule though. There are a number of possible reasons for this. Most strikingly and notwithstanding the views of Bentham, there are many instances where it is difficult to see how any legitimate or useful numerical values might be calculated. One legal argument may be more probable than the other and be seen as such by jurors. How to conceptualise this, let alone give it numerical value, remains a very live area of debate (Dawid, Musio and Murtas, 2017).

The Principle of Indifference

Both Knight (1921) and Keynes (1921) made reference to the principle of indifference in their reviews. This idea had previously described as the principle of non-sufficient reason and was a long-established idea in probability theory. Put at its simplest, this suggests that in the absence of grounds for assigning unequal probabilities, it is appropriate to assign an equal probability for events. If we do not have good reasons to think otherwise, then the principle says that events are assumed to be equally probable. There is an intuitive appeal to this idea but problems with it were identified and its limitations were soon recognised (Bernoulli, 1954). Unmodified the principle quickly leads to logical paradoxes and inconsistent conclusions. In his work on probability, Keynes (1921) illustrates this with a simple example using the colour of book covers. Here, in the absence of other grounds, the probability of a book cover being black or red would each be assigned an equal probability of 0.5. On the same basis, the probability of a book cover being blue or red would be assumed to be equal at 0.5. Extending this logic in unmodified form leads these probabilities being extended with the paradoxical conclusion that the probability of a book cover being blue, or red or black is 0.5 (Keynes, 1921). As Keynes noted, this paradox is clearly nonsense and in fact can be very easily resolved. However, in resolving this, additional constraints on the principle of indifference are needed. This is not in fact a trivial observation in relation to risk where the principle of indifference has often been applied mechanistically, without additional constraints, meaning that adequate allowance for the limitations to the principle are not made. It is worth stressing the point made by Keynes (1921) and others that the probability of a proposition about which we have no further information will not always be 0.5, something that is often neglected in practice. In fact, applying the principle of indifference requires a number of direct judgements and these must be made in advance, to determine which characteristics are felt to be relevant and which can be excluded.

Types of Probability

The preceding discussion has touched on some of the complexity involved in the concept of probability. For the moment, it is also worth stressing the importance of two broad but differing conceptions of probability. These different views strongly influence the way that ideas of probability are applied and may be interpreted. The first of these is commonly described as relative frequency, frequentist or 'objective' probability. The other is commonly described as knowledge-based, 'subjective' or Bayesian probability.

Relative Frequency Probability

This approach dates from the earliest work available on probability and was clearly understood by Bernoulli (1654–1705) and Arbuthnot (1667–1735). Its development though can be seen to derive largely from later work by Cournot (1843), Ellis (1844) and Venn (1866). In elementary terms, the central idea here is that probability is based on groups of events. Estimating the probability of an outcome at an individual level comes from looking for information about a relevant group. Such a probability will in turn have a degree of uncertainty around it. The power of this approach lies in the ability to identify, or imagine, such groups, with judgement of probabilities in turn resting on how valid our knowledge of these defined groups is.

This conception of probability fitted well with ideas based on early gambling paradigms. An early example of the application of this approach is also given by Arbuthnot (1710) who used statistical tables that had then been recently developed, to try to address the practical question of the differential birth rate for male children and their observed higher death rate. Using an 82-year sample of London population records, Arbuthnot estimated a very low probability that the observed differences were the result of random chance. Such thinking and the application of relative frequency probabilities was very far ahead of its time.

It has now become widespread, forming the basis of a wide range of hypothesis testing across social and natural sciences.

This approach to probability though is open to a number of criticisms, ranging from the fundamental to the practical. These include the fact that such a conception of probability excludes other concepts of probability, based on induction or analogy. The probability that witnesses evidence is true is one example of this. For most advocates of relative frequency approaches, such questions are not ones that probability can sensibly answer. It can be argued they are either true or false propositions with no underlying random process. Since probabilities of this kind cannot be quantified as a ratio, based on such an underlying process, they are not probability questions. This self-imposed limitation has been repeatedly challenged by those who have argued that probability is not identical to statistical frequency, even though this is central to the concept. Such views have been associated with quite different conceptions of probability generally described as 'subjective' or 'knowledge based'.

Knowledge-Based Probability

The idea of knowledge-based probabilities addresses just this type of case, where there are logical rather than numeric grounds to favour one alternative over others. Here the probability of a proposition can be seen as reflecting degrees of belief about something. More technically, it can be seen to be linked to a reference class, where the truth-frequency relationship may be known within wide or narrow limits (Keynes, 1921). This may take away the need for the kinds of numerical ratios seen in relative frequency probability and replace these with notions of more or less. Alternatively, it may involve replacing such ratios with knowledge-based estimates that may be updated in light of accumulating information. In contrast to relative frequency views of probability, which focus on ratios with high levels of inter-subjective agreement, knowledge-based probability is concerned with efforts to measure likelihood through the eyes of an assessor. Efforts of this kind will be informed by the available knowledge an assessor has access to. The approach therefore does not need to refer to underlying populations of similar events. It has the major advantage that it always allows probability to be specified (Lindley, 1985).

This approach to probability rests on theory developed independently by de Finetti (1930, 1974) and Ramsey (1931). It includes methods that relate degrees of belief to different reference points, such as odds or stakes in gambling or alternatively by non-gambling points of reference. A common illustrative example used here has been the drawing of coloured balls from an opaque container. To take a simple example of this, in the case of three successes from a series of ten observations, it may be possible to assign a probability for A of $3/10$ or $P(A) = 0.3$.

Importantly, this is not based on an estimate of the true underlying probability for a hypothetical population of similar events. Rather, it reflects an assessment of a degree of belief about the uncertainty related to the occurrence of A. Such a method may be appropriate where the observations are judged relevant to assessing uncertainty around A and this uncertainty is not deemed to be large.

In the context of risk, such assumptions may not be true though. Situations are often unique and the distinction between aleatory uncertainty (intrinsic randomness) and epistemic uncertainty (lack of knowledge) may be unclear. Here, more sophisticated 'Bayesian' methods may be used. A simple example of this involves ascribing an initial probability on the basis of available knowledge and modifying this in light of further experience or findings. This Bayesian updating approach can be understood by again using a simple example based on a gambling paradigm. This involves a dice game where if you throw any number between 1 and 5, you win £6,000, but if you throw a 6, you lose £6,000. Based on a single throw, how might this information be dealt with? Here, a Bayesian approach might suggest defining a prior distribution for the probability of throwing a six, based on beliefs about the situation. The probabilities here are knowledge based and it could reasonably be concluded that the game is unlikely to be fair. A value of 1/6 for throwing a six would represent a fair die, alternatively a value of ½ or 1 might be specified on the assumption of a loaded die. Table 1.1 sets out a knowledge-based probability distribution, called a prior distribution in Bayesian terms. This starts from a reasonable assumption of bias in the game.

So, here, the initial assumption is that there is a 0.25 probability that the die will always fall on a 6, a 0.25 probability that it will fall on a 6 nine out of ten times, a 0.25 probability that it will fall on a 6 half the time and a 0.25 probability that it is a fair die. This can be updated using Bayes formula to give a posterior distribution in light of emerging evidence. Here, the die is thrown and does not show a 6. The initial distribution can then be updated to the one shown in Table 1.2. Here, the probability that the die will always be a six becomes zero: having obtained another value, it is now not possible that the die always lands on a six. The likelihood of the die being very biased reduces markedly to 0.07, whilst the probability of it being moderately biased increases a little and the probability of it being fair more than doubles.

Table 1.1 Bayesian prior distribution for p

p'	$P(p = p')$
1	0.25
9/10	0.25
1/2	0.25
1/6	0.25

Table 1.2 Bayesian posterior distribution for p

p'	P (p = p' given X=0)
1	0
9/10	0.07
1/2	0.35
1/6	0.58

Table 1.3 A simplified Bayesian network with 2 conditions

	Drought present/ disease present (%)	Drought present/ disease absent (%)	Drought absent/disease present (%)	Drought absent/disease absent (%)
Loss of leaves present	95	85	90	2
Loss of leaves absent	5	15	10	98

This kind of updating can continue to be repeated, leading to revised probability estimates as more information becomes available. The appeal of such approaches to real-world problems is largely self-evident. It is possible to start with estimates based on a given idea or hypothesis and continually update these in light of emerging evidence. Unsurprisingly, Bayesian methods have been developed and used extensively across the natural and social sciences. Table 1.3 shows an example taken from the biological sciences of how this approach might be applied. This illustrates a Bayesian network looking at the probability of disease, drought and loss of leaves. Here, it is possible to set out a conditional probability table, based on what is known about these factors. To define the aleatory uncertainty here using a relative frequency approach would require a hypothetical infinite population of similar conditions. In reality, such a construction is not likely to be meaningful. There is in reality no large set of 'identical' and independent instances of droughts and of disease, where some elements are fixed and some are free to vary. In cases such as this, defining aleatory uncertainty using a relative frequency approach therefore requires constructions that are not likely to be meaningful and, in some instances, may be difficult to imagine. In contexts such as industrial quality control, comparing crop yields or predicting weather patterns, such hypothetical populations can make intuitive sense. In other instances, for example, terrorist incidents or self-inflicted deaths, they do not, and attempts to adapt relative frequency approaches to such cases can appear tortured (Fischbacher-Smith, 2016).

Problems with Knowledge-Based Probability

Knowledge-based probability has been subject to a number of criticisms. Several of these are discussed in later chapters and range from detailed methodological issues, through to a complete rejection of the idea of knowledge-based probability as being unscientific and unjustified. Certainly, in many real-world situations, there will be a lack of information and knowledge with which to determine knowledge-based probabilities. Comparisons with related observations may be difficult, meaning that instead hypothetical thought-constructed systems may have to be relied on. Background information can be used to justify these but here the intervening steps involved are often opaque and may be difficult to justify, with traditional scientific methods being difficult to apply.

Applying Probability

The role of probability in directing behaviour has been of interest for centuries, with much of the early work in this area being theologically driven. For example, Jesuit thinking suggested that actions with the lowest probability of success may be justified, where the results are the best possible. In contrast, the Port Royal Philosophers (1861) and John Locke (1664) rejected this view, seeing the dimensions of probability and outcome as interacting, with each needing to be evaluated against the other. The growth of utilitarian philosophy from the 19th century onwards adopted a view that stressed a balance in the form of the 'greatest good of the greatest number' in both the short and long term (Bentham, 1827). However, subject to later refinements (Mill, 1863), this suggested some form of arithmetic relationship between probability and outcomes was possible and useful. Although the language in this area has changed dramatically over the centuries, the key philosophical themes raised have remained very much alive (though often unacknowledged) in current thought and practice (Daston, 1988).

Descriptive and Inferential Statistics

Statistics can be divided into two main forms: descriptive and inferential. These two are clearly linked, with the descriptive leading on to the inferential. In moving from description to inference, there will generally need to be an effort to deal with extraneous information, such as the sampling used or the conditions of observation. A simple example here might be the use of a correlation coefficient as an inferential statistic calculated on the basis of two sets of descriptive statistics. This process will though leave open numerous aspects of interest that may not be amenable to numerical statistical description.

Many general insights into the relationship between these two forms of statistic have long been evident. The development and application of these appeared relatively late in the history of human thought, with the growth of the use of both argued to reflect a break from dominant Platonic views in western thought during the 17th and 18th centuries and the decline of ideas of unconditional truth (Keynes, 1921). This change also occurred alongside a decline in the use of torture as a forensic means of divining the truth. It was only by the 17th and 18th centuries that formal and large-scale production of descriptive statistics was seen in Europe (Daston, 1988). This included work such as that of Halley (1693) who developed early mortality tables, leading to the identification of what he termed 'partial associations', or what would now be called correlations. This referred to the finding that regular patterns emerged from these descriptive statistics. In addition, it was observed that these often became more marked as the numbers analysed increased, leading Poisson (1837) to develop a 'law of great numbers' to refer to a discoverable system within apparent randomness. He suggested that some constant causes were always present and that these would normally become clear in the long run of observations. This idea was taken up by Quetelet (1842) who undertook seminal work in statistics, greatly developing and formalising such ideas and undertaking applied work, in areas such as the normal distribution of height in people and the regularity of suicides within populations.

The idea of a law of large numbers is central to notions of using descriptive statistics to draw inferences. It can reasonably be argued that early work greatly overstated this, with any degree of association based on large numbers being seen as a stable finding. Parallels were drawn between such associations and the findings that were emerging in the natural sciences. In reality, stability of this kind does not appear to be universal as suggested, or even typical, meaning that it cannot routinely be assumed. In turn, this led to the gradual discovery that in some instances, it was not possible to predict individual cases at all but only regularity with given sets of information (Keynes, 1921). This important observation has been largely neglected in forensic practice despite its striking relevance.

Conclusion

Probability is then not a straightforward concept. It is relational in nature and an event can only be probable within a given context, which, in turn, needs to be determined, by means of analysis and judgment. There is no single concept of probability, and probability theory is both a complex and dynamic area of research, which can be divided into at least two major distinctive approaches. One of these is based on the notion of relative frequencies and is often described as 'objective' probability. Drawing on the idea of probability as a proportion, it is based on a reference to a larger often hypothetical population. The other approach to probability is often described as knowledge based or 'subjective' or Bayesian probability. Here probability is seen in terms of degrees of belief, rather than by reference to a population. Both approaches to probability are clearly relevant to and have strongly influenced work in the area of risk. Within forensic practice though, somewhat curiously, the use of knowledge-based probability appears to have been largely neglected. Indeed, a sense of these very different conceptions of probability has not always been evident at all in approaches to risk assessment within forensic practice.

The Language of Risk   2

Risk assessment has been defined and described in various ways and as with the notion of risk itself, there is no universally agreed terminology. The many definitions proposed have themselves been strongly influenced by thinking on risk more broadly and the perspectives adopted. Two recent definitions are illustrative of this highlighting the contrasts in approach. The UK Government Treasury Orange Book, for example, describes risk assessment as:

> ...*uncertainty of outcome, whether positive opportunity or negative threat, of actions and events. The risk has to be assessed in respect of the combination of the likelihood of something happening, and the impact which arises if it does actually happen.*
>
> HM Treasury (2004)

By contrast, the International Organisation for Standardization (ISO) (2009) standards produced by the International Organisation for Standardization describes risk assessment as the:

> ...*overall process of risk identification (3.5.1), risk analysis (3.6.1) and risk evaluation (3.7).*
>
> ISO (2009)

These two definitions are based on very different ways of seeing risk and its assessment. The former can be seen as reflecting a largely economic approach, focused on estimates of risk as a combined valuation of likelihood and impact.

DOI: 10.4324/9781003108665-3

This aligns with the views on risk developed by Knight (1921) and to a range of later work across economics, health, engineering, insurance and the natural sciences. The ISO approach by contrast adopts a much broader perspective, seeing risk assessment as part of a more extensive process, involving extensive work in the identification, analysis and evaluation of risk. This approach fits better with the views expressed by Keynes (1921). Examples of each of these contrasting definitions could be multiplied but the key point here is that each reflects a difference of emphasis in risk assessment and how it is approached. This in turn influences the way risks are understood and the methods used to answer questions about risk.

Terminology in the area of risk is similarly varied, often as a function of these fundamentally differing views of risk and the fact that it is an area that cuts across so many disciplines and areas of practice. Similar problems have arisen in different fields and settings, with very different traditions and conventions emerging. These have not always been informed either by the history of work in this area, or by the work undertaken in other fields. A tendency towards silo thinking in some disciplines and settings has been evident, with a great deal of reinvention of work already undertaken. Risk is an area where the wheel has been reinvented many times, often being called different names and being described in different ways. Isolated thinking has also resulted in continued use of concepts and methods that have often been improved on or superseded elsewhere, and here forensic practice is perhaps one of the more serious exemplars of poor practice. The idea that risks can be assessed simply as a function of relative frequency and impact alone draw heavily from increasingly outdated models, that had dominated thinking. Such simple models are still advocated by some, in areas such as economic risk, although even here developments in the area have resulted in increasing criticism of such a limited view (Thaler, 2000). The idea that the kinds of risks seen in forensic practice can be assessed in this way is not convincing.

A variety of language has often been used to describe identical or overlapping concepts around risk, with individual disciplines tending to develop their own terminology to describe risk. This has perhaps inevitably led to confusion and the independent repetition of errors. Here, though it can credibly be suggested that across many disciplines, there has been significant convergence in recent years, with a growing interchange of ideas, greater consensus and less reinvention. Development of formal frameworks and standards have clear limitations but have aided in this process. The International Organization for Standardization (ISO) (2018) and International Risk Governance Council (IRGC) (2005) frameworks are examples of this process. Unfortunately, forensic practice has on the whole remained largely isolated from these developments and there has

```
                                          ┌─ Planning
                   ┌─ Risk Assessment ────┼─ Risk Analysis
Risk Management ───┤         ↕
                   └─ Risk Acceptability ─── Risk Treatment
```

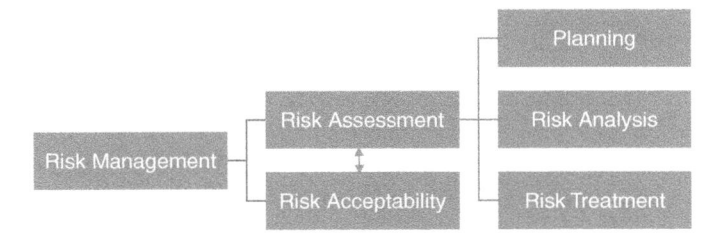

Figure 2.1 A simple model of risk terminology.

remained a strong attachment to outdated and often idiosyncratic ideas that have tended to draw on simple models of risk. It seems important to move on from this, with greater learning from other disciplines and practice settings, seeing risk assessment as part of a wider process. This process approach to risk can be thought of in terms of a number of interacting stages or phases or processes (Rowe, 1975; Fischbacher-Smith, Irwin and Fischbacher-Smith, 2010). The precise way that these are divided and described varies in detail, but a number of key concepts are central to this. Figure 2.1 sets out a simplified model summarising these.

This model defines risk management as an overarching and controlling process. This is simplified here as involving two linked areas, risk assessment and risk acceptability. Risk assessment is itself divided into sub-parts; here, it has been broken down into phases of planning, analysis and treatment. Within this framework, risk assessment can be seen to form part of a much wider systemic approach concerned with understanding and managing risks. Current forensic practice has markedly drifted away from this with a growing focus on producing assessments of likelihood for broadly defined risks. The idea of risk analysis is generally absent or largely neglected in forensic practice, with a direct jump to making probabilistic assessments of outcomes. The idea of risk evaluation forms an important part of analysis and generally links to the difficult area of value judgements, about the acceptability of risks (Rowe, 1975; Irwin, Smith and Griffiths, 1982; Fischbacher-Smith, Irwin and Fischbacher-Smith, 2010). The idea of risk treatment can be contentious but it has been widely used in other areas of risk. Oddly it is rarely seen in forensic practice, where the idea seems to be generally conflated with risk management. It is treated as a distinct area here for several reasons. The most important of these is that risk treatment forms only part of risk management (International Organisation for Standardization 2009; Aven, 2016). This aspect of risk is defined here as involving consideration of the various ways in which risks may be mitigated through the use of interventions or barriers.

Risk Assessment

The term risk assessment is used here to refer to efforts involved in trying to provide estimates of likelihood of events and the consequences of these. This builds on risk analysis and risk evaluation processes and, in turn, will guide risk treatment considerations. The view put forward here is that effective risk assessment rests on the foundation of good quality analysis and evaluation. Any attempts to jump directly to risk assessment in the absence of these is seen as misguided and poor practice that will generally be less effective. Within forensic practice, this has been a growing problem in how risk is dealt with. There has been what appears to be a growing trend towards neglecting analysis and evaluation, moving hastily to make probabilistic estimates of risk. Within forensic practice, this seems to have involved two main approaches: One adopting a quantitative methodology, normally in the form of relative frequency probability of an outcome and the other involving qualitative descriptions of likelihood of outcomes.

The largely neglected processes of risk analysis and evaluation provides a broad-based picture of risk, which will include views on the causes and consequences of risk. This enables the development of better and more focused risk assessment in the form of the likelihood of outcomes and their consequences. This can be described symbolically as (A, C, P, K) where A refers to the event, C, the consequences, P, the probabilistic assessment and K, the knowledge this is based on (Aven, 2013). The inclusion of K in the terms here frames any risk assessment, making clear the relationship between the values derived and the knowledge used to produce them. The provision of estimates of probability (P) has increasingly come to dominate forensic practice, despite the fact that developing such estimates in isolation excludes other aspects of relevance. A broader 'risk picture' allows for consideration of the risk or risks being considered (A) as well as what might be the acceptable limits around these. These are also framed by what is known or can be inferred (K), and, in turn, this provides important information about the nature of the values derived for likelihood and consequences. This goes beyond data expressed as probabilities or expected values, as these may hide important assumptions and suppositions from scrutiny. A focus exclusively on probabilistic data may, particularly in cases where knowledge is weak or lacking, lead to very inaccurate or misleading expectations. This is not to discount the role of the probabilistic assessment, rather it is to stress the need to understand this simply as part of a much more extensive process of dealing with risk as effectively as possible.

Probabilistic risk assessment gives a focus that is concerned with how likely events, chains of events and consequences are. Within many areas of risk, this has tended to be focused on likely financial costs or financial costs in association with other values. This appears largely driven by methods deriving from economics and management. In other areas, estimates of probability may concern significant harms, such as environmental degradation, injury or death of patients in health settings. However, economic and managerial approaches have become increasingly influential here as well, in seeking to apply financial values in particular ways. Estimates of such losses can capture some aspects of uncertainty associated with adverse events, but this is clearly a limited view. Additionally, such probabilistic assessments are incomplete without consideration of how robust they are and how sensitive they are to changes. This involves consideration of the extent that results depend on the conditions present and assumptions used to produce estimates of likelihood as well as what it would take for conclusions to significantly change.

Risk Treatment

The term 'risk treatment' refers here to the overall process of selecting and implementing measures thought to mitigate risk. This can be described as involving potentially overlapping efforts to avoid, reduce, optimise or transfer risks (Aven, Baraldi, Flage and Zio, 2014). These in turn can be systematically compared using a variety of methods, which would include widely used techniques such as cost–benefit and cost-effectiveness analysis, as well as non-economic measures of changes to risk. Avoidance of risks is an obvious strategy and this refers to not doing activities that are linked to risk. Mountain climbing is an example of a high-risk activity and the risk associated with it can be 'treated' by using avoidance: simply by not going into the mountains at all. However, avoidance as a way to treat risk may not be a desirable or desired strategy and may not be possible at all. The acceptance of some degree of risk may be unavoidable or be seen to have balancing advantages. In situations where decisions are taken to accept a level of risk, then risk treatment may involve efforts to alter the level or impacts of risk. This may be in the form of barriers or interventions to reduce risk, in the example of mountain climbing, the use of specialist safety equipment and procedures, or the provision of specialist training. Optimisation in turn can be seen as involving efforts to minimise negative and maximise positive consequences. An example here might be the provision of needle exchanges for intravenous users of illegal drugs, where a lower overall balance of risks may be achieved with the aim of reducing harms as opposed to 'zero tolerance' where users may be less likely to seek help. The idea of risk treatment by transfer typically refers to moving the risk to others and here a common example is insuring financially against negative outcomes. Within forensic practice, a clear example might be moving some of those under community supervision into prison or secure hospital settings.

A natural starting point with risk treatment has been to focus on those areas thought to have the greatest impact on risk. In common sense terms, there is little point in directing considerable efforts to address areas that make a marginal contribution to risk, when even a large impact on this will have little effect in reducing risk. By contrast, even a small impact on a major contributor to risk may yield significant overall reductions. The process of risk treatment can be applied systematically to allow meaningful comparisons, and again, there are a range of methods for doing this, which have been developed across many contexts. One example of this involves analysis of the existing solutions as a base case, followed by efforts to identify approaches that could reduce this by say 10%, 25% and 50%. Possible measures and solutions to achieve these levels of reduction can be developed, set out and evaluated. In some cases, these kinds of measures may have only positive effects, but more typically, they will have both positive and negative effects. A topical example of this would be the use of vaccinations to prevent disease. There are a range of positive effects from vaccination to do with infection, disease progression, recovery and transmission to others. However, there are also negative effects such as the occurrence of rare adverse effects. Vaccinations may also act differently for particular populations, such as older adults, children and those with pre-existing vulnerabilities. As a result, there is a need to consider the interaction of the effects of risk treatments and strike an appropriate balance for individuals and populations when considering risks. A broad and thorough analysis of risk treatment is therefore seen as central to the overall process of effective risk management.

Dose Response

An important aspect of risk treatment is captured by the term 'dose response', which typically refers to the relationship between level of treatment and effects. The relationship between the intensity of an exposure to an infectious agent, and its effect on a living organism would be an example of dose response. So too would be the link between the dose of a therapeutic drug of a known quantity and the average response to this, which may or may not be known. For any dose, there will be a degree of uncertainty (U) around this, with respect to how likely an individual will be to show a response similar to the group average. This is typically considered by means of some form of probability estimate based on available knowledge (K). Two linked aspects are likely to contribute to such variation: exposure effects and vulnerability. The former relates to the effects of exposure to environmental effects. Here, an example might be exposure to high levels of air pollution and the interaction of this with the hypothetical illness. Vulnerability refers to individual variation and how these may interact with the illness. For example, a history of asthma may interact with the disease and indeed may also interact with environmental effects, such as air pollution to increase the severity of effects. For this reason, it is common in areas such as epidemiology to talk of risk and vulnerability analysis rather than risk alone.

Dose effects clearly have application to some areas of practice. The use of various forms of drug treatment to address areas such as delusional belief or severely depressed mood provide clear examples of this. However, the notion has been extended in some areas to refer to broader treatment regimes. Taking the example of depression, this might include environmental changes to increase levels of activity as part of a regimen of treatment, with more activity equating to an increased dose (Dunn, Trivedi, Kampert et al., 2005). Within some areas of forensic practice, a variation on this terminology has developed, which refers to 'dose' rather than 'dose response' and uses this term in a distinct and idiosyncratic way. Here the term has been modified to refer to group-based risk treatments, using measures of input to define 'dosage'. So, for example, the number of group sessions becomes the 'prescribed dosage', with a troubling historical trend that appears to suggest a linear association between the level of such inputs and outcomes (Mailloux, Abracen, Serin et al., 2003). Use in this way seems to be a significant, confusing and unhelpful divergence from the traditional idea of dose response, as it has been applied to the understanding of links between psychotherapeutic contact and outcomes in forensic practice (Hansen, Lambert and Forman, 2002). The importation and misapplication of this terminology in forensic practice, perhaps reflects a wider developing tendency of adopting scientific terminology from elsewhere, as a marketing method that suggests rather stronger scientific foundations than those that actually exist.

Risk Management

Risk management has been defined as all the coordinated activities to direct and control an organisation with respect to risk (ISO, 2009). As such, it covers both internal and external organisational environments. Risk management describes the initial identification of the need to consider risks, through to the process of evaluating and feeding back outcomes (Rath, 2007). This use of the term is very different from that commonly seen in forensic practice, where it is used more narrowly and with a routine conflation with risk treatment. It is suggested here that the clear separation of these two related concepts is significant and important from a practice viewpoint. It can be illustrated by again taking the topical example of vaccination for infectious diseases. Here the use of COVID-19 vaccines with 70-year-old males with asthma may be an easy clinical decision to make. Its use in an 18-year-old female professional athlete would be more closely balanced. In the latter case, it may serve to reduce risk at a population level but the balance of risks for the individual would be more closely aligned. Vaccination for a child of 15 would raise similar balance of risk issues and additional issues around consent. Questions of this type, along with many others, are informed by risk treatment but fall within the province of risk management. The confusion of risk treatment with risk management in forensic practice can be seen to have had harmful effects. It can be seen as having led to a neglect of important issues in risk management, such as the identification of risks and interacting risks. It may also have contributed to a failure to focus on risk evaluation and effective risk communication.

Cautionary and Precautionary Principles

There are a variety of ways of thinking about risk management in more detail, involving differing levels of structure. General guides such as the cautionary and precautionary principles are often used here and provide a good starting point. Essentially, these concern thresholds for risk. Representing qualitatively different levels of caution as a function of the extent to which risks involve severe outcomes, high levels of uncertainty or both. The cautionary principle is often illustrated with the example of insurance, such as the case of home insurance. Here, a range of measures will often be present to ensure a low probability of fire. However, people may still insure against fire to avoid the risk of complete loss. Within risk management events that have serious consequences and a significant degree of uncertainty are seen to suggest the need for cautionary measures to be taken, or that the activity should avoided. In its simplest form, the precautionary principle builds on this and concerns activities that threaten areas such as human health or the environment. Here, precautionary measures may be taken, even where causal relationships have not been fully established. Archetypal examples of the precautionary principle might include areas such as bans on genetic modifications to living organisms or on the creation of chemical compounds that are not broken down in the natural environment. Here, the severity of outcomes is such that much more aggressive risk management may be seen as necessary.

More formal frameworks can be applied in using these principles and these have clear relevance and potential application to forensic practice. A commonly used approach is called As Low As Reasonably Possible (ALARP), a framework designed to focus judgements and risk management decisions on risk treatments to reduce risk to the lowest possible level within 'reasonable' constraints. The application of such methods may have a useful role in focusing on the process of risk management. However, use of these formal frameworks has also been criticised on a number of grounds, including the concern that they can drive mechanistic decision-making. The use of such frameworks has also been criticised for using numerical values or 'metrics' in managerial jargon, to make decisions at the expense of wider consideration of the risk picture. In applying these methods to practice and policy it has been observed that none of the methods available approach the level of precision needed to justify the mechanistic use of numerical values in such a way (Aven and Renn, 2009a; Aven, Baraldi, Flage and Zio, 2014).

Robustness and Resilience

Risk resilience and risk robustness are related concepts and have a wide application across the area of risk. Both have been largely neglected in forensic practice (Towl, 2015). Yet they involve important aspects of risk management. At its simplest, risk robustness concerns the ability to cope with anticipated deviations from normal functioning. A simple forensic example would be how well community forensic mental health services respond to the deterioration in a patient's mental health. Risk resilience can be seen to refer to the ability to withstand unexpected events or surprises. Here, a topical example would be how well forensic services have responded to the effects of pandemic infections. Robustness and resilience can themselves be broken down further to distinguish between risks that are linked to a particular activity and risk linked to constraints around that activity such as organisational or technological limits.

Risk and Protective Factors

It is common in forensic practice to talk about risk and protective factors. Risk factors being defined as anything thought to increase the likelihood of an adverse outcome and protective factors as anything that reduces the likelihood. In echoing early thinking on risk, these are often broken down into 'static' and 'dynamic' factors, referring to unchangeable and changeable characteristics. This terminology has the advantage of being simple and easy to explain. It does though have a number of significant disadvantages and serious weaknesses. It represents a significant divergence from the approaches used in other areas, where more precise operational definitions are favoured as being fundamental to scientific methods. This is further complicated by the adoption of terminology that appears specific to forensic practice with the unhelpful use of the term 'criminogenic risk factor'. This has been used to describe things that appear closely associated with the risk of criminal convictions or alternatively with criminal behaviours. The term appears to have originally developed from research in criminology, which suggested that some environments were associated with high levels of recorded crime and anti-social behaviours. These areas tended to show high levels of economic deprivation and lacked social resources. This pattern was shorthanded using the term 'criminogenic' to describe these kinds of environments (Mays, 1968; Wikström and Treiber, 2009). The use of the term genic can be taken to suggest that problem behaviours emerged as a result of interaction between individuals and these damaging environments. This idea was subsequently modified to incorporate prisons, as a particular type of damaging environment from which higher levels of criminality might emerge, as a result of these interaction effects. More recent use in forensic practice has seen this concept altered beyond recognition, with a primary stress on internal and individual characteristics rather than a stress on environmental characteristics and interactional effects (Fass, Heilbrun, DeMatteo and Fretz, 2008; Howard, 2009). Such change can be legitimately criticised as fundamentally changing and unhelpfully simplifying the original concept. It also appears to give primacy, in the absence of adequate evidence, to individual psychological characteristics whilst neglecting environmental effects, such as deprivation and poverty, and interactional effects between the individual and environments (Crighton and Towl, 2008; Farrington, 2017).

The use of terminology in this area has been looked at in detail, drawing on good practice from other areas such as epidemiology (Kraemer, Kazdin, Offord et al., 1997; Monahan, Steadman, Silver et al., 2001). Here, the importance of using consistent and operationally defined language has been well recognised. Using psychiatry as an exemplar, Kraemer et al. (1997) began by drawing a clear distinction between correlates and risk factors with a correlate being something that is systematically related to a given outcome of interest but that has not been shown to precede it. Correlates would then include phenomena that accompany or follow something, termed concomitants and outcomes. These correlates can be further divided into fixed and variable risk markers. Fixed markers here refer to unchangeable characteristics such as race, whilst variable markers refer to things that do change such as age.

Risk factors are defined as something systematically related to a given outcome of interest but that, unlike a correlate, has been shown to precede it. These factors can also be sub-divided into fixed and variable types, and here, a further distinction between variable and causal risk factors can be suggested as important. The former refers to things that can be changed, such as an individual's level of education. However, the term causal risk factor is restricted to variable risk factors where such manipulation can be shown to change the outcome. The example often given of a causal risk factor in forensic practice, perhaps because it is one of the few known, is substance use.

Work by Kraemer, Stice, Kazdin et al. (2001) looked in more depth at the nature of risk factors, drawing on work in other areas such as epidemiology (Rothman, Greenland and Lash, 2008). In particular, the ways in which interactions of risk indicators and risk factors could be described was reviewed, with a framework of five types of interactions being proposed:

1 Proxy
2 Overlapping
3 Independent
4 Mediators
5 Moderators

These are perhaps most easily understood using the practice examples given by Kraemer et al. (2001) to illustrate them. The notion of proxy risk factors concerns the correlates of 'strong' risk factors such as the correlation between inadequate parenting and attention deficit hyperactivity disorder. Any of the components of 'inadequate parenting' such as the use of physical punishment may act as a proxy for this broader concept. Such proxy factors may in turn be aggregated, in an effort to gain better insights into what the causal processes might be.

Overlapping risk factors involve situations where two different measures strongly tap into the same construct but where neither has temporal precedence. In this sense, they overlap, hence the description. An example here, drawn from psychometrics, is the use of two widely used measures of depressed mood: the Hamilton Depression Rating Scale (Hamilton, 1960) and the Beck Depression Inventory (Beck and Steer, 1984). High scores on both assessments are risk factors for a subsequent suicide attempt and it appears likely that they are tapping into the same overall construct of depressed mood. As such, they would significantly overlap. The idea here is that by using such overlapping measures, incremental improvements in the measurement of the shared construct may be achieved. Independent risk factors by contrast are those that are uncorrelated and where there is no temporal precedence (one does not necessarily precede the other). The example given here uses female sex and non-white ethnicity as independent risk factors for developing obesity. Neither has temporal precedence and they are not correlated with each other, so both are independent risk factors for incidence of obesity (Kraemer et al., 2001).

The distinction between mediator and moderator risk factors is perhaps less obvious but is arguably of particular importance in many areas of forensic practice. The nature of a mediator was illustrated by Kraemer et al. (2001) using the example of phenylketonuria. This is an inherited metabolic disease and its adverse effects are mediated by an elevated level of a specific enzyme in the blood stream. The elevated levels of this enzyme result in harmful neuropsychological effects, which may in turn be measured by lower scores on standardised psychological tests. A moderator here specifies under what conditions another variable will act to give a particular outcome. For example, female sex and early puberty have been suggested as risk factors for the occurrence of panic disorder. Here sex temporally precedes early puberty and is uncorrelated with it. There is though some evidence that early puberty is more significant for females than males, with reference to panic disorder. Sex is seen to moderate the effect of early puberty (Kraemer et al., 2001).

Conclusion

The language used to address risk in forensic practice can be critiqued on several grounds. It has increasingly diverged from that seen in other areas of risk and from good practice in a number of ways. Most strikingly, there has been a failure to use adequate operational definitions. Definitions typically used in forensic practice have at times been so broad that they are of little clinical use and have impeded research and development. There has been a striking and prolonged failure to draw from research from the social and natural sciences, including highly and directly relevant areas such as epidemiology, to improve practice. Such siloed thinking is puzzling, given the quality of work available to draw on. It perhaps reflects an increasing isolation of forensic practice from the evidence base and wider thinking about risk. Improving practice is likely to rest in large part on a reversal of this trend and the adoption of more precise and mainstream terminology for thinking about risk.

Current Practice in Risk

Actuarial and Algorithmic Approaches

3

Current forensic practice in the area of risk has become increasingly focused on using what have been called risk assessment instruments (RAIs) or less commonly, 'tools' to develop probabilistic assessments of risk. These can be divided into two types, both of which have been contrasted with what has been inaccurately called 'unstructured' clinical judgement. One type, often called actuarial, statistical or algorithmic RAIs, relies on some kind of formal analysis, such as inferential statistics, typically to produce numerical estimates of probability. The other, often called structured clinical, structured judgement or protocol-based RAIs, is based on a checklist approach, which yields qualitative estimates of likelihood. Both types of RAI are seen across a range of areas of forensic practice, with an extensive and growing array of such instruments having been developed and marketed, particularly since the 1980s. In turn, this has given rise to a particular and misleading language of 'generational change', used to describe these RAIs.

The focus below is on the actuarial or algorithmic assessments that draw on formal analysis to combine and analyse data. Use of this type of RAI has been advocated as a supplement to, or replacement for, human decision-making. The grounding in formal methods and the increasingly automated form of these, based on structured decision rules or algorithms, has been repeatedly put forward as a significant advantage. The method has long been advocated as a more accurate alternative to human judgement, avoiding inherent biases and systematic errors that people may be subject to (Lundberg, 1926; Sarbin, 1944). The use of these RAIs in forensic practice has become more diverse

DOI: 10.4324/9781003108665-4

in recent years and they are now a common feature in three major areas of practice:

1 Policing
2 Sentencing and conditional release
3 Decision-making in relation to risk treatment

Advocates for actuarial and algorithmic RAIs have made several arguments in support of their use, without necessarily agreeing with the range of application. The most salient of these perhaps being that the method results in more accurate and therefore better decisions, compared with any available alternatives. An analogy drawn here has been with various forms of commercial activity that rely heavily on these methods. Historically, the insurance industry was often used as an, illustrative, example of the success of actuarial and algorithmic methods. More current and widely reported examples would include the use of algorithmic methods for decision-making based on large amounts of data, used by internet-based companies. Proponents of actuarial and algorithmic approaches have stressed the fallibility of human judgement and decision-making, with the demonstration of vulnerability to a number of systematic biases or errors adding to this argument (Kahneman, Slovic and Tversky, 1982). These failings in judgement have been seen as deriving from a reliance on simple heuristics or 'rules of thumb', leading in turn to the observed systematic errors and biases. Replacement of these with formal analyses are seen as the means of reducing this, with algorithmic methods acting as an antidote to people's heuristics and biases.

The area of crime prevention and policing is illustrative of the growing use of algorithmic RAIs, where use is suggested as a means of using probabilistic risk assessment to help eliminate individual biases (Saunders, Hunt and Hollywood, 2016; Slobogin, 2017). Police officers, it is argued, will suffer from the same heuristic decision-making and associated biases as anyone else. Relying on these simple decision-making rules will lead them astray. By contrast, actuarial and algorithmic approaches are able to direct resources towards areas and individuals who in fact present the highest probability of criminal or anti-social behaviour or of being a victim of crime. Practices such as stopping and searching individuals may therefore be targeted more accurately, using numerical predictions based on algorithmic methods, for example, identifying those most likely to be carrying weapons. This avoids stopping and searching low-risk individuals, which, in turn, may reduce adverse impacts of policing on the majority. There has in recent years been a very marked increase in the use of this approach, developed largely by academic and commercial organisations. These in turn may be linked to a range of automated facial recognition algorithms, removing the need to even know a person's identity before assessing risks.

These kinds of RAIs may also be seen in courts settings, being used for sentencing purposes. More formalised versions of this practice have been termed evidence-based sentencing, and this involves the use of these methods to inform the process of criminal sentencing. This approach has developed in North America, where it has been used to identify low-risk offenders during sentencing. Here, this has been seen as one practical way to begin the process of unwinding mass incarceration, particularly in the United States. The use of algorithms in this manner is seen as offsetting bias and as a counter to political and other pressures experienced by judges who are often elected. However, less systematic use of actuarial and algorithmic methods is common in other jurisdictions. Within the United Kingdom, for example, algorithmic risk assessments are commonly seen as part of pre-sentencing reports completed for the courts. Here, the use of actuarial information is argued to provide a means of addressing long-standing issues of unfairness in the criminal justice system and also in relation to civil detention linked to mental health. In both cases, it is evident that some groups are being treated more harshly than others. The poor, uneducated and some ethnic groups have been faring particularly badly, as reflected in disproportionate levels of punishment and incarceration. The use of actuarial methods here is suggested as a means of systematically rectifying this by identifying risk and diverting low-risk individuals away from custodial sentences (Casey, Warren and Elek, 2011).

A large part of forensic practice involves decisions about the interactions between risk as both probability and consequences and risk treatment and how these impact on issues such as arrest, imprisonment, conditional release and supervision. The failings in these areas have a long history and have been extensively and repeatedly documented. An early example of this is a study from the 1920s that looked at those who offended whilst on parole (Burgess, 1928). This research highlighted the strikingly poor predictive accuracy of the Parole Board at that time, despite the inclusion of expert members such as lawyers and psychiatrists. This led to the suggestion that more systematic approaches to decision-making about parole, based on the development of predictive actuarial tables. The use of such RAIs, it was argued, could significantly improve the levels of accuracy seen (Lundberg, 1926). Analysing this further, Sarbin (1944) hypothesised that in making assessments of risk, individuals were in fact using empirical methods to make comparisons between past and present data. They were, however, he argued, doing this in a manner that introduced errors into the process. Because of the limitations of human cognition, such as the limited capacity to recall previous data sets, it was suggested that human assessors would always perform more poorly than algorithms. These initial ideas, that errors were due to problems with recall and drawing on corrupted information, proved to be incorrect. Later experimental research suggested quite different causes and indeed these early ideas were challenged and corrected sometime later (Meehl, 1954). In reviewing the area, Meehl stressed a fundamental distinction between the process of gathering data and the process of combining it. For Meehl, the combination of data was the main difficulty with human judgements and in relation to data gathering, he adopted a broad-based view, accepting a wide range of clinical and other data might provide useful information for processing. Once gathered, however, he argued that algorithmic decision-making would, given equal amounts of data, always be more accurate. This led on to what quickly came to be characterised, rather crassly, as a 'clinical' versus 'statistical' debate about the best means of probabilistic risk assessment.

Use of Actuarial and Algorithmic Approaches in Practice

There has been around a century of systematic work to develop these actuarial approaches to risk. Some examples of actuarial and algorithmic methods currently in use are outlined below, to illustrate the ways in which this has been applied in current practice.

Policing

The use of algorithms in policing and crime prevention can be seen to address one of four main areas: the prediction of crime; predictions around who is likely to offend; methods for identifying likely perpetrators of crimes, and prediction of likely victims. Each type of assessment may be used at different points in organisations or systems and with different levels of complexity. The application of algorithms to process a range of inputs has increasingly been used internationally, often in partnership with commercial providers or academic institutions. One example of this has been the approach adopted by the Chicago Police Department in North America (Saunders, Hunt and Hollywood, 2016). This was initially called the Strategic Subject List (SSL) or was more informally called the 'Heat List'. Following significant criticisms, it was subsequently revised and renamed the Subject Assessment and Information Dashboard. A sub-division of this assessment designed to predict victimisation was developed and called the Crime and Victimisation Risk Model (CVRM). This approach can be seen as a form of profiling, although here the aim is to profile victims of crime rather than develop offender profiles (Fox and Farrington, 2018).

These algorithms had been developed by the police in collaboration with the Illinois Institute of Technology, and drew on a range of statistical methods for mapping and assessing risk. This was done on the basis of a range of data sampled with the aim of developing a risk picture for individuals that could aid policing decisions.

Individuals could for example be placed into different risk tiers, generated by the CVRM. The CVRM being an algorithm that estimates individual risk of becoming a victim or possible offender in a shooting or homicide in the next 18 months, based on risk factors drawn from a person's recent criminal or victimisation history. This was reported to be based on six data items, with these given in order of importance as:

1. Victim of a shooting incident
2. Age during latest arrest
3. Victim of an aggravated battery or assault
4. Trend in criminal activity
5. Arrests for unlawful use of a weapon
6. Arrests for violent offences

Based on a weighted combination of this information, an individual could be placed into a risk tier that ranged from 'very low' to 'very high'. This is, of course, very different from providing a numeric probability of an outcome. Higher-risk tiers represent greater risk for future involvement as either a victim, or an offender, in a shooting or homicide.

The available detail about the psychometric characteristics of this group of assessments is to date limited. Information on areas such as how reliably different assessors code data was not initially evident. Neither was information on the validity of predictions, typically seen in other areas where such methods have been used. There was a general lack of information concerning development samples and the routinely reported psychometric properties of RAIs. The reasons for this are unclear, but in general, levels of reporting appears lower where assessments are covered by issues of commercial confidentiality where RAIs are seen as commercial or intellectual property or where they are seen as intelligence assets. Evaluation of the methods used in Chicago was though subsequently undertaken and this yielded often disappointing results. These contrasted markedly with the often-impressive claims made for similar commercially marketed algorithms. A quasi-experimental evaluation conducted into the predictive policing algorithm used by Chicago's police department, the SSL, reported an increased likelihood of arrest for a shooting in those identified as higher risk but no difference in rates of becoming a victim of a homicide or shooting (Saunders, Hunt and Hollywood, 2016).

Sentencing and Conditional Release

The use of this type of RAI was seen relatively early in the area of conditional release of sentenced offenders being used to inform sentencing and release from mental health detention slightly later. An example of this kind of RAI taken from England and Wales is the Offender Group Reconviction Scale and this is currently in its third revision (OGRS-3) (Howard, Francis, Soothill and Humphreys, 2009). This now forms part of a broader assessment conducted by correctional services called the Offender Assessment System (OASys), which is based quite closely on the Level of Service Inventory Revised (LSI-R) developed in Canada (Fass, Heilbrun, DeMatteo and Fretz, 2008) and now provides at least two additional algorithmic scores, the OASys General Predictor (OGP) and OASys Violence Predictor (OVP) scores, both of which are based largely on similar items and work in a similar manner to the more established OGRS-3. The OGRS-3 algorithm is designed to give the percentage reconviction rates within a 12- or 24-month period in the community, for those having similar characteristics to the individual being assessed. This is based on a number of risk factors and indicators that are input, normally by a probation officer. The algorithm is based on a relatively large development sample and the numeric values are placed into descriptive bands ranging from 'low' to 'very high'. This typically forms part of the information available to sentencers or to those assessing suitability for conditional release.

Once completed, the OGRS-3 RAI provides a numerical prediction for a broad range of criminal reoffending. It has been described as being based largely on 'static' risk factors and indicators and was developed in England and Wales, initially for use by prison, probation and youth justice staff. As noted above, it forms part of a broader OASys system of assessment, which is described as including a range of changeable or 'dynamic' factors as part of the assessment. However, there is little guidance on how much of this information should be integrated with the actuarial estimates derived from the OGRS-3. The empirical basis of the OGRS is rather better than many other algorithmic RAIs, having been developed using a sample of 71,519 convicted offenders in England and Wales who received non-custodial sentences and a sample of 7,675 who received custodial sentences. The developers reported that this group was divided using a 60/40 split into calibration and validation datasets respectively (Howard, Francis, Soothill and Humphreys, 2009). Data from the UK Police National Computer (PNC) was used to trace reoffending over 12- and 24-month time frames. Reoffending was defined as a recordable offence, meaning those who had an offence proven within the follow-up plus an additional three-month confirmation time, which included those accepting a police caution, warning or reprimand or being found guilty in a court. Some offending will clearly not be included here with 'reconviction' being used as a proxy measure for the true rate of 'reoffending'. Having selected predictor variables, largely on the grounds of parsimony and ease of use in practice, the developers used an ordinal logistic regression model, with the same factors used for 12- and 24-month predictions.

The OGRS-3 includes six factors within the regression model:

1 Reoffending within one or two years
2 The COPAS rate
3 Sanctioning history – current sanction
4 Age and sex
5 Principal current offence

The COPAS rate is reported to be the Logarithm of the number of sanctions the individual has received divided by ten, plus the years between the first and current sanction.

The OGRS-3 and its previous iterations share a number of limitations, clearly recognised by the developers. These include the difficulties associated with going from group-based (nomothetic) data to individual (idiographic) predictions, and the validity of such individual predictions. As with similar RAIs, this method also has difficulty in dealing with high-impact low-frequency events, which may undermine algorithm-based predictions at an individual level. In addition, concerns have been raised about the use of a single OGRS algorithm across both female and male offenders and across different ethnic groups. Here, there is no certainty that predictions made are equally valid. There is also little public data on the reliability of the scoring of the OGRS-3 but, given that the items tend to be straightforward and the algorithmic analysis is automated, this seems likely to be relatively good. This is in contrast to the OASys more generally, where levels of agreement between assessors, particularly in some areas of assessment, tended to be strikingly poor (Debidin, 2009; Moore, 2015).

There is limited independent research available on predictive validity of the current iteration of the OGRS with much of the evidence base relating to the earlier iterations of the algorithm. Here, however, the evidence has generally been positive. Yang, Wong and Coid (2010) reported a detailed examination of RAIs, based on a sample of 1,955 cases with an Area Under the Curve (AUC) statistic of 0.71 for the OGRS, with an effect size of 0.78. This suggested that the OGRS algorithm performed well and indeed better than the range of other RAIs studied.

Risk Treatment

Efforts to determine who needs treatment was one of the first uses for RAIs and it is perhaps the least contentious, with RAIs like the OGRS-3 being routinely used for the allocation of individuals, to various forms of risk treatment. Use here is clearly analogous to actuarial or algorithmic methods used in areas such as medicine and epidemiology. Here, treatments are directed towards those who are believed likely to benefit most and equally importantly, not towards those who are unlikely to benefit. Typically, this might involve prioritising those most likely to become seriously unwell or providing treatments to those with specific causal risk factors. If one takes the COVID-19 pandemic as a topical illustration of this, mass vaccination efforts were initially directed at those at highest risk of death or serious injury from the disease at least in those states with well-developed public health systems. Primarily, this meant targeting older age groups and those with pre-existing vulnerabilities, on the basis of risk. Those with risks greater than any likely benefits were not initially vaccinated at all (Budd, Miller, Manning et al., 2020). By analogy, within forensic practice, risk treatments are typically directed in a similar manner, for example, at those felt to present the highest risk of reoffending, with those who present low levels of risk being left untreated.

The Static-99 provides an example of such use and is an actuarial tool designed to assess the risk of sexual violence in adults. It has been developed for use with sexual offenders and consists of ten items that are scored numerically:

1 Age (18–24.99 or 25+)
2 Ever having lived with a lover for two years or more
3 Any convictions for non-sexual violence
4 Any convictions
5 Prior sexual charges (0, 1–2, 3–5, 6+) or convictions (0, 1, 2–3, 4+)
6 Prior sentencing dates (3 or less, 4+)
7 Convictions for non-contact sexual offences
8 Unrelated victims
9 Strangers as victims
10 Any male victims

Based on the scoring of these items, the individual being assessed are placed into one of four categories ranging from 'low' to 'high' risk (Harris, Phenix, Hanson and Thornton, 2003). As with other actuarial and algorithmic approaches, this allows comparison of that individual with a group of others with similar identified characteristics, yielding numerical estimates for reoffending.

The level of reliability for the Static-99 has been reported. This data was based on 55 cases of assessment, completed independently as part of civil commitment hearings in North America. Here, a 91% level of agreement across item ratings was reported along with an Intraclass Correlation Coefficient (ICC) of 0.87 for the total scores (Hanson, 2001). However, independent assessments of the reliability of this RAI have been less impressive than those originally reported with, for example, an ICC of 0.63 (Ducro and Pham, 2006).

The predictive validity of the Static-99 has been reported based on 42 studies covering 13,288 cases, using the AUC statistic. Here, a value of 0.70 has been reported across studies in North America and Europe. However, there has been significant variation between studies, with some reporting lower levels of predictive validity, with a value of only 0.50, equivalent to random chance, for one group studied (Långström, 2004). In turn, such findings have led to a focus on carefully matching the use of this assessment to populations similar to the development sample, here adult, male, predominantly white, convicted sexual offenders, who have been released from secure hospital and prison settings in North America and Northern Europe.

The Violence Risk Appraisal Guide (VRAG) (Harris, Rice and Quinsey, 1993) and the later revised version (VRAG-R) (Rice, Harris and Lang, 2013) provides a common example, of an actuarial RAI used to address non-sexual violence in convicted mentally disordered offenders in Canada. Related algorithms have subsequently been developed to assess the risk of sexual violence and violence towards intimate partners. The VRAG relies on an actuarial scoring method using a number of scored items as input. It typically consists of 12 items that are defined in detail and are scored by the assessor positively or inversely:

1 Living with both parents to the age of 16
2 Elementary school maladjustment
3 History of alcohol problems
4 Marital status (at the time of or prior to index offence)
5 Criminal history score for nonviolent offences prior to the index offence
6 Failure on prior conditional release (includes parole or probation violation or revocation, failure to comply, bail violation, and any new arrest while on conditional release)
7 Age at index offence
8 Victim injury (for index offence; the most serious is scored)
9 Any female victim (for index offence)
10 Meets DSM criteria for any personality disorder (must be made by appropriately licensed or certified professional)
11 Meets DSM criteria for schizophrenia (must be made by appropriately licensed or certified professional)
12 Psychopathy checklist (PCL) score (if available)

It can be seen to differ from the OGRS-3 and to a large extent the Static-99 in the nature of these risk factors, some of which involve dynamic or changeable characteristics, requiring skilled assessment. It is also perhaps worth highlighting that one item, the PCL, is itself a detailed clinical assessment involving the assessment and scoring of the individual over 20 areas proposed as describing the construct of 'psychopathy' (Thomson, 2021). This aspect of the VRAG has been modified in the later revised version that does not require full completion of this assessment, but, instead, relies on the facet of this, which is primarily focused on prior criminal behaviours as an input. Individuals are scored numerically and allocated to different risk categories based on this score. In turn, these allocations provide a probability of recidivism over a given time frame, here seven or ten years.

The psychometric properties are claimed to be relatively good for the VRAG assessment. The initial development of this RAI is reported to have involved two independent assessors, who rated a sample of 20 cases. A Pearson correlation coefficient was calculated, to estimate agreement between the assessors, which was reported as 0.90 (Harris, Rice and Quinsey, 1993). The standard error of measurement was reported to be 4.1, equating to approximately half the width of one of the VRAG's descriptive categories for risk (curiously referred to as 'bins'). The assessment developers reported that the calculated 95% confidence intervals became wider as the scores on the VRAG increased but that the probability of the evaluations differing here by one or more categories, was very low. Subsequent independent studies have though yielded rather more mixed results. A study by Edens, Penson, Ruchensky et al. (2016) for example, reported an ICC of 0.66 between paired assessors, with individuals being placed in the same risk category in 68% of cases.

The validity of the VRAG has typically been reported using the AUC statistic and here the developers reported a value of 0.76 for violent recidivism. A further 35 studies that did not have overlapping samples reported a similar value of 0.72 (Rice and Harris, 2005). The VRAG developers also reported a good level of generalisation for the VRAG, although sometimes with smaller effect sizes across different types of violent outcomes, very serious violence, self-reported violence, general recidivism and time to failure (Quinsey, Harris, Rice and Cormier, 2006). Here, as well, independent studies have yielded more mixed results in terms of lower AUC estimates of 0.66 and poorer levels of generalisation (Coid, Yang, Ullrich et al., 2009; Yang, Wong and Coid, 2010).

The Case for Using Actuarial and Algorithmic RAIs

It seems fair to say that arguments in favour of this type of RAI rest on the central hypothesis that the formal combination of data performs significantly better than approaches based on human judgement (Meehl, 1954; Dawes, Faust and Meehl, 1989). This idea has been evident across many different fields and has been the subject of often heated debate. Many of the counter arguments posed against this view have been criticised for misunderstanding the method, such as conflating data gathering and data combination. Other critiques have been seen as largely self-serving ways to justify work that, whilst well rewarded, was largely or even wholly pointless. Advocates of this approach have stressed that the prediction schemes used should be the ones that introduce the smallest error for each individual (Meehl, 1996). In a review paper, Grove (2005) summarises this view, which requires a process of maximising expected utility, addressing in turn professional requirements to maximise the benefits and minimise the harms around decisions. In choosing methods with lower levels of utility, it is argued, practitioners would be directly cutting across this fundamental ethical requirement (Meehl, 1956; Grove, 2005).

The actuarial and algorithmic approaches outlined above serve to highlight a number of the inherent strengths and weaknesses. Given adequate development, they tend to be relatively easy to score, once the relevant data has been gathered. A strongly argued position in favour of this approach is that they can be more effective than often more resource-intensive alternatives. In relation to areas such as policing and sentencing, use is stressed as a better way to deploy limited resources as well as being fairer. Time and effort are focused, according to this viewpoint, on those places where they are needed, such as places where crime is more likely. Similarly, those who do not need to be imprisoned on grounds of risk can be diverted towards community sentences. More broadly, rationality, logic and the utility of these methods is seen as providing the basis for their wider use. The power of algorithmic methods in this respect is vividly illustrated by their use in large-scale computing applications using the internet. Here, they have been able to process billions of data points to guide predictions at relatively low cost, greatly improving on the power of early actuarial methods. However, arguments equating this method with cost-effectiveness are somewhat undercut by the form of RAIs used in forensic practice. It is the case that some RAIs of this type fit the description of being highly cost-effective, with the OGRS-3 providing an example of an algorithmic RAI that combines routinely gathered information and uses computing power to process this quickly. However, RAIs like the VRAG and VRAG-R contrast markedly with this, showing that some RAIs of this type are neither cheap nor quick to use, involving the collection of large amounts of specific data. These may in fact be more resource-intensive than alternative methods. The use of methods such as the 'Heat List' and its subsequent revisions in policing, may also in practice impose additional demands on police staff, necessitating formal assessments that they would not otherwise complete.

However, once the data to be input has been gathered, RAIs of this type have in common a reliance on the formal combination of this. Taking the algorithm for the OGRS-3, this yields numerical values for the likelihood of reconviction, in much the same way that an actuary might calculate an insurance premium. Both are based on numerical estimates of risk of an adverse event, a criminal offence or an insurance claim, based on various characteristics. Such values and the data they are based on, it is argued, are generally clear and can be open to scrutiny. When an individual is described as 'high' risk using RAI like the OGRS-3 or VRAG-R, this has a clear meaning, with high levels of inter-subjective agreement. Advocates of actuarial and algorithmic methods stress that, as a function of this transparency, any biases can be identified and corrected much more easily than the biases in human judgement, which often remain hidden.

Conclusion

Actuarial and algorithmic RAIs involve the application of formal analysis to defined risk and protective factors and indicators. They have been widely applied across a range of forensic practice, from policing to conditional release decision-making. Advocates argue that they provide a powerful means of forming probabilistic risk assessments that can be highly reliable and valid: doing this in a fairer way.

Current Practice in Risk Structured Clinical Judgement Approaches

4

Structured clinical judgement approaches to risk assessment are often also described as structured professional judgement, protocol-based or checklist risk assessment instruments (RAIs). Currently, they provide the main alternative approach to algorithmic RAIs in forensic practice and have some similarities to these RAIs, as well as a number of fundamental differences. Essentially, they are checklists that provide varying degrees of structure, that can be used by forensic practitioners to aid in the assessment of risk. They involve a process of recording information about pre-defined items, increasingly with the option to add additional, individually tailored items. These items are included on the basis of being thought to be associated with a given event and are used in an effort to more accurately predict these defined outcomes. The events that are the focus of prediction are typically adverse events, for example, incidents of sexual violence. However, this is not a fundamental requirement and assessing the likelihood of positive events, or framing assessment in terms of factors and indicators that reduce risk, is equally possible although this has been less common. This later approach has been seen to a limited extent in forensic practice, with one example of this being the structured assessment of protective factors (SAPROF) for violence (de Vries Robbé, de Vogel and de Spa, 2011). However, a majority of checklist RAIs have retained a focus on adverse events, using a mix of items, felt to be risk factors and risk indicators, to yield probabilistic estimates of risk.

Individual checklist RAIs vary significantly in terms of the type and amount of information gathered as well as the extent to which this process is structured and constrained for assessors. By definition though, all RAIs of this kind provide structure and requirements for the minimum of what is to be considered.

DOI: 10.4324/9781003108665-5

Most also provide operationalised definitions around the coding of individual items and of probabilistic risk categories. Some may also include the results of actuarial or algorithmic assessments within their structure and, as with some of these RAIs, checklist-based RAIs may also include detailed clinical assessments as items.

The structured checklist approach differs from actuarial and algorithmic methods in a number of ways. One fundamental difference is the way in which this information is treated. The process of collecting information may often be similar for the two types of RAI and indeed many of the items included may be the same or overlapping. However, once the information is gathered, algorithmic RAIs combine this using some kind of formal approach, typically based on inferential statistics. Commonly, in forensic practice, all of the data collected is subject to a form of regression analysis that looks in a systematic way at covariance. Structured checklist RAIs by contrast, involve the assessor combining the information to derive their own probabilistic estimates. This may involve differing levels of guidance on how to do this but the assessor, ultimately, retains the flexibility to determine their own estimate of likelihood. In addition, RAIs of this type have increasingly allowed assessors greater flexibility to include additional items or information, something that is not possible with algorithmic RAIs. Accordingly, structured checklist RAIs do not give final numeric estimates of risk and confidence ranges for these. They do involve probabilistic assessments of risk for a given event or outcome. However, these are qualitative estimates, more closely aligned with the conceptions of legal probability discussed by Keynes (1921). This typically involves assigning a verbal description of probability such as 'high', 'low' or 'moderate to high', with empirical evidence seen as potentially contributing to but not determining such estimates of risk. Structured checklist RAIs also differ from actuarial or algorithmic assessments by incorporating qualitative assessment of the nature of more than one outcome, such as the likely severity and assessed imminence of events.

The use of structured checklist RAIs has largely displaced expert clinical assessments and actuarial or algorithmic RAIs as the dominant methodology in many areas of forensic practice. This seems in part a function of these RAIs being seen as more flexible and also more acceptable to practitioners and decision-makers, compared with clinical judgement or the use of algorithmic approaches. Use has progressively expanded into policing and crime prevention, criminal and civil legal settings and correctional settings. Individual checklist RAIs have been developed to inform assessment of risk, across a wide and growing range of areas. Some recent efforts have been made to deal with this rapid growth by reviewing these RAIs in terms of the quality of development, with the aim of ensuring basic quality standards. An example of this is given by the Scottish Government that established a body to review RAIs in this way (Risk Management Authority, 2016). This body was in many respects intended to be an analogue of review bodies set up to consider efficacy and cost considerations in areas such as pharmaceutical and healthcare products. Such reviews have suggested dramatic growth in the availability of checklist RAIs, with recent suggestions of more than 400 (and growing) being available (Scurich, 2016). However, there is extensive overlap here, with many of these RAIs covering similar areas. Although the availability of checklist RAIs has progressively expanded into new areas, most recently with application of the method in efforts to assess the risk of terrorist events motivated by religious or political beliefs (Smith, 2018).

The use of checklist RAIs in forensic practice is based on the fundamental idea that people are not good at making accurate decisions about risk unaided. Something that is argued to extend to experts as much as non-expert judges. This is generally common ground with advocates of algorithmic RAIs: the solutions proposed, however, are very different. In the use of checklist RAIs, the role of providing structure in the gathering of information is central to the method. This is seen as improving accuracy and, in the absence of such a structure, it is suggested that the reliability of assessments will tend to be poor. This in turn will negatively impact on the validity of any assessment. Here a curious distinction is sometimes drawn between this use of checklists and what is misleadingly termed 'unstructured clinical assessment'. A more appropriate distinction might be between the different forms of structure used and how constrained or unconstrained these are, in relation to data gathering and use in forming probabilistic risk assessments (Monahan and Skeem, 2016).

Structured checklist RAIs do vary in the extent of the structure and guidance provided for gathering information and estimating the likelihood of outcomes. All, however, retain a degree of flexibility. As noted, this has increasingly taken the form of allowing consideration of additional information but even where this is not the case, the method allows high levels of flexibility in the manner that information can be evaluated and integrated to reach probabilistic estimates of risk. This flexibility is seen by advocates of the approach as a fundamental strength. One of the arguments for this view has been that this addresses a major weakness of actuarial or algorithmic RAIs. This concerns the well-recognised problem of low-frequency high impact events. It is widely recognised that these are a significant problem for such RAIs and that formal analysis does not generally deal well with these. The flexibility of structured checklist RAIs by contrast means that they do have the ability to consider such events. In forensic practice, this might include examples such as offenders with high actuarial risk of violence towards others, who go on to develop severely debilitating illnesses, removing their capacity to exhibit particular risks. Here, actuarial or algorithmic RAIs will typically suggest similar levels of risk, at odds with the individual case characteristics. Checklist RAIs can much more easily accommodate information of this kind.

As well as providing flexibility, advocates of checklist RAIs tend to stress that they provide a clear focus on risk factors and indicators, based on evidence. By directing practitioners to look at these factors and not on extraneous information, the method is argued to produce more accurate predictions than would otherwise be achieved. To take an illustrative example, the idea is that by considering multiple correlates of parental violence towards children, it will be possible to say which parents are more likely to commit serious assaults. The combination and weightings of these correlates is not done using formal logic such as inferential statistical analyses but is undertaken by the assessor. This integration is not complicated by factors and indicators uncorrelated with the outcome of concern and which may generate errors or bias in the process.

Claims of this kind have led to a number of debates about whether checklist RAIs perform better or worse than actuarial or algorithmic RAIs. Within forensic practice this has generally focused on the question of which form of probabilistic risk assessment is more accurate: often characterised as a 'clinical' versus 'actuarial' debate. The measure of success here has often been seen in terms of which approach performs best using statistical measures such as the Area Under the Curve (AUC) statistic to arbitrate. Advocates of using formal methods to integrate the data on risk have generally been unimpressed by the development of structured judgement RAIs and seeing them as open to the same failings as unconstrained expert judgements. The use of checklist RAIs is criticised as, at best, only partially correcting for this and so being inferior to the use of methods based on formal analysis. In addition, attention has been drawn to the fact that even simple algorithms can achieve comparable, or greater, levels of accuracy than elaborate structured checklist RAIs (Grove, 2005). In response, advocates of checklist RAIs have stressed the greater flexibility, capacity to focus on individual needs and characteristics and ability to focus risk treatment that the method gives (Andrews and Bonta, 2007).

Checklist RAIs have been developed significantly over time. These changes have been described by advocates of the checklist approach using a language of 'new generations' of assessment. Here 'first generation' has been used to refer to assessments based on unconstrained and unaided human judgement. The 'second generation' of RAIs is described as involving early methods that used fixed characteristics of individuals, to develop predictive algorithms. Early predictors used in decision-making for parole stand out as a clear example here. The 'third generation' refers to assessments that began to incorporate assessment of needs as well as seeking to predict risk and, in doing this, introduced the consideration of changeable characteristics. These have been largely replaced by 'fourth generation' RAIs that have expanded the extent of individual assessments, based on a mix of fixed and changeable risk factors and indicators. The 'fifth generation' of RAIs are those that have begun to automate the process of assessment, using machine learning and artificial intelligence to try to predict events in real time (Garrett and Monahan, 2020). It remains unclear how far these changes have in fact improved on the results obtained from the much simpler RAIs used earlier (Kroner, Mills and Reddon, 2005).

Use in Practice

Arguably the development and application of checklist RAIs lagged behind that of algorithm-based approaches. It has, however, seen dramatic growth in recent years, with the use of checklists RAIs increasingly displacing expert assessments and algorithmic RAIs in day-to-day practice. These structured checklists appear to have developed initially in the less contentious area of selection for treatment, identifying higher risk individuals who may be more likely to benefit from particular interventions. As with algorithmic RAIs, many were initially developed to more accurately identify those felt to be in need of treatment linked to mental ill-health and dangerousness (Cocozza and Steadman, 1978). As with algorithmic RAIs, they have also seen a progressive extension in use, with the methodology now commonly seen across wide areas of forensic practice. Much of this can be described by looking at three broad areas: policing, sentencing and conditional release and decision-making in relation to risk treatment. Development of checklist RAIs in these areas have been undertaken by a wide range of organisations, including academic, state and commercial providers. This has resulted in a large amount of duplication, with competing RAIs often addressing the same areas of risk. However, a relatively small number of RAIs are seen regularly and have become increasingly dominant in an increasingly commercial model of delivery. Some of these are used here to illustrate current practice.

Policing

Checklist RAIs have largely been used in policing and crime prevention to predict those most likely to offend and those most likely to be victims of crime. The use of checklist RAIs to do this has tended to focus on more serious forms of criminal behaviour, often based on legal categories of offence. The reason for this appears largely to be the result of the costs of administration, with the method tending to be more resource-intensive than algorithmic approaches. Examples of the areas where checklist RAIs have been used would include assessments of risk for family violence, intimate partner violence and terrorism offences.

Taking the example of violence towards intimate partners, this is an area where police services have often faced serious criticisms. The spousal assault risk assessment (SARA) now in its third revision (SARA 3) is a checklist RAI developed in Canada. The SARA was described as assessing the risk of violence towards spouses or intimate partners and as being suitable for use by a wide range of practitioners (Kropp and Hart, 2015). The assessment has undergone a number of major revisions since its inception, resulting in the current version. In addition, shortened versions of the SARA were developed, leading to a piloting of a specific police version of the SARA and the development of the brief spousal assault form for the evaluation of risk abbreviated as the B-SAFER (Kropp, Hart and Belfrage, 2020). This checklist RAI was designed for more rapid use, typically by staff working in policing or community settings, where there was unlikely to be time to complete full SARA assessments.

The SARA 3 involves a six-step process for completion and is designed to be used by experienced assessors. It is now routinely used in correctional settings, primarily by probation officers. The B-SAFER version is designed to be suited to a wider range of practitioners (Storey and Strand, 2013). Assessors using the SARA 3 should, according to the developers, have experience of both risk assessment and the evidence base on intimate partner violence to use these RAIs. Some areas of assessment are also explicitly limited to those with relevant mental health experience and training. The six steps involved in completing the SARA are as follows:

1. Identification of perpetrators and victims (potential victims).
2. Assessment of risk factors.
3. Assessment of the relevance of risk factors.
4. An outline of distinct risk scenarios.
5. A description of management plans.
6. Conclusions with case priority level, risk of serious physical harm, imminence, other risks and case review requirements being set out.

There are 24 'risk factors' identified within step two of the process, and these are divided into three broad groups, covering the nature of the violence, the characteristics of the person being assessed and the characteristics of any potential victims. Each of these items is given an operational definition set out in manual form. The B-SAFER reduces this down to consideration of seven 'risk factors':

1. History of spousal violence
2. Life-threatening spousal violence
3. Escalation of spousal violence
4. Attitudes supportive of spousal violence

5   General anti-social behaviour
6   Failure to obey court orders
7   Mental disorder

This reduction is reported to have followed an analysis of the redundancy in risk factors conducted in Scotland but involving 1,768 men on probation and 1,010 offenders detained in Canadian federal prisons. Using exploratory and confirmatory analysis, the original risk factors were reduced to the seven listed above. These were described as adequately modelling the larger group of factors. The developers also went on to pilot test a police version of the SARA in Sweden and from this developed a ten-item version of the B-SAFER, covering ten areas divided into two sections (Kropp, Hart and Belfrage, 2020). The first section addressed items linked to 'spousal assault':

1   Serious physical/sexual violence
2   Serious violent threats, ideation or intent
3   Escalation of physical/sexual violence or threats/ideation/intent
4   Violations of criminal or civil court orders
5   Negative attitudes about spousal assault
    The second addressed 'psychosocial adjustment':
6   Other serious criminality
7   Relationship problems
8   Employment and/or financial problems
9   Substance abuse
10 Mental disorder

Each of the factors within the SARA or B-SAFER checklist RAIs are evaluated in the same manner as being 'present', 'possibly or partially present' or 'absent'. They may also be omitted if there is a lack of adequate information. Items are assessed and coded for current presentation and historic presence of each area. The final step of the SARA assessment involves drawing on the evaluation of these items to reach conclusions about the level of what is termed 'case priority' but really seems to refer to risk of violence towards intimate partners. This probabilistic assessment of risk is qualitatively rated as 'high', 'moderate' or 'low' as is the potential severity and imminence of risk. There is also provision to identify other risks and to specify review and management arrangements. For the B-SAFER, this is modified to simplify completion and case priority is assessed as 'high/urgent', 'moderate/elevated' or 'low/routine', with the assessment of likelihood of life-threatening violence and imminence coded in the same manner. The assessment also has a greater focus on immediate issues around potential victim safety.

Information on the psychometric properties of the SARA 3 framework and B-SAFER is limited. As with the other checklist RAIs, the regular revisions to the framework have meant that evaluation data on new versions has tended, at least initially, to be provided by the developers. Independent evaluation has inevitably lagged behind each revision. As a result, there tends to be more information on earlier versions, than on current versions of checklist RAIs. The SARA and B-SAFER assessments are similar in this respect, with the reliability of the second revision of the SARA being reported as an intra class correlation (ICC) of 0.68 (in relation to general violence assessment) and 0.87 (for intimate partner violence). The overall level of agreement between assessors was reported to be 0.67 (Kropp and Hart, 2000). The ICC values for the SARA in its current third revision are reported in a small sample study of 30 cases by Ryan (2010). Here, this was reported to be a rather poor 0.40 for the evaluation of case priority, 0.68 for serious physical harm and 0.41 for the imminence of violence: although the small sample sizes mean that these correlations need to be treated with considerable caution.

Data on the predictive validity of the SARA in its current form is also limited and much of the data has related to concurrent validity, essentially correlating the results of the current version with other similar RAIs. The predictive validity of the earlier SARA 2 assessment has though been reported, based on five studies, which included a total of 992 cases. This suggested an AUC of 0.67 (Kropp and Hart, 2000). An independent study by Williams and Houghton (2004) found a marginally lower AUC value of 0.65 for intimate partner violence, based on recidivism in a sample of 434 cases. A small-scale study of 88 offenders also looked at this over an extended follow-up. The AUC statistic was reported to be 0.59 at 12-month follow-up and 0.63 at two years and 0.65 at five years (Grann and Wedin, 2002). Methodological issues again mean that these results need to be treated with caution. The studies taken as a whole, however, suggest that this RAI improved on random chance but not by a large amount. The predictive accuracy of the B-SAFER total score on intimate partner violence has been assessed and here a rather better AUC of 0.70 has been reported by the developers (Storey, Kropp, Hart et al., 2014).

The B-SAFER has gone on to be used in policing cases of intimate partner violence internationally and this has been subject to some independent research. Here the results have been less positive than those reported by the developers, with the risk and victim vulnerability factors reported as only minor contributors to risk assessments. The predictive validity of the assessment in Sweden was reported to be 'low' with an AUC of 0.55 for repeat incidents of intimate partner violence (Svalin, 2018). In addition, the protective actions identified when using the B-SAFER were frequently not put in place and where they were, these did not appear effective in preventing repetition. The reasons for these negative findings were not clear but the researchers stressed the role and importance of effective training in improving the overall police approach to intimate partner violence, rather than simply seeking to predict risk (Svalin, Mellgren, Torstensson Levander and Levander, 2018).

Sentencing and Conditional Release

The risk of sexual violence protocol (RSVP) is a checklist RAI for the assessment of risk of 'sexual violence'. It is routinely used to inform sentencing and conditional release decisions that apply to those convicted of offences involving sexual violence. This RAI comprises six steps that form the assessment process, which are similar to those involved in the SARA 3. A total of 22 'risk factors' for sexual violence are scored. These cover five broad areas: sexual violence history, psychosocial adjustment, mental disorder, social adjustment and manageability. The assessment also incorporates a detailed clinical assessment, in the form of the psychopathy checklist revised (PCL-R) or psychopathy checklist screening version (PCL-SV) as an individual item (Pouls and Jeandarme, 2014). This assessment, addresses the concept of 'psychopathy', characterised as a maladaptive pattern of functioning associated with a lack of empathy, little concern for others and high levels of anti-social behaviours. A high score on this assessment is seen as a risk factor for sexual violence. The RSVP was originally developed in the context of mental health services and, arguably, it retains a strong emphasis on risk treatment issues.

Each of the factors are evaluated as being 'present', 'possibly or partially present' or 'absent'. Some items may also be coded provisionally or omitted if there is a lack of adequate information or the assessors lack relevant experience to confidently assess an area. Items are assessed and coded for current presentation, historic presence and future relevance of each area. The final step of the RSVP assessment involves conclusions about the level of 'case priority' in relation to sexual violence. This can be rated qualitatively as 'high/urgent', 'moderate/elevated' or 'low/routine'; with risk of serious physical harm being rated as 'high', 'moderate' or 'low'. The assessment also includes consideration of whether immediate action is required, other risks are present and what case review requirements should be put in place.

There is limited evidence around the reliability of the RSVP, but a review was provided by Hart and Boer (2014), which summarised published and unpublished studies examining inter-rater reliability. Based on a sample of 50 high-risk convicted sexual offenders under community supervision, they report high inter-rater reliability for two assessors with an ICC for overall case priority of 0.92 (Watt, Hart, Wilson et al., 2006). Another study looked at the reliability of ratings by two assessors of 90 male adult convicted sex offenders, who had completed community-based psychosocial treatment work in Canada. Here the inter-rater reliability for items ranged from 0.62 to 0.92 with a median of 0.84. The ICC1 statistic for agreement on case priority is given as 0.75, with the risk of serious harm being 0.85 and need for immediate action being 0.81 (Watt and Jackson, 2008; Jackson, 2016).

There is also some information about the predictive validity of the RSVP framework. One study, for example, looked at predictive validity of this RAI in a group of 109 identified offenders, who were followed up for a period of between six months and five years (with an average follow-up of 3¼ years). Here, the results were described by the authors as mixed. The RSVP case priority level showed predictive value for sexual recidivism when using a survival analysis. The total scores and summary risk ratings were also reported to have predicted serious and violent offending (Darjee, Russel, Forrest et al., 2016). Using the AUC statistic, it was reported that the RSVP did not effectively predict sexual reoffending, although it was suggested that this may have been moderated by the positive effects of those assessed undertaking sex offender treatment work (Jackson, 2016). Such results are of course complicated by the very low levels of conviction for sexual violence, reflecting the long-known fact that use of convictions to test how effectively sexual violence was predicted needs to be treated with great caution (Abel, Becker, Mittelman et al., 1987; Towl and Walker, 2019).

Risk Treatment

Checklist RAIs are now widely used in forensic practice to allocate individuals to various forms of risk treatment. Taking the example of violence here, those assessed as 'high' risk would tend to be directed towards interventions felt to be useful in reducing the risk of violent reoffending. The commonly used Historic and Clinical Risk 20 assessment is used here as an example. This assessment is currently in its third revision (HCR-20 V3) (Douglas, Hart, Webster and Belfrage, 2013). This checklist RAI is routinely used to determine allocation to interventions, such as anger management or problem-solving skills work, across health, social care, correctional and other settings. The HCR-20 assessments were initially developed to evaluate the risk of violence in mental health settings in Canada.

The format of the HCR-20 V3 is similar to the two examples already given above. The assessment is made up of 20 items, felt to be associated with the risk of future violence. These are divided into three broad categories: historic, clinical and risk related. The assessment is weighted towards consideration of historic items and there are ten items within this category, whereas there are five each under the clinical and risk sections. The historic items are described as largely 'static' in nature and address previous violence, anti-social behaviour, relationships, unemployment, substance abuse, major mental disorder, personality disorder, trauma, violent attitudes and previous responses to treatment and supervision. Each item is rated as being present, possibly or partially present, absent or not determinable on the basis of the available information. In turn, each of these items are assessed for relevance and rated as either 'low', 'moderate', 'high' or this can be omitted if it cannot be determined. The clinical section of the assessment is concerned with areas described as 'dynamic' being open to change over time or in response to various forms of treatment. These include insight, violent ideation or intent, symptoms of mental disorder, instability and current treatment response. The risk section of the assessment is concerned with aspects relating to how manageable the person may be in different settings and addresses the quality to professional services, living situation, personal support, likely response to supervision and treatment and tendency to experience stress and cope poorly. Both the clinical and risk sections of this structured checklist RAI are scored in the same manner as the history section. In turn, this leads to an overall assessment of case priority for violence being qualitatively described as 'low', 'moderate' or 'high'. Assessors also complete similar assessments in relation to the severity and imminence of violence and identify appropriate review arrangements.

As with the other current frameworks, information is limited about the psychometric properties of the HCR-20 V3, with much more information available for the earlier versions. A study by Belfrage and Douglas (2012) reported that, based on a sample of 35 forensic mental health patients in Sweden, the framework reported to show an excellent level of reliability. The ICC for the historical items was reported to be 0.94, with lower levels for the clinical (0.86) and risk outside an institution (0.75) assessment. A later study of 20 patients by Doyle, Shaw and Coid (2013) found ICC values of 0.72, 0.69 and 0.76 respectively.

Information around the predictive validity of the current version of the HCR-20 is also limited and has tended to rely on experimental designs using historical samples, to model the performance of the assessment. Using this methodology for a sample of 86 forensic mental health patients in the Netherlands, and using a draft version of the HCR-20 V3, the AUC statistic was calculated to be 0.67 at three years post release and 0.77 at one year (de Vries Robbé and de Vogel, 2010). This was described as being in the moderate to large range. A larger prospective study of 387 forensic mental health patients, looked at a one-year cohort of those released from medium secure hospital settings in England and Wales (n = 387). This group was followed up at 6 and 12 months and again a draft version of the HCR-20 V3 was used. At 12 months, the AUC values were reported to be 0.70 for the whole scale and 0.63, 0.70 and 0.63 for the historic, clinical and risk sub-scales respectively. A logistic regression analysis was conducted, and this suggested that the assessment was significantly predictive at 6 and 12 months, even when controlling for age and gender (Doyle, Shaw and Coid, 2013).

The Case for Using Checklist RAIs

A number of reasons have been put forward for the use of checklist RAIs. As with algorithm-based RAIs, they are predicated on the idea that clinicians are not good at assessing risk when they do so in an unconstrained way. Proponents of structured checklist RAIs though have rejected the solution used in algorithmic methods, where human decision is replaced by the application of some kind of formal analysis, normally the use of inferential statistics. A different solution to this difficulty is offered, by advocates of structured checklists, where the use of structure is focused on the information that is gathered and the way in which this is judged by assessors. Advocates of this method have argued that this structuring of data gathering and guidance around the way that this is integrated provides significant gains. The constraints placed on data gathering mean that the levels of agreement between assessors are better. They are also argued to keep assessors focused on risk factors and indicators, rather than extraneous information. In combination, this is argued to significantly improve the accuracy of probabilistic risk assessments.

A further advantage suggested for checklist RAIs runs somewhat counter to the stress on the advantages of consistency touched on above. The flexibility of the approach has also been stressed as a significant advantage over algorithmic RAIs. Most checklist RAIs allow flexibility in the gathering of information, although the extent of this varies across assessments. This allows for the addition of new risk factors or indicators, and this is argued to have clinical utility by avoiding the problems associated with restricting assessors to a completely fixed checklist of items. Two primary gains can be seen as possible results of this. It can provide a means of dealing with a range of different people and settings and not simply those involved in the assessment development. These can be accommodated simply by the addition of relevant areas to the primary framework. A checklist RAI to look at the risk of suicide in prisons in England can then be adapted for use in prisons in Northern Ireland, New York or indeed anywhere else by the addition of risk items informed by the assessor's judgement. Second, the flexibility of checklist RAIs has been proposed as a means of dealing with the problem posed by low-frequency high-impact events. These are a well-recognised problem afflicting algorithmic approaches (Taleb, 2015; Fischbacher-Smith, 2016). They relate to rare events that may have a high impact on individual cases, and here it is suggested the method performs better than algorithm-based approaches. Where such events are evident, they can simply be included by assessors as additional information and factored into the evaluation of probability. The ability to resolve this known difficulty has been seen as an important advantage for checklist RAIs.

Many of these RAIs began simply as lists of risk factors and indicators. The items used tended to be relatively easy to gather and code based on brief operational definitions. In many respects, they looked very much like algorithmic RAIs that they competed with. However, they are fundamentally different. The results of checklist RAIs are integrated using human judgement. Subsequent iterations of this method have seen these assessments becoming increasingly elaborate, covering more items and gathering more information. This has been argued to be a way to incorporate developments in treatment and likely response to treatment, moving beyond probabilistic risk assessment and into risk treatment and management. Some have also been extended to include structured hypothesis generation, with assessors developing hypothetical scenarios around future behaviour. Changes such as these are reflective of developments in current practice. They may be seen as improving the accuracy of risk assessment (Andrews, Bonta and Wormith, 2006; Austin, Coleman, Peyton and Johnson, 2003). The extent to which these changes have resulted in any gains compared with earlier and simpler checklist approaches is, however, unclear.

Conclusion

Checklist RAIs involve the operational definition of a number of risk and protective factors and indicators. These are then integrated by assessors to yield probabilistic estimates of risk. This method has increasingly displaced the use of clinical assessment and algorithmic RAIs across many areas of forensic practice. These assessments have become progressively more complex. Advocates see the method as a powerful and more flexible alternative to algorithmic methods of risk assessment.

Critiques of Current Practice

Socio-Legal Perspectives

5

The influence of risk in forensic practice can be seen to have risen and fallen significantly over time, with early enthusiasm for risk-based approaches in areas of civil and criminal law and utilitarian philosophical ideas being displaced by ideas of retribution and deterrence. This has often reflected changes, nationally and internationally, in mental health and corrections policy. Resurgence of ideas of risk in forensic settings appears to have in large part been a reflection of these wider trends, with risk becoming an increasingly central concept across many areas. Development in science and technology has generated many novel risks that needed to be dealt with and, in parallel, led to dramatic improvements in the ability to measure and cope with these. Questions of risk have now become central across many areas of the social and natural sciences and the technologies that derive from them. Notions of risk are now intrinsic to areas as diverse as the working of financial institutions, engineering, biology, atmospheric physics and climate change. As social and technical structures have become more complex, the sense that the dangers inherent in them need to be assessed and reduced has continued to increase. Perhaps the most significant parallel for forensic practice has been developments in the biological sciences in general and medicine, in particular. Here questions of risk have increasingly supplemented, or even supplanted, notions of diagnosis and treatment. Ideas of people being at 'high risk' of disease are now routine in a way that would likely have surprised earlier generations of physicians and surgeons.

Concern with questions of risk leads on logically to a need to be able to produce estimates of likelihood. Initially, this was based, often of necessity, on unconstrained human judgements made by 'experts', a method often described as 'clinical' judgement. For novel risks, there is no alternative to this, and it is the way in which such risks come to be understood, addressed and in turn become routine. To take an engineering example of this, in the 18th century, it was not known how to safely build bridges covering very wide spans. A number of distinguished engineers, working from first principles, gradually learned how to do this using suspension bridges, although not without considerable costs in failed attempts. The principles of building this kind of bridge safely are now well understood and routinely applied by engineers, based on well-established models, drawing on areas such as mathematics, mechanics and materials science. These models enable the risks involved to be estimated accurately and reduced systematically, making failures in this area rare.

In forensic practice, experts often appeared, like the 18th-century engineers, to be poor at assessing risks. Large differences between expert assessors were evident and poor predictions of risk were often seen and could be demonstrated experimentally (Meehl, 1954). This led on to concerted efforts to improve performance and, as seen earlier, this has involved the adoption of methods that have increasingly constrained individual judgements about risk. A variety of structured methods of assessing risk have been developed to reduce the level of disagreement between assessors and produce more accurate estimates than unconstrained judgements. A wide array of risk assessment instruments (RAIs) have been developed, with an increasing focus on broad categories of risks, some of which have been described in earlier chapters. A wide variety of RAIs have seen use in forensic practice and this has included use in mental health settings, courts, policing, crime prevention, child protection, corrections and others. A large and growing number of these RAIs have been developed and marketed for use, making comprehensive coverage of these impractical. Many though overlap in terms of the risk concerned, content and approach. In looking at this, a few relatively well-known examples from current forensic practice have been picked, from a wide range of similar instruments. These have been chosen to help explain key concerns and are used to illustrate legal and social policy criticisms. This includes the Historical and Clinical Risk 20 (HCR-20) (Douglas, Guy, Reeves and Weir, 2005): Oxford Risk of Recidivism (OxRec) (Braverman, Doernberg, Runge and Howard, 2016): Chicago Police Department predictive policing pilot / 'heat' list (Saunders, Hunt and Hollywood, 2016); the policing algorithm Beware (Robinson, 2017); Correctional Offender Management Profiling for Alternate Sanctions (COMPAS) (Washington, 2018) and the Level of Service Inventory Revised (LSI-R) (Fass, Heilbrun, DeMatteo and Fretz, 2008). The way that these and other RAIs have been used in forensic practice has given rise to a large number of legitimate challenges and criticisms, from what can generally be characterised as socio-legal perspectives. This of course covers a lot of ground and includes critiques of many of the ideas and assumptions that underpin current practice as well as the ways that RAIs have been used in practice. In an effort to make the discussion of these clearer and more coherent, these have been broken down into three, potentially overlapping, areas: fairness, accuracy and impact.

Fairness

Legal notions of 'fit' go to the heart of fairness and concern how well any given evidence fits the legal question or questions being addressed. This is seen as an important aspect of fairness, although the concept goes beyond this and certainly also involves issues of accuracy and utility. Using evidence that does not fit the question well is seen to be fundamentally unfair. In addition to 'fit', the idea of fairness also extends into questions of systemic biases in assessment of risk. In these respects, the current use of RAIs in forensic practice has raised many questions, from theoretical to highly practical concerns.

The most fundamental question raised about fairness is perhaps whether it is right to punish people for what they might do, rather than what they have done. Using notions of risk, operationalised through the use of RAIs, introduces just this kind of probabilistic thinking into legal decision-making. At a technical level, the accuracy of RAIs is a legitimate concern. If these were 100% accurate, then such a concern would still arise but would be easier to address. Evidently though, this is not the case. In essence, RAIs provide estimates of likelihood and whether the claims made by assessment developers are justified or not, they do not reach or even approach perfect accuracy. This imprecision in turn gives rise to questions about the utility of RAIs, with concerns about whether the value in using these methods justifies the costs. In considering this, a number of unintended effects arising from the use of RAIs have been raised, including the impacts on wider policy and practice as well as on the individuals who may be the subject of these RAIs.

Impacts from using concepts of risk can be both positive and negative but the way in which current practice has developed, as well as the systemic changes made, has raised concerns. Worryingly, such a change has often taken place in the absence of any adequate public discussion and debate, as part of an increasingly market-based system of development and implementation. Here, the way RAIs are used to answer legal questions has been criticised for often failing to adequately meet fundamental legal requirements. For example, it has been suggested by Slobogin (2017, 2018) that they need to address the legal issue at stake and lead on to the least restrictive means of achieving a particular goal, such as suggesting less severe forms of risk treatment. It is far from clear that such requirements are being met in many areas of forensic practice.

Ideas of fairness are a central tenet of legal thinking and cannot be adequately captured at a conceptual level in statistical terms. This has often been neglected in the work developing RAIs, where technical considerations often appear to have taken precedence over other considerations. Ethical and policy concerns often appear to have been neglected or to be, at best, secondary considerations here. Questions of fairness have rarely been made explicit. There is, however, a substantial body of scholarship and research as well as a wide range of views evident in this area. These extend from arguments in favour of purely retributive models of justice, through to advocacy of utilitarian approaches, with debates often focused on ideas such as the dignity of the person and human rights. These are clearly distinct from but related to discrimination and are of central importance in forensic practice. The idea of dignity of the person, as it applies to legal punishment, can be seen in a widely used quotation from a legal philosopher and advocate of retribution-based punishments: "[u]nless the person actually made the wrongful choice he was predicted to make, he ought not to be condemned for that choice – and hence should not suffer punishment for it" (von Hirsch, 1985). Taken literally, this would rule out any role for risk in the context of legal punishment, stressing as it does the role of retribution over any utilitarian considerations. From this viewpoint, the use of RAIs can be criticised as fundamentally wrong, leading to the punishment of people for what they might do, rather than what they have done. Retributive views of justice allow for legal punishment based only on acts, although they may also allow for some enhancement of punishment, based on prior acts. Beyond this focus on current or past acts, they reject imposing punishment for potential acts as a breach of that person's innate dignity, or their right to be treated with respect as a person. The growth in the use of RAIs to inform legal decision-making has gained support from those advocates of more utilitarian views of law, with its stress on the impact of punishment, rather than retribution. Where punishment is likely to have a positive effect, it might be justified and here questions of risk become important (Epstein, 1989).

Considerations of risk have been extended widely across forensic practice and are now commonly seen in areas such as sentencing and detention, where estimates of risk, in criminal as well as civil mental health settings, may be considered. Historically, courts have often appeared reluctant to adopt risk-based approaches, whilst accepting it as a necessity in a small minority. Policy makers have shown much less reluctance, as is illustrated by the introduction and subsequent abolition of Indeterminate Public protection (IPP) sentences in England and Wales, along with similar provisions seen internationally (Bettinson and Dingwall, 2013). Courts in the UK had long held powers to impose indeterminate sentences on those convicted of serious offences, based on ideas of risk. These had, however, been used quite sparingly in criminal contexts. The

IPP sentence can be seen as mirroring civil mental health law provisions, where patients deemed to be dangerous and in need of treatment could be indefinitely detained to receive treatment. The IPP sentence represented a wide-ranging application of this kind of thinking to criminal law: probably rather wider than was anticipated, at least at a political level. These IPP sentences have been criticised reversing the normal burden of proof, with individuals sentenced in this way needing to prove they did not present an unacceptable risk (Rose, 2012). They were also criticised as requiring prisoners to complete treatment to reduce risk, where such treatment was not available. Critics could suggest that sentences of this kind represented the expansion of psychological and psychiatric models of control from civil to criminal law.

The fairness of extending ideas of risk to criminal law has been defended on a number of grounds. These have included a stress on the public protection role of criminal law. The argument has also been made that the concept of punishing only acts and not individuals had never been the reality. In all areas of forensic practice, there are systematic and systemic biases, acting to undermine the fundamental idea of retributive justice, that of punishing only actions. Well documented biases around race, sex and social class in the criminal justice system show this starkly, although they are generally viewed as undesirable and something to be eliminated as far as possible. The general principle of punishing acts is widely accepted as fundamental to justice, but utilitarian approaches take the view that risk and risk treatment have a place by focusing on the utility of punishment. Punishment is viewed in this way in terms of how effective it is. Different sentences for similar acts may be legitimate on the grounds of risk. In fact, the reality is that legal systems have all tended to involve a mixture of retributive and utilitarian thinking. Punishments are typically seen to have elements of retribution and elements that are linked to risk. The use of extended sentences in the UK provides a clear example of this, where the person is subject to a retributive element and an extended risk-based part of the sentence. Here, individuals may be released into the community but remain subject to supervision, treatment requirements and recall to prison custody if this is viewed as necessary on risk grounds. As such, their sentence does not end with completion of the retributive element.

Still on the theme of fairness in punishment, many RAIs have been criticised for the inclusion of areas that are inappropriate legally and ethically, or that act as proxies for such items. Examples would include characteristics, such as race and income, used as part of the OxRec RAI (Braverman, Doernberg, Runge and Howard, 2016). The use of proxy items that may involve such characteristics, such as community or neighbourhood characteristics, have also been extensively criticised. The use of such items may result in individuals being assessed and determined to be at higher risk on the basis of characteristics they have little or no control over. Using this as a basis for punishment, it is argued, is fundamentally unfair and, in many legal systems, prohibited. People do not determine what race they were born into and cannot affect whether they are born into a poor family or a rich one. Similarly, individuals may have no scope to choose whether they live in high- or low-crime areas. Using such items to assess someone as being at higher risk and hence punishing them more severely, can be criticised as unfair in terms of both discrimination and also breaching their dignity as a person. The defence for using such characteristics has largely been empirical and utilitarian. Where race is an effective predictor of a subsequent event then, it has been argued, it would be irrational to exclude it, in pursuit of some theoretical notion of fairness. Likewise, items such as social class, poverty, immigration status and sex may all be effective statistical predictors. Removing such information will, it is suggested, yield predictions that are less accurate, less useful and so less fair.

A concern that emerges from this debate is that neglecting issues of risk, in favour exclusively of what someone has done, introduces different but equally serious biases. An example given here is that of a violent young male and an older female with a treatable mental health problem (Slobogin, 2018). In this example, the older woman is significantly more likely to respond to risk treatment work. Giving exactly the same punishment to both may be a philosophically pure approach, but it is less obvious, in this case, that it is a fair one. This has supported a number of suggestions for compromise, with solutions based on modifications to the idea of fairness. Often these suggest that some factors should be absolutely excluded from consideration, whilst others might still be used but to moderate rather than determine punishments. Race is perhaps the most striking and widely discussed example, where it has been argued that such discrimination should be rejected, even where it is claimed to be predictively useful. Other factors, it is suggested, should be carefully balanced in terms of how much they incrementally add to the validity of the risk assessment and how much they impact on fairness. A decision to include factors such as sex and age may be made, as these may be significant predictors for some outcomes, without seeming to be excessively unfair (Monahan and Skeem, 2016; Scurich and Monahan, 2016; Monahan, 2017a). Others like marital status and employment status may not be included, as they add little incremental validity and so appear unfair. Additionally, a focus on changeable areas, ideally with a demonstrated causal relationship, have been suggested as a means of making RAIs fairer. Here items are legitimated as being something that the person has agency over such as illicit drug use. An obvious difficulty here though is the shortage of known causal risk factors for a range of criminal behaviours and the slow progress in identifying these (Monahan and Skeem, 2016; Farrington, 2017). This is in part a reflection of the poor state of theoretical understanding, model development and effective research in this area. However, research into areas such as violence and illicit drug use, alcohol use and impulse control suggests that given the motivation to do so, it is clearly possible to identify causal factors.

The BEWARE RAI provides a useful illustration of some of the criticisms around fairness in using concepts of risk in forensic practice. This is an algorithmic RAI, marketed as a means of predicting rare events. It was designed to assess the risk of serious injury to frontline police staff, following response to emergency (911) calls for police assistance in the US. The low frequency of such events has been highlighted using data for 2014, from the area where this RAI was deployed. Out of 408,718 emergency calls made, 363 were reported to result in this kind of serious incident (Slobogin, 2018). There are well-known difficulties associated with empirical predictions of rare events. Such rarity makes it difficult to adequately develop algorithms and also make it difficult for any algorithm to perform well. This gives rise to questions about how algorithms can be developed given such low frequencies, since this typically involves using a broader range of incidents, or drawing on a wider area than for the events being predicted. So, in developing algorithms, these might be based on less serious violence, or use national rather than local or regional development samples providing larger samples of data. However, this methodology can be reasonably criticised as giving rise to algorithms that may be less relevant to predicting the outcomes of concern, drawing into question the level of accuracy. Answers to such questions are not available for this algorithm, as much of the detail of development and how data is collected and processed are not public, meaning that independent research and evaluation is limited. Indeed, it has been reported that the police, as the customer, did not in fact know how high-risk scores were being assigned when using this particular RAI (Robinson, 2017). This raises legal and policy questions around the fairness of using closed algorithms in this way, how these might be evaluated and also where accountability lies when they might be used blindly.

Critiques based on fairness have often stressed the need for transparency around how RAIs work and here a lack of transparency and accountability has at times been evident. This may be especially true where RAIs have been used in the private sphere, such as workplace settings or the monitoring of privately owned spaces, or for 'intelligence' purposes. Commercial providers have generally funded private development of RAIs and so have protected their intellectual property rights through commercial confidentiality. However, this may prevent the scrutiny of issues of fairness in relation to the items, factors, weighting and the processing methods used. Whether these introduce various forms of unfair treatment is often not transparent or open to independent scrutiny and research. Concerns that the Chicago 'heat list' RAI was discriminating in this way were raised and led to a number of changes. However, this was a public algorithm, where its characteristics were available for scrutiny by independent researchers. The Chicago Police Department removed items that it was felt could not be ethically or legally defended but this only happened because of the openness to scrutiny shown.

Taking this argument further, it has been suggested that items based on things that individuals have little control over should also be removed from RAIs. An example here would be removal of items such as an individual's home area. There are costs to this, where such information contributes significantly to the accuracy of the RAI. Taking the example of knife crime in major UK cities, policing efforts have tended to be directed to areas where such offences are more common. These tend to be areas that are poorer and information about poverty and deprivation may have predictive value. Removing such information can be criticised as reducing predictive accuracy and directing efforts away from where they are needed. It could be argued that conducting patrols in affluent rural areas, in pursuit of an ideal of fairness, is itself unfair on potential victims of knife crime in poorer urban areas.

A strong critique in relation to the use of risk-based approaches is put forward by Harcourt (2015) who argues that the use of RAIs has led to increasingly marked racial disparities, with risk acting to amplify rather than reduce existing biases in legal systems. Pioneering research published in the 1980s is referenced as providing insights into this and is not encouraging. This looked at the process of deinstitutionalisation from US mental hospitals that took place largely from the 1960s. The findings showed that the focus of civil law detention in mental hospitals changed from one that had been focused on treatment to one focused on risk in the form of 'dangerousness'. As this happened, the proportion of 'non-white' patients detained on the grounds of dangerousness increased, with the proportion going up from 18.3% in 1968 to 31.7% in 1978. The percentage of white patients being admitted to mental hospitals also decreased from 81.7% to 68.3% in the same time period (Steadman, Monahan, Duffee and Hartstone, 1984). Comparable effects in other areas are clearly a significant risk, as, for example, efforts have begun to unwind the vast expense of using mass imprisonment in North America and elsewhere (Byrne, Pattavina and Taxman, 2015). Where race is used directly, or via proxy measures within RAIs, it seems likely that some groups will be disadvantaged and come to form a larger proportion of those held in custody on the grounds of risk. This argument is put bluntly by Harcourt (2015) who suggests that, in the context of North America, risk has become a proxy for race. As such, it has often provided a justification for unequal rates of incarceration and the mass imprisonment of young black men. The heavy weighting often given to risk items such as previous formally recorded criminality is often justified on the basis that past behaviour predicts future behaviour well. This may be true but official convictions also involve known systemic biases that are correlated with race, educational disadvantage and poverty. This has been described as label bias and the use of formal measures, such as arrests and convictions, are recognised as an example of this in forensic practice (Goel, Shroff, Skeem and Slobogin, 2021). These concerns have, however, often received little attention in practice settings. As a result, the use of many RAIs can be criticised as entrenching and strengthening existing racial and other disparities, cloaking these in scientific objectivity and reducing the scope for legal appeal against them.

The inclusion of socio-demographic factors as part of RAIs has led to concerns about equal treatment. As noted above, algorithmic and checklist RAIs can directly, or via proxy measures, use characteristics that may be seen as unacceptable or illegal in other contexts. It seems reasonable to assume that forensic practitioners would not set out to promote disadvantages in this way, on the grounds of characteristics such as race, lack of formal education or being poor. Yet variables that are proxies for these characteristics are routinely used in RAIs to determine levels of risk. The HCR-20, for example, includes detailed consideration of 'living circumstances' whilst the current OxRec relies on items such as disposable income, race and neighbourhood deprivation to predict risk. Items or proxies assessing social background, or family criminality, are common in a range of RAIs, yet these are areas the individual often has no control over or indeed takes responsibility for. If you are unlucky enough to be born into a poor area, with high levels of crime and violence, or forced to live in such an area, it is argued that cannot reasonably be said to reflect on you as an individual. The likelihood of contact with the criminal justice in such circumstances is also higher. Avoiding arrest or conviction may have more to do with luck than individual conduct. The opposite is also clearly true, with good fortune and privilege being no moral reflection on its beneficiaries. Yet many RAIs tap directly or indirectly into such areas, constructing this as 'risk' and then often defending such practice on narrow empirical grounds. There has been a surprising lack of focus on, or discussion of, this form of systemic discrimination within forensic practice (Braverman, Doernberg, Runge and Howard, 2016; Slobogin, 2017).

Scholars, largely from legal and social policy backgrounds, have not been so reticent. Starr (2014), for example, looked at the issues around sex and risk, noting that many sex biases have been evident across criminal and civil justice systems and only recently have these come to be seen as undesirable in many. The discussion around and use of RAIs in forensic practice has seemed largely unaffected by these changes, with a continuing focus on sex as an empirically strong predictor in areas such as violence. As with race, this discrimination has been defended on empirical grounds and here the analogy with motor insurance is perhaps useful. Women as a group present a lower risk for claims than men. Yet this clear actuarial distinction has been legally challenged and rejected on equal treatment grounds, with it being argued that people are not entitled to more favourable treatment on the grounds of their sex. The insurance example is one where women may have been more favourably treated than men but as Starr (2014) notes, there are many examples of more unfavourable treatment. This has led to the argument that the general principle of equality should apply to both favourable and unfavourable treatment. The counter argument put forward stresses that treating men and women similarly in relation to areas such as violence incurs substantial costs. It would in many cases involve treating women more harshly (Skeem, Monahan and Lowenkamp, 2016). It may also involve directing inappropriate risk treatment on the grounds of fairness. The analogy sometimes used here has been the idea of not using sex to inform allocation to risk-based medical treatment. Any effort to ignore sex in areas such as screening for uterine or prostate cancers would be generally rejected as absurd.

Such debates involve broader points that are relevant to many legal systems and have increasingly stressed the importance of individual rights. The rights of an individual are, in most legal systems, seen as trumping those of group characteristics. The use of RAIs is criticised as typically reversing this, involving average values for groups in decision-making. Statistical discrimination of this kind has historically been resisted by courts as unfair: generally being seen as involving a move away from treating each person as a unique individual with their own intrinsic human rights. Some group generalisations have, however, been allowed. These have been the exceptions to the general rule and have also been circumscribed. However, they are important. An example of this would be laws around alcohol use and car driving, common across many legal systems. In the UK, for example, these are based on measured levels of blood alcohol. There has been no tolerance for the idea that different levels might apply to subgroups, such as men, or to individuals based on higher or lower physiological tolerance for alcohol. This is despite the known differential effects of alcohol. Here, it has been seen as fair to act based on group characteristics, rather than individual characteristics.

Across most of forensic practice, risk has always been an important consideration in a variety of ways, and this undoubtedly includes applications such as sentencing. The increased and increasing use of RAIs, however, may have distorted practice, reducing other considerations. It has been suggested that this change has shifted the balance away from concepts such as retribution, deterrence and treatment towards an ever-greater focus on risk assessment in isolation. This has generated a range of contrasting views of this, both positive and negative. On the positive side, the identification and diversion of low-risk individuals from custodial sentences have been identified as important. An emphasis on risk is also proposed as a means of unwinding mass incarceration and offsetting increasingly punitive views (Garret and Monahan, 2020). More negatively, the way in which risk can hide many areas of concern around equal treatment has been stressed. The lack of transparency around these mean that effective appeals against them are often difficult. It seems fair comment that within mainstream forensic practice, these issues have not generally been given adequate thought.

A further issue of fairness with RAIs is that in using this technology, the outcomes of interest may themselves be changed. This is perhaps easiest to illustrate with reference to the use of policing RAIs. It is reasonable to assume that police staff responding to an emergency call will alter their approach to an individual when advised that they present a 'high' risk. Regardless of how valid or invalid such a prediction is, it could be argued that it would be irrational for front line staff not to react to this information in some way. The effects though may be to increase the risk of harm, to public and officers alike. Here, the prediction may alter the nature of the response in an adverse way (Robinson, 2017). This can be seen as fundamentally unfair on those requesting help. When combined with technology such as automated facial recognition, algorithmic RAIs do not even require any contact with a person before flagging them as high risk and automatically directing an approach to them, based on this characterisation. This is put forward as a strength of such RAIs with claims that they can direct attention to higher-risk individuals and situations, so reducing the need for intrusive approaches to those presenting a low risk. Decisions therefore become 'data driven' and focused, reducing prejudice and biases that might otherwise influence decision-making. People's biased and often irrational decision-making processes are substituted with rational empirically based indicators, directing efforts towards greater and more imminent risks. Such a Panglossian view masks serious concerns that are further amplified by the development of very high-speed computing at a comparatively low cost. Such applications of RAIs often appear to fall outside the scope of current legal controls, which have increasingly fallen behind technology. This may in practice provide apparently objective methods of harassing particular communities, or individuals, subverting traditional protections such as the need for reasonable suspicion of wrongdoing before interfering in someone's life.

The discussion above can be criticised for often comparing RAIs to hypothetical and idealised systems of law. Anyone working in the forensic practice quickly learns that this is not the reality. There are long-standing issues, across criminal and civil justice systems internationally, that affect the way an individual is treated. These include caste biases in India, social class biases in the UK, the racial biases that have been vividly illustrated in North America, Australia and Europe, to take just a few examples. Legal systems tend on the whole to treat the poor and uneducated more harshly than the wealthy and educated. There are areas of criminal and civil justice systems where injustice is blatant.

The rates of prosecution and conviction for sexual violence and violence against women in the UK provide a particularly shocking, although not unique, example of this. Often these effects are driven by policies and the characteristics of those making decisions. The use of RAIs is often seen as a means to redress this, even though they may include items and proxies for income, education, employment status, reliance on state benefits, job skills, race and so on. In doing this, they have been criticised for simply making systemic biases less obvious rather than less present. Across much of the world, there has been a drive to reduce the impact of such disparities. The effectiveness of these efforts is disputed but there is wide agreement that people should not be punished or spared punishment based on who they are. The use of RAIs here has been criticised as triggering additional or unequal and so unfair punishments rather than, as many advocates hoped, ensuring greater equality and fairness in sentencing. Some advocates of RAIs have suggested as a solution that risk should be used only in mitigation (Couzens, 2011). This would present difficulties in practice and whilst risk information may be used in mitigation for some, it has been argued it is unlikely that it would not also be used to increase punishments for others (Starr and Rehavi, 2013). The notion that those making decisions would only weight assessments of low risk and setting aside assessments of high risk would be difficult to ensure in practice.

Accuracy

The term accuracy is used here to refer to how effective RAIs are in predicting outcomes. This can be seen to largely involve two statistical concepts: reliability and validity. These are a common source of confusion, since these terms are distinct from their use in normal language. In essence, reliability can be seen as the extent to which different assessments will agree in the face of changes, such as being conducted by different assessors, under different conditions of assessment or the passage of time. This conflicts with common dictionary definitions of reliability with a stress on trustworthiness and which in many ways are closer to notions of statistical validity. Validity can be generally characterised as how well RAIs measure what they claim to. This can be estimated in various ways but the most important form in forensic practice tends to be predictive validity.

Commonly, a small number of inferential statistics are used to assess the characteristics of RAIs, although there has been some recent widening of the measures used. The most commonly seen inferential statistics tend to be the use of correlation coefficients to assess reliability and the Area Under the Curve (AUC) statistic to assess data fitting and sometimes predictive validity. Briefly put, correlation coefficients are a means of looking formally at covariance, with a value of 1 representing a perfect relationship or covariance and 0 representing no relationship or covariance. The AUC statistic was originally developed in the context of signal detection technology such as radar and sonar. It involves plotting the true positive rate over the false positive rate. An AUC value of 0.5 therefore equates half the observations falling above the line and half below it, equivalent to random chance such as tossing a fair two-sided coin repeatedly. Any value above 0.5 suggests a better than chance performance, up to a maximum value of 1, which would be perfect detection; values below 0.5 equate to a performance that is poorer than chance (Mossman, 1994).

The AUC statistic has been widely used to evaluate the accuracy of RAIs and these have been reported to fall within a relatively narrow band. When independently evaluated, they have tended to cluster around a value of 0.70 with a ceiling of around 0.75 (Yang, Wong and Coid, 2010; Coid, Yang, Ullrich et al., 2011). For a typical RAI used in forensic practice to assess reconviction, this can be interpreted as suggesting that around 70% of those reconvicted will have received a higher score than someone who is not reconvicted (Slobogin, 2018). This level of performance does not appear to be improved by the added complexity of later versions of RAIs. Indeed, some of the most complex RAIs have performed more poorly than simpler ones. This has led to the suggestion that this may be a result of drawing on a small number of relatively good correlates across different RAIs (Yang, Wong and Coid, 2010).

This level of accuracy is better than chance but is poorer than that seen in many other areas of risk assessment. It has also raised concerns about whether this is sufficient for use in legal decision-making. In determining how someone should be punished, these limited levels of accuracy do not fit easily with criminal law standards of likelihood, such as proof beyond reasonable doubt. Punishments for criminal offences have profoundly serious implications for individuals and for society more widely. There are good reasons why courts have generally adopted such a high bar for imposing criminal punishments. Criminal courts have been reluctant to define this bar numerically, but it seems unlikely that 75% approaches the level of removing reasonable doubt. If they cannot do this, then the suggestion arises that RAIs should not be used for such questions at all. The fairness of imposing criminal punishments, based on RAIs with wide margins of error, has long been seen as a significant concern (Steadman and Coccoza, 1974; Monahan, 1981). The case for using RAIs for civil legal questions, involving judgements on the balance of probability, is more convincing. This is also true of areas such as guiding treatment, where the use of risk-based approaches is less problematic. Most would be comfortable, up to a point, with efforts to focus treatment on those most in need of it, even where the measurement of treatment need is imperfect. The idea of punishing someone based on such limited accuracy would be unlikely to be widely accepted in the same way. These distinctions are important and generate serious ethical questions. It is therefore concerning that they appear to have suffered from growing neglect in the application of RAIs in forensic practice.

The appropriate use of RAIs in forensic practice requires that the psychometric properties are understood and that they are adequate to the task. As a minimum, this suggests that RAIs demonstrate acceptable levels of reliability and predictive validity for a given context. Any RAI that produces very unreliable results is unlikely to be of use. Likewise, one that cannot predict at much better than chance levels may do more harm than good. In relation to this, RAIs need to show they are relevant to the assessment. To take a concrete example, it could be argued that a policing RAI developed in Chicago is not relevant to different cities, say Los Angeles or London. Here, there would be nothing to suggest that the RAI would work as well in the new settings and good reasons to expect that it would not. Use in a new setting that differed significantly from the initial development would not be appropriate and the separate development of RAIs would be necessary. This creates significant challenges for the use of RAIs and here a balance clearly needs to be struck between relevance and development costs (Monahan, Steadman, Applebaum et al., 2006; Goel, Shroff, Skeem and Slobogin, 2021). Any idea that RAIs are widely applicable without alteration is, however, fundamentally misconceived. Even within relatively unitary nations, the roll out of such methods to different settings has been questioned on the grounds of accuracy. Methods developed in London are unlikely to be equally applicable to Belfast, Cardiff, Edinburgh and Manchester. Yet this kind of error is often seen and repeated in the use of RAIs. The application of RAIs in forensic practice often breeches these minimum standards for development. Details of the psychometric properties of RAIs may be opaque and so the accuracy of these is not open to independent research and scrutiny. RAIs that were developed for one setting may be routinely, apparently unthinkingly, applied to quite different settings. Those developed in North American mental health settings being applied to correctional settings and in other nations provides a stark example of this. Poor practices of this kind may in large part be linked to economic factors. Adequate development of RAIs can be an expensive process and it has become increasingly commercially driven, leading to conflicts. Business imperatives may drive wider application of RAIs than can be justified on technical or practice grounds.

In common with other forms of assessment, RAIs will yield four critical outcomes. A result may be a true positive; a false positive; a true negative or a false negative. Using the example of reoffending, a true positive would be someone who is predicted to reoffend and does so. A false positive is where the person is predicted to reoffend but does not. True negatives are where the person is predicted not to reoffend and does not. False negatives are where the person is predicted not to reoffend but does. When using RAIs, it is entirely reasonable, at a logical level, to require the level of true positives found to be sufficient to justify any actions suggested. This important point has often been neglected, or at times apparently misunderstood. At a concrete level, policing algorithms would need to have a sufficient rate of correctly identifying those who go on to commit offences, to justify different levels of intrusive action that interfere with a person's freedom to go about their lives such as stopping, questioning, searching and detention. Similarly, the use of RAIs in making conditional release decisions should be sufficiently accurate, in identifying those who will commit offences, to justify their continued imprisonment. Assessments, which, for example, produce more false positives than true positives, or which generate many false negatives, are likely to do significant harm. Here, the courts in North America have generally been more willing to put numeric values to such considerations than those in Europe and elsewhere. Federal Courts in the US have previously accepted a level of 30% as meeting the test of 'reasonable suspicion' and 50% as sufficient to justify the use of long-term surveillance (Slobogin, 2018). In using RAIs for parole, or in the use policing of private settings, the basis for such decisions is often opaque. In such situations, it is often not obvious what thresholds are being used, what might be seen as acceptable or how accurate the RAIs being used are.

The reporting of these kinds of routine information in forensic practice has often been weak, sometimes to the point of obfuscation. This may include the use of a range of different statistics to describe basic characteristics of RAIs, making comparisons, at best difficult, at worst impossible. Notions of construct validity may be presented as supporting the use of a particular RAI, but this involves calculating the levels of agreement between similar instruments. Whilst this has a clear role in evaluating RAIs, it is unlikely to be the type of validity that is of concern to most of those making decisions. Here, the focus of interest is how consistently, and accurately, future behaviour might be predicted and modified. The US Supreme Court decision in *Addington v. Texas* (441, US. 418, 431–433 (1979)) has been quoted as illustrative of this thinking. In this case, the court set out a requirement for 'clear and convincing' evidence, which it quantified at a 75% level of certainty, for involuntary hospitalisation on the grounds of 'dangerousness' (Slobogin, 2018). By extension, it seems a fair argument that at least this level of certainty should apply to keeping people in prison custody, although this would make the use of many currently used RAIs, at best, marginal.

Individual and Group-Based Predictions

The various areas of forensic practice all have in common, to a greater or lesser extent, a stress on precision. This extends across the language used, to how concepts are defined and the nature of legal tests. The level of precision for RAIs remains a focus for critics looking at application in areas of practice, who have argued that RAIs are not providing anything like the necessary level of precision needed for accurate prediction at the level of individuals. From this perspective, even the most accurate RAIs do not, it is suggested, perform well. The estimate of around 75% discussed above, rests on group predictions, and in moving away from these to individual prediction, accuracy falls. As a result, a lack of accuracy becomes integrated into the legal process, often due to a poor understanding of the RAIs used. This has been illustrated by looking at the use of predictive algorithms in other contexts. Algorithms of this type now form a key feature of internet use, where they often generate what were erroneously assumed by most to be unimportant predictions, such as likely areas of interest for advert placement. There has been a surprising lack of interest in the political propaganda and criminal uses of such methods from within forensic practice, but here, the focus is on the power of the technique to make group and individual predictions.

When using large data sets, any inaccuracies and limitations these algorithms have, at the individual level, are masked. As with the insurance examples given earlier in this text, algorithms here do not need to give accurate individual predictions to be useful; group predictions suffice. By contrast, the decision in 2020 by the Department of Education for England to use an algorithmic approach to allocate examination grades to individuals showed some of the problems with the method when individual predictions are needed. Faced with a need to cancel group examinations in person, as a result of the high levels of COVID-19 infections in the community, algorithmic predictions were to be used to determine grades. The arguments in favour of this approach echoed those often made for the use of algorithmic RAIs in forensic practice. These included the elimination of individual biases shown by teachers in awarding grades, greater accuracy and improved fairness. Despite this, the approach quickly unravelled and there were a few obvious reasons for this. As with RAIs, the algorithms used were in fact simple: in fact, very much simpler than those used in 'big data' applications on the internet. They were also seeking, as with many RAIs, to make individual rather than group-based predictions. The results appeared in some cases to be both arbitrary and unfair, as indeed had been predicted by statisticians. Most seriously though, the use of algorithms in this way had served to formalise many of the existing systemic biases in the education system in England, favouring more affluent groups (Hern, 2020).

In her review, Starr (2014) used the example of predicting height to illustrate some of the problems inherent in this kind of approach to individual predictions. With height, there is a relatively precise model, based on extensive data. Height can also be measured with a good degree of accuracy. Using the US Census data, she noted that the average height of males is reported to be 70 inches, with a standard deviation of 3 inches and a normal distribution of height across the population. For females, the figures were an average height of 65 inches and a standard deviation of 2.5 inches, with height also being normally distributed. It is quite easy to draw samples of varying sizes here and Starr used samples of 20, 200 and 400 to calculate regression equations for gender against height. How closely each of these samples approximates the population average height will involve an element of chance or randomness. The role of this is likely to reduce though, as the sample size increases. Confidence intervals can be calculated for a given sample and these will be smaller for the larger samples. All of which is routinely taught on statistics courses from secondary school onwards. Importantly, however, Starr (2014) noted that this applies to the group averages; it does not apply to the individual values. Here, it is possible to calculate prediction intervals, and these will remain quite wide. They are not narrowed by larger sample sizes in the same way that confidence intervals are. As a result, she argued that even using the larger sample of 400, in trying to predict the height of the next female you met, your best guess would be the average value for the population of women (65 inches). This would not be a very confident prediction but would be the best available. The calculated prediction interval here would be 59.5 to 70.3 inches. So wide in fact that it would be of little practical value, with most women falling within this range. Hence choosing the average value would, given the normal distribution of scores, be the best guess here (Starr, 2014). This, she argued, means that for the kinds of binary decisions made in much of forensic practice, this type of statistic is of limited use, except for extremely high or exceptionally low probabilities, those close to 1 or 0.

This largely explains the use of alternatives designed to assess binary outcomes, such as AUC or less commonly survival analysis. A popular alternative has also been to look at covariance in the form of correlation coefficients between predicted and actual outcomes. For current forms of RAIs as noted, the results here have been generally consistent, yielding ceiling values of around 0.75 for the AUC. The results based on covariance have been similarly consistent and taking the Level of Service Inventory (LSI-R) as an example, a correlation of around 0.35 has been found with reoffending. Such values are clearly better than chance but have been criticised as being rather unimpressive. By way of contrast, Starr (2014) noted that the correlation coefficient for a sample of 400 in the height by sex example above would be 0.65. A key observation here is that whilst current methods show a level of fit to historical data or predictive value, this is often far from compelling, even at a group level. The accuracy of prediction at an individual level is often poor.

There have been several responses to such views. These have included stress on the value of group averages in providing important information for risk estimates (Skeem and Monahan, 2011). An example often used here is one of a forced choice game of Russian Roulette, where one gun has a single loaded chamber and the other has five loaded chambers. The analogy here is between a low-risk group of offenders and a high-risk group. The issue is whether it is rational to ignore the presence of many risk indicators in one of the groups. It is argued that it does not make sense to ignore the information that the average risk of further offending for one group is 17% and for another group, 83%. To do so would, it is suggested, be irrational (Redding, 2009; Skeem and Monahan, 2011).

More utilitarian arguments can also be made in favour of drawing on group average information. These would suggest, amongst other things, the better targeting of resources towards those with greater needs. This raises issues of its own, and in many legal systems, this kind of statistical decision-making has been rejected, on the grounds that it can lead to the severe adverse treatment of individuals. Taking again the example of predicting examination grades by algorithm in England in 2020 (Hern, 2020), a number of candidates would be expected to fail to attend. These candidates clearly would not pass the examination. This is likely to be, at least in part, due to random factors. Non-attendance may occur for many reasons, some of which will have nothing to do with the ability to pass the examination: illness on the day, a family bereavement, transport problems and so on. These are likely to include the kind of low-frequency and high-impact events that have been identified as being problematic for algorithms. Here, the algorithm appeared to award these failing grades to the weakest students at particular examination centres. At an individual level, this was seen, not unreasonably, as being grossly unfair. There is little to suggest that all these individual students would have been the ones who failed to attend the examination.

The use of RAIs has been suggested as a means of addressing many of the biases present in the criminal and civil justice systems. Examples of this have included work on Evidence Based Sentencing (EBS) beginning in North America but spreading more widely. This has itself become a contentious area, and there are a number of reasons for this. In her review of the area, Starr (2014) suggests that there are three primary concerns where RAIs are used to inform sentencing considerations in this manner:

1 That RAIs provide nothing close to precise predictions of individual recidivism.
2 That the evidence RAIs improve on traditional approaches and are less discriminatory are missing.
3 That the current use of RAIs typically fails to address the genuinely useful utilitarian question of how much a given sentence will affect the risk of recidivism.

On taking each in turn, it has been argued that RAIs are primarily a means of giving additional information to inform decision-making. They do not determine sentence or replace traditional judicial and quasi-judicial decision-making. More broadly, RAIs have been defended on the grounds that risk assessment and prediction are not new and have always been a fundamental aspect of sentencing. In looking at the accuracy of RAIs, it is reasonably argued, the appropriate test is not one of perfect prediction but how they perform compared with existing practices. Current use of RAIs makes this process more accurate but also more transparent, allowing for the identification of any biases. Critics have countered that RAIs have increasingly displaced human decision-making, with concepts of 'moral deserts', 'fairness' and 'equity' being replaced with probabilistic estimates (Prescott, Pyle and Starr, 2019).

Internationally, there has been growth in the use of statistical concepts and information. The criminal and civil justice systems have not been immune to this, but the approach has not always been appropriate or well informed (Dawid, Musio and Murtas, 2017). An illustrative example of this is a system called COMPAS, a commercially marketed RAI introduced first in Wisconsin in the US (Brennan, Dieterich and Ehret, 2009; Washington, 2018). This was developed to assist judges at pre-trial in identifying those defendants most likely to fail to comply with bail requirements. The algorithm is reported to have been subsequently extended, without modification, for use in sentencing (Robinson, 2017). Challenges have been made to the use of this RAI but have been impeded by details of the algorithm and the way that it is processed not having been disclosed. This is reported to have led to the Supreme Court in Wisconsin issuing a series of cautions in relation to the use of COMPAS. This suggests that legal systems are often poorly equipped to understand and evaluate RAIs of this kind (Robinson, 2017; Washington, 2018). It is notable that this black-box algorithm has been shown to predict no better than laypeople without legal training and that simple heuristics that rely on the cues of age, gender and previous record predicted equally well, whilst being fully transparent (Angelino, Larus-Stone, Alabi et al., 2018; Dressel and Farid, 2018). Such technology is though often very actively marketed and presentations may be technical in nature, with independent research and evaluations often being unavailable. In addition, Robinson noted that the use of such RAIs often serves to distract from potentially more productive and cost-effective work. For example, finding out why individuals fail to comply with bail, rather than trying to predict who will not. Even simple interventions here, such as sending text messages or making reminder telephone calls, have been shown to markedly increase attendance across a range of areas (Gurol-Urganci, de Jongh, Vodopivec-Jamsek et al., 2013). People simply forget things and for those living the kind of chaotic lives commonly seen in forensic practice, it seems this will be all the more likely. It is perhaps surprising that efforts to predict risk have often taken precedence over simpler methods to treat risk.

This links to broader criticisms of whether the use of RAIs is of sufficient utility to justify use. Here comparisons have been made between RAIs and unaided human decision-making. Excluding some legally questionable risk indicators has been shown to reduce the accuracy of RAIs. The removal of race as an item from RAIs has been reported to lead to a loss of accuracy in the 5–12% range (Petersilia and Turner, 1987). By contrast, however, removal of demographic and socio-economic factors did not appear to impact on accuracy, raising questions about inclusion in the first place. As early as the 1980s, it had been suggested that the average accuracy of predictions based on just past behaviour could outperform RAIs or traditional mental health assessments (Mossman, 1994). This suggests that in areas such as sentencing, approaches based on careful analysis of current and previous offences might be the most effective form of risk assessment. From a legal perspective, it has been argued that this could be preferable to current practice by more closely aligning punishment with acts rather than individual characteristics (Starr, 2014).

It has become received wisdom in much of forensic practice that RAIs always perform better than what have been termed 'unstructured' clinical judgements about risk. As with a lot of received wisdom, this oversimplifies the evidence and does not reflect the views of more thoughtful advocates of such approaches. Claims of the superiority of algorithmic methods over human judgement, for example, rest on a wide range of evidence. A detailed review of this is often quoted in support of rejecting or strongly limiting human decision-making (Grove, Zald, Lebow et al., 2000). The results of this review do not, however, support simple conclusions. In around half of the studies included, human assessments were approximately equal to algorithmic methods, and in around one in ten cases, they performed better. It has been suggested here that these 'clinical' assessments may have been advantaged by access to more data. Given equal access to information, it has been argued, formal approaches would perform as well or better than the informal human combination of information. This is clearly a hypothesis, and as such, open to empirical testing. Where 'clinical' methods perform at similar levels to algorithmic methods, they may indeed involve more information, time, effort and expense. Cutting out areas that may be irrelevant or of marginal relevance may be a means by which algorithmic RAIs can focus resources more productively. Arguments of this kind, however, remain contentious and in her review, Starr (2014) concludes that the view that RAIs outperform 'clinical' assessments has acquired the characteristics of a shibboleth.

At a practice level, the specifics of RAI use and 'clinical' judgement are clearly important. The use of RAIs in the context of mental health assessments, concerned with areas such as compulsory treatment, will involve teams with detailed knowledge of the individual. Here, the use of RAIs may form a small part of a much more extensive process, conducted by people with high levels of expertise and those who know the individual being assessed well. By contrast, assessments in other settings may be quite different. Assessments in correctional or court settings may involve relatively brief and narrow assessments. They may not be undertaken by expert teams and will often be undertaken in less-than-ideal conditions. The growth in use of RAIs can also be seen to be meeting managerial concerns, something highlighted in a review of risk in the context of child protection (Wald and Woolverton, 1990). The use of RAIs there was criticised as being used, or misused, as a means of cost-cutting and rationing of inadequate assessment and support services. Standardised RAIs, it was argued, were being used to replace rather than aid individualised assessments of at-risk children, serving to increase managerial control over processes that were previously a matter of professional judgement and difficult to control and measure as 'metrics' (Wald, 2014; Gambino, 2019). Significantly, RAIs also came to be seen, quite implausibly, as a defence against litigation.

The usefulness of RAIs has also been challenged on the basis that they are often trying to answer the wrong question. The question with genuine utility, it has been suggested, is who will be most affected by various forms of punishment, not who is most likely to be reconvicted. This appears to be a question that can be answered, but it has until recently had limited attention. Even if the central premise is rejected, in forensic practice, it does go to the critical area of risk treatment. This is of central importance in forensic practice and concerns that individuals and groups will tend to have their risk changed by different interventions. Questions of this kind involving the effects of risk treatment are routinely addressed in epidemiology and similar issues are evident when RAIs are used in forensic practice (Harcourt, 2015). In many instances, a higher assessed risk may not equate to more effective risk treatment. An individual identified as high risk may not be more effectively deterred by police actions, or respond more positively to a longer prison sentence. Focusing resources on groups at high risk of reconviction may not have the largest effect on risk. The targeting of groups that are already be marginalised may, in fact, be least likely to deter and be largely ineffective or counterproductive. It is argued here that it is the 'elasticity' of crime, in response to interventions, that matters most (Harcourt, 2015). Much the same argument can be applied to corrections and the ways in which imprisonment might be used to reduce crime. This is distinct from estimating the probability of reconviction and refers to who is most likely to be affected by imprisonment, community supervision and efforts at-risk treatment. There is little reason to think that those at greatest risk of reoffending will be the most responsive. It seems more likely that they may frequently be more 'inelastic' in this respect. Despite this, ideas of incapacitation and specific deterrence have dominated many areas of forensic practice, with questions about elasticity of response to correctional interventions being frequently neglected. Incapacitation seems, at least until recently, to have had a dominant role, supported perhaps by the growing commercial interests in corrections. In the UK, for example, custody is still widely advocated to prevent further offending and improve public protection. Specific deterrence, or the rehabilitative effects from custody itself, appears much less influential. The need to set both against the known adverse effects of imprisonment, such as greater difficulty in finding stable employment on release, have until very recently gained little political or policy attention (Agan and Starr, 2017).

Much of the literature on the utility of RAIs in forensic practice has neglected the question of the effects on recidivism risk from imprisonment. It is sometimes suggested that incarceration per se increases recidivism, but this is of course an overly simplistic analysis, making a spurious comparison between those sent to prison and those not. These two groups are likely to differ on far more than just the sentencing option taken, so simple comparisons like this are not very informative. Even if correctly identified, a higher rate of recidivism alone would not, it is argued, provide convincing support for the idea of targeting imprisonment at higher-risk offenders. It may simply increase already higher levels of risk, except where such offenders are detained permanently. Arguably, this suggests that the greatest utility of RAIs is as a means for directing risk treatment, analogous to the use in medicine and epidemiology. Here, RAIs are not serving to determine punishment. They address less contentious but no less important questions about who is most in need and who is most likely to benefit from interventions to reduce risk (Garrett and Monahan, 2020).

Impact

The impact of RAIs on decision-making has been seen in contrasting ways. Use has been advocated on the basis that they can offset human and systemic biases. Alternatively, they have been suggested to provide marginal gains, serving to inform decision-making. The former view sees them as providing a check or anchor against the biases that decison-makers are prone to as well as the political and other pressures they may be under. The use of RAIs, it has been observed, does not prevent normal forms of mitigation being put forward and that information about risk may provide additional mitigation (Couzens, 2011).

A point perhaps worth stressing here is that in discussing the usefulness of RAIs in forensic practice, they need to be seen as a form of technology. The presentation of the results of such technology implies a basis in science, lending weight to the results. Such technology can though be built in the absence of scientific understanding. Predicting the motion of the stars was achieved long before anyone understood the true motion of the planets. The ability to reach even modest levels of prediction can therefore be misleading. In many of the areas where RAIs are used, the level of scientific understanding and theory is at best poor. This may be compounded by errors within the technology being less obvious than individual prejudices. Closed algorithms and methods of analysis mean that even independent experts may be unable to identify biases and errors. Meanwhile, the results of RAIs with qualitative descriptions such as 'high' or 'low' risk may influence the views of decison-makers, even where they explicitly reject risk-based approaches.

Conclusion

In drawing together the socio-legal criticisms of risk assessment outlined above, it is worth noting that the influence of risk has grown consistently across forensic practice, with use now widespread in some areas. Initially developed as a means of directing risk treatments, assessments of risk have expanded into diverse and very different areas of practice, such as policing, child protection, sentencing and conditional release from detention. It is now common for RAIs, or multiple RAIs, to be used to inform risk-based decision-making in many legal contexts. These changes took place with little in the way of informed public discussion or debate, even though such a transition raises serious legal, ethical and policy concerns. The appeal of RAIs, as part of this process, appears to have been at least twofold. They have been put forward as relatively simple, technical and 'scientific' solutions to complex questions. They have also been sold as a means of making more accurate and fairer decisions more cheaply, eliminating many of the biases that have bedevilled these areas for centuries. In many ways, they have also appealed to an increasingly managerialist approach.

The use of RAIs has been criticised from a range of socio-legal perspectives and also from within forensic practice, where it has been seen as part of the displacing of complex skills in policing, clinical and correctional work. These changes have been progressive and have occurred in parallel with the exponential growth of data gathering and algorithmic analysis, which has been so profitable in the commercial sphere. The extension of such methods to forensic practice gives rise to serious ethical and policy questions. The main challenges discussed in this chapter relate to questions of fairness, accuracy and utility remain. At a fundamental level, the use of RAIs has been criticised as being unfair to individuals using risk to punish individuals for what they might do, rather than what they have done. This may be compounded by the use in RAIs of individual characteristics to estimate risk that are ethically and legally dubious, with race and wealth providing clear examples of this. This cuts across notions of equal treatment. Such concerns appear to have driven legal challenge. The accuracy of RAIs in making predictions about individuals has become a focus for criticism, with suggestions that RAIs frequently fall below acceptable standard for use in areas of forensic practice.

Critiques of Current Practice

Risk Analysis Perspectives

6

One of the most striking aspects of current forensic practice is the extent to which it has become isolated, both from other disciplines concerned with risk and from its own research base. This broad field of research and practice development has been captured here under the shorthand term of 'risk analysis', which is used to cover a very wide range of expertise across areas of science, mathematics and technology. The way that risk is conceptualised and dealt with in practice has benefited enormously from such a wide range of disciplines taking an interest in risk. It also reflects the fact that risk is not, in any sense, a trivial or easy problem to deal with (Irwin, Smith and Griffiths, 1982; Fischbacher-Smith, Irwin and Fischbacher-Smith, 2010; Fischbacher-Smith, 2016). The isolation of thinking in forensic practice is in stark contrast to many other areas and has been associated with a dominance of often very narrow and simplistic approaches. It seems a reasonable observation that there has been a consistent failure to apply such learning and research to current forensic practice. The aim of this chapter is therefore to look at some of the main criticisms that arise from looking at current forensic practice through this critical lens.

As a starting point, perhaps the most obvious and striking issue is with the terminology and language used to think about risk. Within forensic practice this has been varied, vague, inconsistent and increasingly out of step with research and practice developments in other areas. This appears largely to be a reflection of the intellectual isolation referred to above, driving a lack of exchange of ideas from both research and from other applied settings. The reasons for this are not immediately obvious, although the use of language seems important here. This may have influenced the way fundamental aspects of risk have been thought about, directing what has been considered and what has been

DOI: 10.4324/9781003108665-7

neglected or ignored. This does not, however, explain the developing isolation of practice from its direct evidence base. The effects of increasing marketisation of forensic practice here may also have been a factor, introducing a range of unhelpful incentives and drivers. To take one example, approaches suggested from research may cut across commercial imperatives, suggesting methods with heavy up-front development costs, needing highly skilled staff. In contrast, the use of generic algorithms and checklists can be marketed, as apparently cheap technological alternatives that can be administered in a mechanistic way, by less skilled staff. The impact of political drivers on the development and marketing of risk assessment should also not be underestimated.

There is in practice no commonly agreed language of risk, although many other disciplines have given this more attention than has been typical in forensic practice. A striking difference here has been the way in which risk is seen in other areas as involving a number of interacting stages or phases. These may be described in a variety of ways but typically include ideas such as analysis and evaluation that have been increasingly neglected in forensic practice. The idea that assessing risk forms part of a more complex and iterative process is far from novel in the research evidence base (Towl and Crighton, 1996, 1997; Monahan, Steadman, Silver et al., 2001; Smith and Fischbacher, 2009), but such ideas have suffered a progressive decline in practice. They have been displaced by an increasingly narrow focus on probabilistic risk assessment in isolation.

A serious criticism that arises from this shift in forensic practice is the neglect of key aspects of risk. Important ideas of risk analysis, risk evaluation and risk treatment have been largely lost from practice or have been conflated with other ideas. Risk analysis now appears to be routinely seen, in much of forensic practice, as synonymous with risk assessment. Notions of risk treatment are routinely and unhelpfully conflated with risk management. Questions of risk evaluation appear to have largely disappeared. It seems a well-founded criticism that forensic practice has also become increasingly focused on a narrow view of risk assessment, which sees this as a process of giving a point estimate of the likelihood of adverse events. This approach opens up a wide range of legitimate criticism. Most fundamentally, it can be seen as a profound misunderstanding of the nature of risk and the best ways to address questions of risk (Towl and Crighton, 1996, 1997; Monahan, Steadman, Silver et al., 2001; Fischbacher-Smith, 2016). In developing such a focus, the opportunity for a wider analysis and better understanding are, to a great extent, lost.

The negative effects of this can perhaps best be illustrated by looking more closely at current forensic practice and the dominance of two approaches discussed earlier. In both, Risk Assessment Instruments (RAIs) are used to provide estimates of likelihood at a given point in time. One approach involves the wide application of algorithmic methods and these are generally based on simple inferential statistics such as covariance and linear regression. The alternative involves the use of structured checklists that generally address broadly defined adverse events such as sexual violence. Both produce estimates of the likelihood of adverse events. One is in the form of numerical values, whilst the later provides qualitative descriptive estimates. Both methods have come to be applied in increasingly mechanistic ways that are out of step with other disciplines and the use of scientific approaches more generally. Both can be criticised as providing crude and simplistic views of risk that, whilst they may be of some managerial or bureaucratic value, are deeply flawed. In comparison with the work undertaken by risk analysts in other fields, most are notable for an obvious lack of sophistication and failure to integrate research and practice.

The very breadth of disciplines with an interest in risk means that similar concepts have often been given different names. Many ideas have been independently discovered and rediscovered and methods duplicated. Arguably, however, in well-developed fields, there has been a coming together of ideas and agreement that risk assessment is best considered as part of a process. For present purposes, the model adopted here is one that treats risk as being divisible into distinct but interacting parts, or stages or phases (Renn, 2008; Aven, 2015). This is illustrated in Figure 6.1, which gives a simplified representation of these different aspects that can be applied to risk problems. The phases outlined should

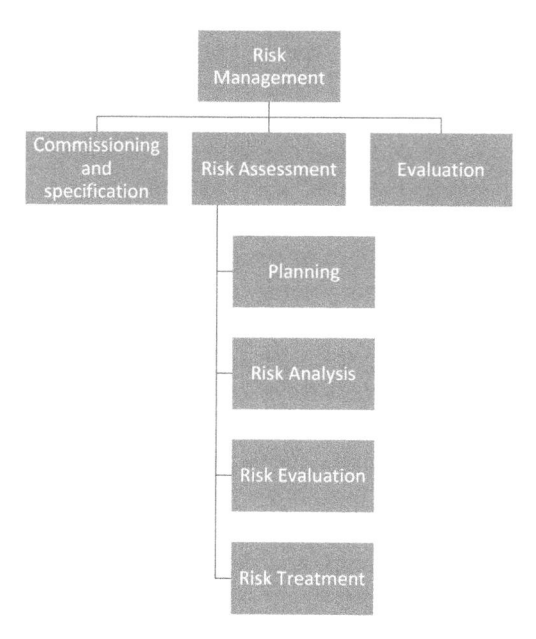

Figure 6.1 Aspects of risk analysis.

not be seen as a linear process but rather one that involves interactions between the various parts.

A few key points emerge from this pictorial representation of risk assessment and perhaps the most notable of these is that it is seen as only representing a small part of a more extensive process. Risk assessment is not seen as an activity that can be sensibly conducted in isolation but an interacting part of a wider problem of analysis, evaluation and management. A second striking difference from forensic practice is the way that risk management is seen. Here, it is clearly seen to be a separate and overarching process, concerned with motivation, control, integration and evaluation. Within forensic practice, the term is often used simply to refer to efforts to reduce risk. The term risk analysis is rarely seen in routine forensic practice, and where it is, the term is often confused with risk assessment, which here is seen as distinct from analysis. For many other disciplines, risk analysis is seen as a major, and often the major, part of the processes of dealing with questions around risk, with other activities flowing from this process, with its stress on detailed understanding. Finally, it is worth noting that the concept of risk treatment is here separated out as a distinct area. As noted, this is frequently conflated with risk management in forensic practice, possibly as a result of adopting odd managerialist terminology from healthcare on 'patient management'. This is something that would be viewed from a risk analysis perspective as inappropriate and unhelpful. The separation of risk treatment is commonly seen in many other areas of risk analysis and is adopted here as having significant advantages, focusing attention on a detailed analysis of both risk barriers and interventions.

The overall objective of this process can be seen as the production of an informative 'picture' of risk. This captures the assumptions used, quantitative or qualitative analyses of events, potential responses and issues of acceptability and tolerability of risk. This is widely seen as an essential foundation. In this respect, however, much of current forensic practice does not fare well. Risk analysis is frequently absent and even where some analysis is undertaken, this often appears cursory and superficial, with the two currently dominant RAI approaches encouraging a sense that risk assessment is a stand-alone process. Risk analysis is in reality a major area of research and practice in its own right (Aven, 2015) and it allows for consideration of a range of potential approaches, with a wide variety of structured and semi-structured techniques available to aid in this. The stress placed on detailed analysis at this point is consistent with the application of scientific method to risk. At a practical level, it is helpful to those conducting the analysis, risk managers and stakeholders. So fundamental is the idea of analysis that stress is often placed on how it can be undertaken and repeated at various points in the lifetime of individual risks or systems. Put bluntly, many others involved in the area of risk would view its absence as a critical failing. Akin perhaps to trying to build a house, without first putting in foundations and services, creating an at best very limited and fragile structure.

Still on the theme of the language of risk, forensic practitioners seem to have been increasingly reluctant to address the area of risk evaluation. Risk inevitably raises questions about how acceptable risks are and the limits of tolerance. This is a simpler issue in some settings than others (Fischbacher-Smith, 2016). In some engineering or economic contexts, it is possible to think of examples where acceptability and the range of tolerance might be relatively easily set out. More typically, this is not the case and evaluations may be very different based on viewpoint. Those bearing the risk and the costs involved may take a very different view from experts who do not. This seems particularly salient for many areas of forensic practice and perhaps explains in part the increasing reticence to address such questions. Here the resort to vague non-numerical estimates of risk, that are open to varied interpretations, allow such questions to be fudged. Even actuarial estimates of risk may leave the questions around evaluation of risk open, or for others to grapple with. The critique flowing from this is that such failures are an unacceptable practice and a negation of professional responsibility. Others can and do deal with comparable challenges, often with severe potential outcomes. Questions of risk evaluation can be and also need to be addressed, as part of the process of dealing with risk in forensic practice (Towl and Crighton, 1996; 1997). In dealing with risk evaluation, analysts have often adopted ideas around the need for escalating levels of caution and what the appropriate thresholds for risk acceptance might be for these. In doing this, a concept of different and escalating levels of caution has been used, with 'cautionary' and 'precautionary' principles reflecting this. In neglecting these, the implicit assumptions that must inevitably be made by practitioners tend to remain opaque and so open to interpretation and misinterpretation by others.

The manner in which risk treatment is dealt with in forensic practice is perhaps the most surprising. The term is widely used in other contexts. It is increasingly rare to see the term used in forensic practice, where a routine conflation of risk treatment and risk management has developed: something that is clear in a number of checklists RAIs in forensic practice. This would though be seen as a significant failing in many other disciplines, where the separation of risk treatment is seen as a central aspect of risk analysis. Risk treatment is seen as capturing a variety of methods and processes that may be shown to modify risk, through avoidance, reduction, optimisation, transfer or retention (Lyon and Popov, 2019). The view adopted here is that such separation is justified and helpful. It is of value to see risk management separately from this, having an overall controlling function. The term risk management is therefore seen as best reserved for activities that surround and direct the process of thinking about and dealing with a given risk, from start to finish. This view of risk management has been helpfully summarised as the process of balancing the conflicts inherent in dealing with opportunities, losses, accidents and disasters (Aven, Vinnem and Wiencke, 2007). It will therefore typically include processes of goal setting, preference setting and the specification of relevant measurements. All of the other processes described in Figure 6.1 can be seen to feed into this, essentially acting as decision support. For complex risk problems, this also provides the framework for considering differing expert analyses and assessments, as well as consideration of the distinctions between 'risk agents' and 'risk absorbing systems'. These later concepts have also been largely neglected in forensic practice, where the focus has tended to be increasingly on individuals as risk agents, at the expense of broader systemic considerations.

Risk Management

The breadth of the term risk management, as used in other contexts, is important because it leads to consideration of the full range of efforts to analyse, assess, treat and accept risks. Importantly, this means that, as a formal process, it captures the full range of activities around a risk problem. The common use in forensic practice contrasts markedly with this and tends to generally or exclusively narrow the focus on to some areas of risk treatment. Largely as a function of this, the main objective of risk management is often erroneously taken in practice to be one of risk reduction. A moment of thought shows that this is not a correct or indeed helpful application of the term. In many areas, a sole focus on risk reduction simply means not undertaking the activities identified. Drawing on forensic practice, for example, might suggest never giving parole for serious offenders, or always using constant observation with any patient expressing suicidal ideas. In other areas, similar concerns would apply. The easiest way to reduce the risks associated with space flight, such as accidents and fatalities, would be simply not to do it. People evidently do not understand risk management in this way, nor do they manage risks in this way in daily life by treating elimination of risk as the sole driver. Risk management is more accurately seen as being concerned with striking appropriate balances, across a range of concerns. For example, considerable but not unlimited resources are expended managing the risks associated with aviation at an acceptable level. These need to be managed by striking a balance with other considerations such as the perceived gains and costs of aviation.

In his review of the area, Hopkin (2018) includes a number of common definitions of risk management, including the definition adopted by the U.K. Treasury which sees risk management as "All the processes involved in identifying, assessing and judging risks, assigning ownership, taking actions to mitigate or anticipate them, and monitoring and reviewing progress". The International Organisation for Standards (ISO) (2009) manages a pithier definition of risk management as the "Co-ordinated activities to direct and control an organisation with regard to risk". These definitions have in common the sense that risk management encompasses all the other areas of risk, from commissioning risk analysis through evaluating and feeding back outcomes to the consideration of human factors and the way these impact on risk. Taking the example from forensic practice of community supervision of potential offenders, there will be a wide variety of risks to be managed. These will differ between individuals and very different considerations will arise in managing terrorist offenders and sexually violent offenders in the community. Some risks will be linked to and interact with the use of technology such as that used for monitoring purposes. Critics might note that much of this is lost when risk management comes to be seen too narrowly as simply risk treatment.

On adopting this notion of risk management, it can be sub-divided and described in various ways, and this may differ across general and specialist areas such as patient safety in healthcare settings. Such descriptions tend to involve various stages and these may be represented in the form of flow-charts or other pictorial representations. All, however, tend to cover the same broad ground and here simpler presentations are often seen as better. They would typically include an initial stage of work looking at the overarching risk appetite and then the strategy for addressing this. Following on from this are efforts to incorporate and improve decisions around risk and integrating this into the day-to-day working or 'operations' of the organisation. A further aspect of risk management is focused on identifying and managing cross-organisational risks and taking opportunities for improvement. The final aspect can be seen as relating to feedback, or the use of learning from experience, to improve the way resources are used to achieve outcomes (Thompson and Graham, 1996; Aven, 2010; Hopkin, 2018). This process may often involve making a formal distinction between 'risk agents' and 'risk systems' as an aid to risk management. To take a simple example from forensic practice, an individual being managed in the community on parole may be seen as a 'risk agent' whereas the organisational system involved in their supervision and support may be seen as a 'risk system'. Much of forensic practice can be criticised for neglecting these two concepts with arguably an undue focus on individuals as risk agents at the expense of looking at the complex area of risk systems and systemic change. This neglect of risk management is perhaps more understandable in some areas of forensic practice than others. It does, however, give rise to significant criticisms, as arguably it has served to close down many points of engagement and development in the broad processes of managing risk. It may also have contributed to a growing tendency to focus exclusively on risk reduction, at the expense of considering the positive aspects of risk.

Risk Analysis

Risk analysis can itself be further divided into a number of parts, depending on the complexity of the area being assessed. For large projects, it is common to break down planning, assessment, treatment and evaluation stages further. For example, planning this might involve looking separately at strategic, financial and operational aspects (Aven, 2012, 2015). For less complex issues, this may not be necessary and may indeed serve no useful purpose and simply overcomplicate the process. The aim of all the parts that form risk analysis is to provide a sufficiently informative picture to address the issue at hand as well as identifying alternative approaches. The level of detail needed to meet this goal will vary. The level of analysis associated with risks of large-scale terrorist events is likely (or at least should) be very different from that associated with risks to an individual. Adequate risk analysis also allows for the identification and specification of important conditions and assumptions that may have been made and how these might influence risk management. Drawing these pictures can, in many respects, be seen to parallel the scientist–practitioner model advocated and used within applied psychology (Shapiro, 2002). This stresses the importance of detailed specification, analysis, assessment and formulation of problems before progressing to treatment and evaluation.

Current forensic practice is open to the criticism that it seriously fails in this respect. Where any risk analysis is done, this tends to be implicit rather than explicit. The use of simple algorithms and checklist RAIs often promote an immediate jump to probabilistic assessment. The process of drawing an adequate picture of the risk, or risks, being assessed is frequently absent. At best, this tends to be cursory and inadequate, leading to assessment being made on weak or absent foundations. This in turn leads to risk treatment that may be similarly lacking in foundation and when considering issues of the acceptability and tolerability of risks that are left unaddressed, stakeholders have little visibility afforded to them. Arguably, this is closely associated with the common practice of adopting broad legal categories as the basis for risk assessments. Much of forensic practice has come to be associated simply with conducting risk assessment of remarkably broad areas. An example of this might be efforts to assess the risk of 'sexual violence', a concept of behaviour so broad that it must surely be of severely limited value in risk terms. Legal categories of this kind were developed for very different purposes concerning the administration of justice. Even on the most cursory analysis, such categories involve distinct and non-overlapping forms of risk, sharing only an implied motive. The development and marketing of various standardised forms of RAI in forensic practice can be seen to have exacerbated this trend. These have typically stressed risk assessment based on broad areas of risk, often drawing implicitly or explicitly on legal categories.

Measuring Risk

The measurement of risk in forensic practice is also open to a number of significant criticisms, having fallen out of step with other fields. As a starting point, it is widely accepted that addressing risk does need some way to deal with the distribution of data. Probability theory has often proved useful here, serving as a formal means of doing this, leading to its use across many areas of practice (Clemen and Winkler, 1999). In comparison with many other areas concerned with risk, however, the use of this in forensic practice can be criticised as being unduly simple and isolated from specialist expertise in the area. There have been robust debates within statistics between advocates of relative frequency and knowledge-based concepts of probability and even as these have abated, similar arguments have become apparent across many areas of risk analysis (Sagoff, 2004). Such debate seems to have been largely absent from forensic practice, where relative frequency conceptions of probability appear often to be treated as if they were the only conception of probability.

As discussed earlier, such 'frequentist' probability involves estimating an unknown within certain limits. These estimates are seen as varying as a result of random variation in samples, with the impact of this variation assumed to reduce as the size of samples increase and approaches infinity. It is perhaps worth noting in passing that Bernoulli undertook work in this area that remained incomplete at the time of his death; yet, in his correspondence, he did not appear to believe this approach was a suitable one for real-world problems. Later theorists have been rather more optimistic, but others have shared his reservations about the application of the approach (Fine, 2014). Within forensic practice, such concerns have often gone largely unacknowledged. A commonly seen alternative to frequentist approaches in risk analysis has been the use of knowledge-based probabilities, drawing on Bayesian methods (Ferson, 2005; Lindley, 2006). As a fundamentally different approach to probability, this does not posit hypothetical populations of similar events, meaning that knowledge-based probabilities can generally be specified. There are a number of different possible interpretations of this concept and as discussed elsewhere, such probabilities can be seen as a degree of belief (de Finetti, 1974). Surprisingly perhaps, attempts to use these approaches to probability have at least until recently declined across forensic practice.

In a detailed review of approaches to risk, Aven (2010) suggests that an unduly narrow view of risk, equating it with probability, is fundamentally misconceived. More recent work in many areas of risk analysis has suggested that this is not an adequate way of expressing risk, which in fact needs to go beyond statements of probability. In his review of the area, Aven (2010) uses a hypothetical case of treatment (T) for a disease to illustrate this argument. Here the probability of T having a positive effect (P) is assessed based on the available evidence, with a value of 0.80 for the estimate P* (the * indicating this to be an estimated value). However, P* cannot claim to adequately capture the situation. This estimated probability fails to address uncertainties caused by using data that are not directly relevant to individual patients, who are likely to respond differently. As a result, the use of P* and the calculation of confidence intervals around this value alone, are not adequate to describe risk. In such cases, it is argued that risk assessment needs to go beyond this, with consideration of its individual relevance (Renn, 2008).

A practical example of this is provided in a study of the assessment of the risk of health problems in divers working on oil production installations in the North Sea, between the United Kingdom and Norway (Aven, Vinnen and Wiencke, 2007). Assessments of risk were conducted in the 1970s to derive probability-based assessments of risk. These had suggested that the risks of health problems were low, with estimated probabilities of serious health problems developing calculated to be around 1%. These assessments drew on the knowledge of health problems in divers then available. The mathematical rigour and sophistication of the methods used, however, served to obscure something important as there was a large amount of uncertainty arising from the novel working conditions. This novelty made the conditions very different from those present in the historic data. Analysis of the evidence base here did not indicate a high probability of health issues, giving poor and, in fact, very misleading predictions. Divers in this environment went on to experience high levels of health problems that emerged over the following decades. Comparable difficulties arise in forensic practice where a focus on probabilities calculated using historic data may be similarly misleading, in light of environmental change and novelty. In an apparent effort to avoid this kind of difficulty, others have sought to move away from drawing on probability theory to focus largely or exclusively on uncertainty. The U.K. Cabinet Office (2002) provides an illustrative example of this, defining risk in terms of uncertainty of actions, outcomes and events. This approach can be seen to focus in part on Knight's distinction between risk and uncertainty. It has a superficial appeal, apparently getting around the difficulties with defining risk in terms of accurate expected values or probability distributions. As noted, these can be difficult to obtain and to accurately estimate. Simply relying on notions of uncertainty, however, generates a raft of difficulties of its own. Most strikingly, it opens up the obvious question of what is meant by uncertainty within such a vague definition.

It can be argued that two definitions have largely dominated recent thinking around risk. Both are similar in their essentials, but differ in detail. One defines risk as a situation or event where something of human value is at stake and the outcome is uncertain (Rosa, 1998). The other sees risk as an uncertain consequence of an event or activity with respect to something of human value (International Risk Governance Council, 2005). Both rest on an assumption that 'risk' exists as an 'objective' state of the world, independent of perception or knowledge of what is at risk or the likelihood of it (Rosa, 1998). Risk analysis here is needed to determine the issues, uncertainty and values.

A variety of structured methods have been developed to aid in this. These range from using simple diagrams, as aids to analysis, through to much more sophisticated methods. The former includes simple pictorial representations to provide a preliminary analysis, whilst the later build on this with increasing levels of complexity and formal analysis (Card, Ward and Clarkson, 2012). These methods can, however, be roughly divided into three groups and all are rarely seen in forensic practice:

1   Simplified qualitative analysis
2   Standard qualitative and/or quantitative analysis
3   Model-based and primarily quantitative methods

Simplified Qualitative Analysis

It is important to stress that a simple overview of historic data does not, in itself, constitute a risk analysis. A more structured form of evaluation is required to justify such a description, along with a clear focus on future events. Qualitative analysis at this level does not need to always be particularly sophisticated. It may involve a structured process of group or individual analysis such as 'brainstorming' or the use of simple diagrams to provide a preliminary sketch of the problem.

Standard Qualitative and/or Quantitative Analysis

There is a range of standardised approaches to risk analysis that may be exclusively qualitative or a mix of quantitative and qualitative analysis. Each have strengths and weaknesses, and there is no perfect or 'one size fits all' method.

Many have developed to address specific types of risk or working environments; others are more generic. Take, for example, two comparatively well-known and widely used frameworks: the hazard and operability analysis (HAZOP) and the structured what if technique (SWIFT). These can be seen as related approaches suitable for addressing a range of risks.

HAZOP is an inductive technique used to analyse risk in a "bottom-up" manner. Analysing risks with this method involves trying to predict deviations from what might be seen as safe conditions. It depends heavily on the level of skill and knowledge of the expert, or experts, involved. The method can be divided into phases involving definition and preparation, examination and documentation and follow-up of the analysis. The definition and preparation phase includes specifying risks along with detailed considerations of what information and data to gather, how to record and report this consistently. The examination and documentation phase in HAZOP involves breaking the problem down systematically and specifying deviations from normal or safe functioning. Causes and consequences of such deviations would be formally assessed here, with the aim of identifying likely patterns of difficulty and potential indicators. The use of these as a means of detecting and preventing problems would be formally considered, as would possible mitigating conditions or actions. This phase of HAZOP leads to the identification of relevant actions to address risk. The final follow-up phase of HAZOP covers the formal recording of the work undertaken and creation of a feedback loop, allowing the analysis to be compared with real-world outcomes. Such feedback allows for a process of correction and modification.

HAZOP has been used in areas as diverse as ecology, pharmaceutical trials and healthcare safety, where analysts are often presented with complex pictures of risk, involving many interacting elements. The method, however, has been little used in forensic practice (Fiorentini and Marmo, 2019). The reasons for this are not obvious and such techniques appear to have clear relevance to many of the more complex problems seen in forensic practice. Here, the use of highly structured analysis may serve multiple functions, serving to draw out a range of risks and interactions between these, rather than focusing on single obvious risks. The formality also means that all of the assumptions and presumptions are made more transparent. The use of detailed structure also encourages the drawing out of various threads to issues, reducing the tendency to jump too quickly to solutions. Finally, such methods stress the importance of feedback, ensuring that solutions chosen are effective but also critically that they continue to be so. Large parts of forensic practice can be criticised for failing badly in this respect, with a lack of effective feedback from the level of individual practitioners, through to large-scale systems.

Methods such as HAZOP can also be criticised in a number of ways. They are complex and labour-intensive to use, requiring high levels of training and expert input to be effective. Done poorly, they may fall victim to the term GIGO from the early days of computer programming, which stands for 'Garbage In Garbage Out'. Complexity itself is an issue of concern with the parts of such analyses being broken down in ever-increasing detail, suggesting a potentially infinite regress. This can clearly be of value, up to a point, when faced with complex types of risk problems, such as large-scale clinical trials. A line does, however, need to be drawn and more is not always better in analysing risk. The scale and expense of such methods is also hard to justify for many risk problems, where it can be seen as unduly expensive, slow and bureaucratic. Such methods may be essential for a large-scale vaccine clinical trial but be excessive for improving patient safety in a primary care health centre. In forensic practice, it may be essential for analysis of risk from terrorist attacks but be seen as inappropriately complex for analysing other risks.

The SWIFT methodology aimed to address some of these concerns and it has come to be widely used in healthcare contexts such as patient safety, because it provides a much simpler and quicker structure for risk analysis. Methodologically, SWIFT structures are associated with analysing risk. This is done by identifying hazards and risks associated with them and then asking a series of questions about each. The method is much less bureaucratic than approaches such as HAZOP and such simplified methods streamline the analysis process, whilst retaining a degree of structure. Frameworks of this kind can be used by groups or individuals as a means of guiding their analysis of risks.

Model-Based and Primarily Quantitative Methods

Event tree analysis and fault tree analysis are two related examples of approaches that use branching questions to analyse risk. Analytic methods of this kind are widely applied to complex risk problems and are used extensively across the social and natural sciences. These methods give a logical picture of events that surround a risk and are based on the assumption that multiple causes of an event are possible. The reference to trees reflects the branching picture of events that they yield. A serious criticism of much forensic practice has been the consistent failure to take on board such techniques. This may, in part at least, be a function of failing to distinguish adequately between risk analysis and risk assessment. It might also be linked to the fact that such techniques require high levels of expertise and hence investment. Complex analytic methods of this kind are known to forensic practice, however, having been researched, developed and tested in areas of direct application (Monahan et al., 2001).

Treating Risk as an Expected Value

Current approaches to risk in forensic practice appear to be heavily influenced by early work in economics and management. Methods from areas such as econometrics have been adopted, wittingly or unwittingly. The pervasive nature of this influence may go some way to accounting for much current practice but given the assumptions that often underpinned these approaches, such influence is surprising. More surprising still is the extent to which they have continued to displace ideas and methods from other areas of the social and natural sciences. On the face of it, work in areas such as epidemiology, ecology and climate change has a lot to contribute to improving work on issues of risk in forensic practice. Yet, the uptake of ideas from these areas into mainstream forensic practice appears to have been limited and declining.

This is important because the way that risk is thought about greatly influences the manner in which it is analysed, evaluated, assessed and treated. This is illustrated by the stress on ideas of expected value (E[V]) to describe risk, which derives in part from economic models of risk and the misapplication of the influential ideas on risk developed by Knight (1921). Knight was explicit in directing his work on risk to the economics of profit, and as a result, the idea of E[V] was of central relevance. The idea also had the attributes of being relatively easy to describe and understand. It had often been used in the past to describe the outcomes of the games of chance, which provided much of the foundation of early probability theory. Some risk analysts, however, have been critical of using this in many other areas where risk is concerned, noting that the kinds of gambling paradigms chosen by early probability theorists were not chosen randomly. Whilst they may or may not have reflected the author's love of gambling, they did provide atypical and relatively straightforward examples of probability, allowing for the calculation of statistics such as E[V]. To take a straightforward example of this, if you were to throw a die 600 times (or 600 dice once), it is relatively straightforward to calculate an E[V] for this procedure. The arithmetic is simply $(100 \times 1) + (100 \times 2) + (100 \times 3) + (100 \times 4) + (100 \times 5) + (100 \times 6)$, all divided by 600. This gives an expected value of 3.5. This straightforward concept has gone on to be widely applied to issues of risk, based on the assumption that rational decision making about risk involves maximising the E[V]. The application of this to the area of profit addressed by Knight (1921) is clear. Its use for other areas of risk has been strongly challenged, almost from its inception. The idea was seen as inappropriate by Bernoulli (1954) who dismissed it in favour of more complex ideas of expected utility (E[U]) rather than value. He suggested that E[V] was not an appropriate measure here, given that individuals differ in their views around risk and uncertainty, making E[U] a more appropriate measure.

There are in fact a range of studies suggesting that people to do not act to maximise E[V] in the manner suggested and these are discussed in more detail in the next chapter. For the moment, it is sufficient to observe that people act quite differently from the models based on ideas of E[V] and also E[U]. A number of hypotheses have been put forward to account for this, including the suggestion that people tend to be 'risk averse' or that people are prone to make irrational decisions based on characteristic biases. The risk aversion view is often illustrated by using examples based on E[V] and a hypothetical game of 'Roulette'. This has been touched on previously and it typically involves a person being faced with a probabilistic judgement, such as a six-chambered gun with one loaded chamber. Where the gun fires, they are told they will lose £24 million, and where it does not, they win £6 million. Most people choose not to play this hypothetical game and choose instead a guaranteed win of £0.5 million. This is taken as illustrating risk aversion or irrationality, as the E[V] is simple to calculate at £1 million. The idea of preferring a guaranteed payment of £0.5 million over an E[V] of twice as much, it is argued, is not rational. Why not play the game when you would expect to win £1 million in the long run? People not doing so feed into ideas that the decision making here is irrational. The idea of utility put forward by Bernoulli (1954) goes some way to addressing this, but does not fully resolve the issue, as indeed he clearly recognised. In this example, how could a win of £1 million be reasonably seen to have lower utility than half that amount?

In response, alternative approaches, again drawn largely from economics, have been developed. These are normally described as 'portfolio' models or approaches and they have come to be identified with large areas of financial risk. Fundamentally, this model works on the assumption that pooling independent risks is an effective means of reducing risk. Broadly, it works from the starting point that if enough independent 'games' of this type are played, then this 'risk aversion' may be overcome. Taking the same paradigm, it is argued that playing this 'game' 100 times (or with 100 guns) will serve to reduce the likelihood of a major loss to very low levels. The potential losses would of course be much larger, running to £2,400 million but, it is argued, the probability of this loss would be much lower (1/6 raised to the power of 100). This is a level of probability equating to an event being almost impossible. By analogy, it is argued that the use of such 'portfolio' approaches in other areas, act in a similar manner to reduce risk. As the number of trials or events increases, then the uncertainties will decrease. Even here, however, most people remain unconvinced, leading to suggestions that risk aversion and irrationality in decision making are even deeper seated and have more serious implications.

There are in fact a few major problems with such portfolio approaches and they have been extensively critiqued by risk analysts (Sinha, Chandra and Biswas,

2018). Most obviously and most critically perhaps, events in the real world are rarely independent of each other in the manner suggested. Where they are not independent, then what is observed will not converge on the expected value in the way suggested and the probability of the event will not reduce to near impossibility. The roulette example above is also very unusual, in that the likelihood of all the outcomes is known and all the variance is accounted for, something that will rarely if ever be true in real-world examples and certainly not in forensic practice. Finally, risk analysts have pointed out that an adequate approach to risk assessment needs to take account of the potential for very large losses (Fischbacher-Smith, 2010; Taleb, 2015). This is likely to be even more true where such a portfolio approach is involved and potential losses in this example could reach £2,400 million, with the lack of independence meaning that the assumption of very low risk is spurious. A particularly striking real-world example of the failings of this approach is provided by the financial collapse of 2008 (Taleb, 2015). The causes were of course complex but a large element appears to have been the use of inappropriate risk models. Many financial institutions appeared to rely on just this kind of portfolio analysis to manage risks outlined above, with catastrophic implications.

Examples that draw out the difficulties with using E[V] as the basis for assessing risk in forensic practice are relatively easy to identify. Incidents of terrorism provide one clear example. Here the event being considered may have a number of carefully defined and analysed characteristics. These may overlap with other types of terrorist events, or may have no overlaps at all beyond the broad motive for the act. The potential losses here, however, might be extreme and difficult to accurately estimate in terms of expected losses. What predictions are available will generally be based on historic information, which may be of little relevance or be inadequate, leading to wide variation in estimates (Taleb, 2015; Fischbacher-Smith, 2016). There is, fundamentally, a high level of uncertainty around such phenomena. Analysis, evaluation and assessment of risk based on ideas of E[V] or E[U] are therefore unlikely to be useful, having the capacity to deviate greatly from actual events and losses.

Criticisms of Using Relative Frequency Probability

Linked to the criticism of treating risk as an expected value is the criticism around seeing risk as a relative frequency or 'objective' probability. A crucial distinction here is the view of probability that is adopted. Indeed, within forensic practice, there often appears to be an implicit assumption that there is a single agreed form of probability. The view of probability that is typically adopted takes probability to be something objective, reflecting some physical reality. This contrasts with the major alternative body of thinking, which sees probability as being knowledge-based or 'subjective', representing not physical reality but degrees of belief about the world. Approaches based on relative frequency ideas of probability, treat it as applicable to repeatable events that involve uncertainty. This view is widely taught to social and natural science students alike and was widely popularised by Fisher (1955) who developed a number of techniques to assess probability. Much of Fisher's work was in the biological sciences, looking at the area of crop yields and the effects of varied interventions on these. Here, an important question was whether differences were attributable to random fluctuations or to the interventions, although the techniques devised have been widely applied. By contrast, subjective or knowledge-based approaches to probability generally start from the position that probability of any event, where there is uncertainty, involves statements about degrees of belief.

As with E[V], enthusiasm for objective probability has perhaps been greatest in the area of economics. Arguably, there has also been a largely uncritical acceptance of this in some other areas of the social sciences. In other areas, however, the adoption of objective probability has been more critically received. As noted earlier, Knight (1921) stressed a distinction between risk and uncertainty, arguing that risk applied only to events where an objective probability distribution could be defined. Uncertainty involved events where this was not the case, which, in fact covers many areas likely to be of interest. In practice, this distinction has been variously received by risk analysts. Some have seen value in the distinction, for example, in terms of the psychological study of risk and the way people address issues of uncertainty (Fischbacher-Smith, Irwin and Fischbacher-Smith, 2010; Mousavi and Gigerenzer, 2014). Others have been much more critical, seeing this distinction as misconceived. Critics have suggested that Knight's views on categories of decision problems remains useful but his distinction between risk and uncertainty does not, arguing that it excludes nearly all areas of likely interest (Aven, 2010). Where subjective notions of probability are adopted, it is argued that Knight's definition of risk becomes meaningless. This view is though misleading and Knight's definition of uncertainty was more complex than suggested by such an analysis. It included situations where the mutually exclusive and exhaustive set of future events and consequences (or state space) cannot be known. Without this state space no probability distribution can be constructed with probabilities that add up to one. In such conditions Savage (1954) made clear that his Bayesian decision theory was not applicable to uncertainty, where heuristics are the best we have (Gigernzer and Engel, 2006).

As an alternative, three classifications of risk problem have been suggested: first, those unusual situations where an 'objective' or relative frequency probability distribution can be established, second situations of more or less complete ignorance and third, situations falling between these two extremes (Aven, 2010). Another alternative suggested looks at risk problems in terms of dimensions, with risk problems categorised in terms of complexity (linear to complex), uncertainty (low to high) and ambiguity (low to high) (International Risk Governance Council, 2005; Aven and Renn, 2009b). The dimension of complex to linear refers to how difficult it is to identify causal links between potential causal agents and observed events. In some cases, this may be relatively straightforward, with a linear relationship. Within forensic practice, complexity is likely to be the norm, however, with variations between and within individuals, interaction effects, delays between cause and effect, non-linear effects and so on, adding to complexity. An analogous situation from the natural sciences might be the assessment of complex ecosystems, which present similarly high levels of complexity and uncertainty as a result of such effects.

This dimensional view is concerned with the adequacy and completeness of information around the risk being assessed. This in turn will interact with modelling inaccuracies and the variability of expert judgements. Such concerns are evident in many areas of forensic practice, where the data is typically limited and models are weak, adding to uncertainty. A third approach, which will be looked at in greater detail later, is one that distinguishes between risk, ambiguity and uncertainty. This sees risk as concerning situations where state space and probabilities are known. Ambiguity refers to situations where state space (essentially all possible configurations of a system) is known but objective probabilities are not known and here subjective probabilities, or the principle of indifference, may be helpful. Uncertainty by contrast refers to situations where state space is not known or knowable, and in such cases heuristics may help (Gigerenzer, 2021).

Criticisms of Using Knowledge-Based Probability

Knowledge-based or 'subjective' probabilities have been extensively used by risk analysts (Ferson, 2005; Grêt-Regamey and Straub, 2006). Given the clear relevance of this approach, its limited use in forensic practice is a legitimate criticism and the neglect is surprising (Crighton, 2004; Hodges, 2019). Such methods are typically used where empirical data is not available and may never be available. As such, it provides a means of addressing ambiguity, by formally including information such as expert opinions. Views of such knowledge-based probability tends to be polarised, with staunch advocates and strident critics, although it has been noted that this has calmed down within statistics, even as the debate has emerged in others as they adopt such 'Bayesian' ideas (Ferson, 2005).

Use of knowledge-based probabilities has grown across many areas of risk (Spiegelhalter and Knill-Jones, 1984; Aven, 2012). This typically involves risk analysts specifying a probability to express uncertainty, based on available knowledge. As such, this does not imply an assumption of a true or 'objective' probability, based on a hypothetical infinite population of similar events. This requires identification of relevant expertise in given areas and it may also include processes of formalising the basis for these knowledge-based estimates of probability. In contrast to this growth in use in other areas, the use of knowledge-based probability in forensic practice has seen a progressive decline in use over recent years (Towl and Crighton, 1996; 1997). Where the idea is considered at all, it has tended to be unfavourably contrasted with dominant approaches that are based on relative frequency probability or rely simply on qualitative verbal descriptions of risk.

The use of knowledge-based probabilities is open to a number of legitimate criticisms. One of these is that knowledge-based probability estimates are difficult to challenge. Typically, the only means of doing this is through the accumulation of observational data, but this may not always be possible. Knowledge-based probability also raises difficulties in applying standard measures of reliability and validity. Efforts have been made to address this, with three criteria being suggested: syntactic, pragmatic and calibration (Aven, 2010), and these are outlined in more detail below. The criticisms that such probabilities are unscientific mirrors the more general criticism of such methods, when used as a unified approach to probabilities. The use of expert opinion to establish initial probabilities has been criticised as being arbitrary and unscientific, something that is important given the influence of such inputs on the resulting estimates of probability (Ferson, 2005). In addressing real-world problems, such Bayesian analysis may often become computationally difficult. Illustrations of knowledge-based approaches typically include examples of Bayesian updating, where initial estimates, even if they are arbitrary, are progressively modified by the accumulation of more data. This raises problems itself, in that even completely wrong ideas are never completely rejected but only modified. In real-world examples, the situation may be worse than this, with few trials or only one trial being possible. This means that updating of probabilities in the way envisaged cannot take place, and in such cases, the question arises whether Bayesian methods add anything to expert estimates of probability (Ferson, 2005; Aven, 2015).

Counter views to such criticism have stressed the function of knowledge-based probability methods in building a rational consensus, where alternatives are often not viable (Bedford and Cooke, 2001). In addressing the use of knowledge-based probabilities, Cooke (1991) suggested five principles that underpin effective use: reproducibility, accountability, empirical control, neutrality and fairness. Clearly, this suggests that the use of knowledge-based probabilities in practice is not an easy option, but it in fact often presents a complex challenge (Bedford and Cooke, 2001; Cooke, Marti and Mazzuchi, 2021). For many areas of practical concern, knowledge may be limited or minimal to begin with. As a result, estimates of likelihood, even by experts, may of necessity be arbitrary at least initially. Comparing expert estimates to subsequent observations is one means of improving knowledge-based probabilities, but in practice, this may not be possible or practical. This requires a fall back on constructed models and thought experiments and here traditional scientific methods, involving repeated independent measures of assigned probabilities from the same individual, are typically not possible (Aven, 2010). Regrettably, much of this debate and the developments in the area of knowledge-based probability have been largely neglected within forensic practice.

Syntactic Criterion

The use of syntactic criterion measures has been suggested as one means of improving estimates of knowledge-based probability. The idea here is that such estimates are likely to be better where they are consistent with syntactic rules from axioms involved in probability. This idea is perhaps easier to grasp with a concrete example. Taking A and B as disjoint events, then the assigned probabilities for A and B should equal the sum of the probabilities for A and B. In other words, if probability of A is equal to 0.3 and probability of B is equal to 0.5, it would be reasonable to expect the probability of A and B to be equal to 0.8. Where knowledge-based probabilities are consistent with such rules, it is suggested that they are likely to be more accurate.

Pragmatic Criteria

The notion of pragmatic criteria involves the idea of comparing assigned knowledge-based probabilities with reality. This involves a subjective estimate of how well the knowledge-based probability 'fits' with observations. Such criteria may apply in often-atypical situations, where there is some adequate data for comparison purposes. For example, where the prevalence of a given disease is known in a population, this may serve as criteria to compare knowledge-based probability.

Calibration

This method is extensively used in dealing with risk, but oddly, it is seldom seen within forensic practice. Essentially, it involves eliciting expert judgements in a systematic manner over multiple cases and comparing these with known measures (Martin, Burgman, Fidler et al., 2012). In this way, individual experts can be assessed, or calibrated, in terms of the accuracy of their estimates. There are various levels of sophistication involved in this process and a variety of methods may be used. Additionally, the process can involve giving systematic feedback and reinforcing of assessors for accuracy, as a means of improving calibration. In some contexts, more sophisticated methods may be used to pool the assessments of groups of experts and also calibrate these pooled estimates (Cooke, Marti and Mazzuchi, 2021) as well as providing systematic feedback on performance (Dressel and Farid, 2018).

Calibration presents a number of practical challenges and it is difficult to do meaningfully for low-frequency events. Equally, the evaluation of how good estimated probabilities are often needs to be made at the point of assignment, before observations are made. In areas of forensic practice, however, such considerations seem less relevant. Many common tasks such as the assessment of high-frequency behaviours in fact appear particularly suited to calibration approaches. Here, multiple independent observations will be obtainable and the potential for evaluating assessor accuracy and providing feedback is clearly possible. Countries with unitary systems of criminal and civil justice seem to be ideally suited to using such methods. It is therefore a powerful criticism that so little effort has been made to use such techniques in forensic practice. Indeed, it is rare to even see elementary efforts to establish baseline calibration of knowledge, for example, by considering how accurate assessors' knowledge of base rates for the behaviours being considered are. Meaningful efforts to calibrate the accuracy of probability estimates for expert assessors, including feedback on hit rates, has been almost completely neglected in forensic practice.

Treating Risk as a Product of History

The use of historic data has a central place in questions of risk. In current forensic practice, historic data sets have been used to provide the basis for estimating future risk, to the extent that the approach may be seen as unquestionable. A number of reasons for this are evident, the most important perhaps being that historic data is often correlated with subsequent events, with individuals showing significant behavioural consistency over time (Fox and Farrington, 2016; Farrington, 2021). Over-reliance on historic data as a basis for risk assessment has, however, been criticised from risk analysis perspectives. The relevance of historic data used in forensic practice varies greatly and it has been noted that some frequently used historic information, has little or no relationship to future risk (Coid, Yang, Ullrich et al., 2009, 2011; Skeem and Monahan, 2020). This reflects wider findings within the literature on risk, which suggests that simply seeing risk in terms of historic data is an inadequate approach. Going back to the idea that there are areas of ignorance about given risks, the reliance on historic data may be of no use and may in fact be actively misleading. The terror attacks on the United States on 11 September 2001 illustrate this graphically, with past information giving little indication of the novel forms of attack. There is a need therefore for methods to address risk that move beyond traditional statistical approaches to risk based on historic data.

An uncritical over-reliance on historic data has been identified across a number of fields but only in some has it been as evident and persistent as in forensic practice. To take an example, there is a substantial body of research into climate change, drawing heavily on historic data and this is undoubtedly useful. Work in this area has not, however, proceeded on the basis that historic data will continue to be adequately predictive of future outcomes. Indeed, research has quickly moved on to develop theory-based and dynamic models of change, essential in a system that is both dynamic and non-linear in nature (Schneider, 2004). By contrast, much of forensic practice can be legitimately criticised for neglecting this. Forensic practice has come to be dominated by the use of correlational statistical relationships between historic information of various kinds and broadly defined adverse outcomes, generating limited insights and little in the way of scientific development (Coid et al., 2011). An example here might be efforts to predict individual suicides in forensic settings, based on a limited collection of historical corelates such as depressed mood, previous self-injury, previous self-poisoning, gender, marital status and so on. Efforts to develop algorithms or checklists based on such data have been repeated over time, with this historic data typically being analysed using inferential statistics, estimating how consistently such RAIs can be undertaken and how well they are associated with actual occurrence of suicides. This kind of methodology has clear attractions, in that it is a simple, requiring none of the complex modelling inherent in the example of the climate change research discussed above. It is, however, clearly a severely limited and largely fruitless means of dealing with a risk that is complex, changes over time and occurs at low frequencies (Crighton and Towl, 2008; Walker and Towl, 2016; Towl and Crighton, 2017; Gould, McGeorge and Slade, 2018).

The ease of using historic data to project future risk and its ubiquity has, at least in practice, obscured the significant weaknesses that have been well recognised by researchers and risk analysts (Monahan et al. 2001; Aven, 2010, 2015; Coid et al., 2011). In forensic practice, this has included assumptions around the nature of the data, relating to distribution and the form of the trends. It appears a common assumption that data will be normally distributed and trends will be linear. Such assumptions are by no means obvious and the level of understanding in many areas of forensic practice is simply inadequate to determine this.

Conventional assumptions of this kind, where they are based on historic data, need in fact to be tested and justified.

At a more fundamental level, the use of historic data, as the basis for estimating future risk, has itself been criticised as misplaced or misconceived. Going back to economic risks as an example, it has been observed that historic data necessarily involves limited sampling of information. This may largely or totally exclude extreme observations, even where sampling involves very large amounts of data. As a result, the sampling may prove inadequate to address concerns around extreme observations. The banking collapses of 2008 in North America and Europe graphically illustrated this, with the use of limited historic data being taken to demonstrate the very low probability of the events that unfolded (Greenspan, 2004). These models, however, were based on both a limited time horizon and assumptions that proved to be poorly founded (Rajan, 2006). The use of historic data here served to exclude consideration of important risks. In his critique, Taleb (2015) described the use of statistical methods in this way as 'mediocristan', contrasting this with 'extremistan' approaches, which assume the presence of extreme events, even where they have not been observed historically. This has come to be more popularly termed 'Black Swan' events and links to more fundamental criticisms of historic data as a means of assessing risk. Ideas that echo the earlier thinking around what was termed 'random walk' by Pearson (1905) as well as later ideas around the non-linear nature of many systems, captured under the multidisciplinary notion of chaos theory (Ayers, 1997). In essence, such work raises fundamental issues about the extent and nature of reliance on statistical analysis of historic data to predict future outcomes.

In practice terms, analysis based on historical data can easily become too narrow and so mislead when conducting assessments of risk. The use of traditional statistical methods, based on historical data sets, have been criticised as failing in two key respects here. First, it has been noted that relative frequency probability methods have expressed uncertainties about fictional or hypothetical parameters, rather than actual events. This has acted as an often-unacknowledged limit on the relevance of past data, which does not give adequate attention to possible extreme events (Aven, 2015; Taleb, 2015; Fischbacher-Smith, 2016). Undue emphasis on historic data around risk may increase the chances of missing extreme events but also of missing emerging patterns. Critics have also noted that a focus on historic data has often led, across disciplines, to effort being misdirected towards the prediction of events in environments that have already changed fundamentally (Aven, Vinnen and Wiencke, 2007). Historic predictors of a range of behaviours, including violence towards self or others, are drawn from different environments to those which currently exist or that will exist. The assumption of continued relevance of such predictors is therefore something that needs to be addressed and tested rather than assumed when analysing risk.

Standardisation and Consensus

There are strong arguments for developing a better shared understanding of the concepts used to address risk and perhaps especially around the use of knowledge-based probabilities (Aven, 2010). Such probabilities are highly individual and in the absence of constraints, they may vary widely. Methods for producing a single 'correct' value do not exist and the manner in which this kind of probability estimate is used will differ across contexts. Some values of this kind will be generally accepted and relatively firm, others will be much more uncertain. Forensic practice can be criticised in both of these respects, lacking both a clear understanding of agreed concepts and of knowledge-based probabilities (Torrey, Stanley, Monahan and Steadman, 2008). In an extensive review of this area, Lindley (2006) highlighted the importance of these concerns using two examples. One concerned the common statistical paradigm of flipping a coin, the other a complex real-world problem of a therapeutic trial for a new drug. In the first example, it was argued that a knowledge-based probability that the coin will land on heads could be given as 0.5. This is a firm and generally accepted probability and can in fact be seen as a distinct form of probability. For the drug trial, the probability that the new drug will be effective may similarly be given as 0.5, on the assumption that the new drug is equally likely to succeed or fail. This may be a reasonable starting assumption, but it is a rather different estimate of probability to the one for the coin. Despite both probabilities being based on the available background knowledge and resulting in the same value, it is reasonable to say that the uncertainty around the drug trial is much greater. Most assessors would ascribe a very low probability for obtaining less than 100 heads in 1,000 trials. In a clinical drug trial, however, over 1,000 pairs of patients, less information is available around which patients would benefit from the new drug. This may perform better, worse or the same as existing treatments. The coin tosses are not easily biased but it is well evidenced that drug trials may be (Schott, Pachl, Limbach et al., 2010). Context of this kind is associated with what view is taken on the 'firmness' of any probability estimate and this can be shown more formally using Bayes theorem for updating probabilities (Lindley, 2006). The essential point here being that there is always a need to address background knowledge, as this provides the basis for evaluation but future outcomes and performance of systems may not in fact mirror these historic observations. They may not even be similar to them or the predictions based on historic information. This is not an easy issue to address but such uncertainty needs to be reflected in properly expressing risk (Aven, 2010) and forensic practice can be legitimately criticised for seldom doing this.

Using Models

A fundamental aspect of scientific approaches is the use of models as a way of representing and typically simplifying the world. The aim of this is the development of greater understanding and insights into the area concerned, allowing more precise and testable predictions. At a more prosaic level, models may also be used to enable an appropriate level of analysis, here in the area of risk. Such models need to balance simplifying complexity and maintaining accuracy. An essential task within scientific communities is therefore the development of theoretical models that may lead to better systematic accounts. A major criticism of forensic practice is the lack of efforts to develop such models, or apply those which exist, across a range of areas of interest. This can be seen as part of a wider critique of the inappropriate use of inferential statistics in the social sciences broadly but most acutely perhaps in psychology (Gigerenzer, 2008). There have been exceptions to this, for example, in the area of suicide and violence (Plutchik, Van Praag and Conte, 1989; Plutchik and Van Praag, 1994) or in developing economic models of domestic violence (Farmer and Tiefenthaler, 1997). These examples stand out as clear exceptions to the vast majority of forensic practice, however, and this forms a legitimate and strong criticism of the field. There has been an increasing focus on atheoretical research, showing statistical differences or covariance between samples, with only rare examples of models and theory building being developed.

Conclusion

Here, a number of criticisms of forensic practice have been introduced, arising from multidisciplinary work across what has been broadly termed risk analysis. The most striking criticism is perhaps the extent of isolation of forensic practice from other disciplines and also from its own evidence base. This is clearly illustrated in the use of language around risk in forensic practice, which is often inconsistent with terminology in other areas and often betrays a lack of understanding of other perspectives. A lack of focus on risk analysis and the conflation of this with risk assessment is perhaps the most concerning example of this. The failure to develop an adequate 'picture' of risks before undertaking assessment seems likely to make a difficult task even harder. The scope to learn from the operational aspects of risk analysis in other disciplines is considerable and indeed has been seen in research into forensic practice. This needs to be translated into day-to-day practice in dealing with risk. The lack of sophistication in the way that risk is dealt with in forensic practice gives rise to legitimate criticisms ranging from the use of limited and relatively unsophisticated statistical methods through to the absence of efforts to build models and theory around areas of risk.

Critiques of Current Practice

Psychological Perspectives

Several criticisms of current forensic practice emerge from broadly psychological perspectives. This includes a range of disciplines including amongst others psychology, areas of philosophy, artificial intelligence and medicine. These critiques have tended to stem from a psychological viewpoint that assumes people have an innate ability to deal with risk, because they need to regularly make decisions about risk and uncertainty. The question from this perspective then becomes one of how good people are at doing this and how and when does this innate ability fail us. This contrasts markedly with current forensic practice, where the predominant view has increasingly been one that sees people as being poor at making accurate estimates of risk and therefore in need of ever greater constraints being placed on them, or indeed their replacement in the process. Such views build on research from experimental psychology from the 1970s onwards, in what is often called heuristics and biases research (Lejarraga and Hertwig, 2021). Findings from these studies demonstrated what were seen to be fundamental limitations in human cognition. People often showed difficulty in making complex judgements, including those involving estimates of risk. The results of this work went on to become part of the language of forensic practice and indeed the findings went on to have very marked influence across the social and natural sciences, where references to flaws in human cognition are now commonly seen. The greatest impacts of this work on heuristics and biases, however, seems to have been in the social sciences, in general, and economics, in particular. Here, the idea that people suffer from systematic biases in the way that they think about problems was taken up with enthusiasm by some economists, contributing to the development of behavioural economics as a distinct area of study. This stress on weaknesses in judgement and decision-making

DOI: 10.4324/9781003108665-8

served a useful and important function in economics, particularly in economic models of risk. It served as a potentially useful counterbalance to traditional models that tended, in the face of all the evidence to the contrary, to model people as acting as perfectly rational agents. Work from experimental psychology provided a means of modelling human economic behaviour in a way that was less in conflict with reality.

This research on heuristics and biases supported an extended period in which the focus of attention was on human limitations or fundamental weaknesses in human cognition, in turn supporting efforts to replace human judgement with more structured or constrained decision-making methods. This greatly supported the growth of structured Risk Assessment Instruments (RAIs) that are argued to address these weaknesses, improving accuracy and being both more reliable and more valid than human judgements. If people were already good at assessing risk, then such aids to judgement would not be needed, or would only be needed in specific circumstances. Within forensic practice, this has seen unaided clinical judgements about risk being displaced by the use of the two main types of RAIs discussed earlier. The use of algorithms and checklists-based RAIs were argued to provide a means of correcting these fundamental biases and errors that are present when people make complex decisions about risks. For some, this led on logically to suggestions that such judgements should in turn be automated and made by artificial intelligence systems. The view that human judgement needs to be constrained in this way has gained almost universal acceptance within forensic practice, although the idea of automating people out of the process entirely has been received with less enthusiasm. This assumption has gone on to have marked effects on practice and it therefore warrants more detailed consideration. Questions around whether human decision-making is as flawed as has often been suggested and if so, what form these flaws take, are important from both theoretical and practical viewpoints. This has major implications for the way issues of risk are dealt with but answering these questions requires at least an introductory consideration of some areas of experimental psychology.

It is perhaps helpful to start with a sense of how psychologists and others have thought about and studied questions of human judgement. One major review of the area divided this into four major traditions of study and that framework has been adopted below as a helpful basis for discussing the subject (Gigerenzer, 2006a, 2008):

1   Theories of unbounded rationality
2   Theories of optimisation under constraints
3   Study of cognitive illusions
4   Ecological rationality approaches

The first three of these theories that model human judgment deal with situations of risk. In contrast, the ecological rationality approach can deal with uncertainty, in the sense of the term used by Knight (1921), where optimisation is not feasible.

Unbounded Rationality

Ideas of unbounded rationality have a long history in philosophy, going on to have profound influences on other areas. It can reasonably be argued that such ideas fell out of favour in the natural sciences quite quickly. The influence of such ideas has been more long lasting in the social sciences, in general, and areas of economics, in particular (Holton, 1988; Thaler, 2000). These ideas have also had a major influence on areas of experimental psychology and the applied practice based on this.

Recent ideas of unbounded rationality in the understanding of thinking and decision-making can be traced back, in Western thought, to the ideas of the Laplace (1749–1827). Indeed, much of Laplace's thinking in this area went on to give rise to fundamental statistical concepts that have now come to be routinely used. In developing his thinking in these areas, Laplace drew on the idea of a fully predictable and deterministic universe (Laplace, 1825). These ideas were subsequently modified by others, to stress the use of optimal strategies, maximising outcomes and minimising errors, in place of a presumption of full determinism. The effects of this line of thought can still be clearly seen in models of risk that stress optimisation, in the form of statistical ideas such as expected values, expected utility and cost–benefit analysis in decision-making (Fishburn, 1988). Whilst the changes made over time greatly altered the assumptions of determinism suggested by Laplace, it has been argued that ideas of omniscience and omnipotence have often remained implicit (Simon, 1955; Gigerenzer, 2008). Models of human decision-making and cognition have therefore frequently taken an 'as-if' approach where people are treated as-if they had such characteristics. It is important to note that these do not assume that predictions will always be accurate, nor in general do they try to describe the processes used by people in decision-making. Rather they seek to model the optimal way in which decisions might be made, using formal criteria. These are in turn used to describe and compare the behaviours of such a model.

Optimisation Under Constraints

Optimisation under constraints models are fundamentally similar to the as-if models described above. They differ, however, in getting rid of ideas of omniscience and omnipotence to greater or lesser degrees, by setting various constraints on these. Constraints might include recognition of realities such as the limited capacity of memory, attention, processing and so on. Some models of this kind may also include consideration of costs and time constraints, associated with gathering information for decision-making. Models of this kind have proved to be especially popular in areas such as behavioural economics (Thaler, 2000; Kao and Velupillai, 2015). Here they have tended to fit with attempts to develop traditional econometric models, in an effort to make these more predictive of real behaviours.

Cognitive Illusions

The term cognitive illusion was introduced early on as an alternative way to refer to heuristics and biases research that had emerged in experimental psychology. The term has been controversial, having been suggested as a more accurate description of this work by Cohen (1981). This idea was accepted by one of the leading researchers in the area of heuristics and biases (Wason, 1981) but was rejected by others. This model of cognition is based on studies in cognitive psychology, which demonstrated that people's decision-making deviated from those derived from formal analyses, in systematic ways, hence the term bias. These results were attributed to the use of a number of heuristics, often described as 'rules of thumb'. The use of such heuristics was seen as leading to the observed biases in judgement and decision-making (Tversky and Kahneman, 1973, 1974). Cognitive illusion was coined as a term to challenge a number of the assumptions involved in this research and also to stress parallels with visual illusions research in experimental psychology.

This approach is a largely experimental one and it has focused on deviations from formal methods of analysis in human judgement, giving rise initially to the description of three major heuristics: representativeness, availability and anchoring (also sometimes called anchoring and adjustment). All three have been suggested to be of particular relevance to forensic practice (Neal and Grisso, 2014). Other heuristics have subsequently been added to the research literature over time, for example an affect heuristic (Slovic, Finucane, Peters and MacGregor, 2007). However, it continues to be a focus of debate on how many of these constitute distinct heuristics, rather than simply being different presentations of those initially identified. This work has been very influential within forensic practice where these heuristics have passed into common parlance. Similarly, a marked influence has been seen in areas such as economics, medicine, management and law.

Ecological Rationality

The notion of ecological rationality has also been described, less accurately, as the 'naturalistic decision-making' tradition (Neal and Grisso, 2014). This model is also derived in large part from experimental psychology and starts with the assumption of an evolutionary relationship between mind and environment, proposed by Herbert Simon (1916–2001) in the 1950s (Simon, 1953, 1955). It concerns the question of which environmental conditions a given heuristic can exploit, in order to exceed or match the accuracy of more complex models (Gigerenzer and Gaissmaier, 2011). In considering human cognition, the approach has commonalties with the work of psychologists such as Inhelder and Piaget (1958) but differed in the stress placed on logic as the basis of human thinking. For Simon, as well as those who have followed his ideas, logic is neither necessary nor sufficient for rational behaviour. Ecologically rational approaches do not ascribe the same central role to formal logic that the three other models do. To date, this model of judgement and decision-making and the implications of the research emerging from it has had remarkably little impact on forensic practice (Crighton, 2004, 2021). It has though had more marked and increasing influence in the natural sciences.

Biases Associated with Cognitive Illusions

As noted above, in a review of forensic mental health evaluations, Neal and Grisso (2014) identified the three main biases of representativeness, availability and anchoring as being particularly relevant. Each of these is discussed in more detail below, along with the addition of affect.

Representativeness

The representativeness bias described by Kahneman and Tversky (1972) can be formally defined as the subjective probability of an event or sample being estimated, based on its similarity to a class of events or a typical specimen. An example from practice is given in a brief vignette of a patient found not guilty by reason of insanity, set out in Neal and Grisso (2014). The summary is designed to describe a patient who would typically be identified as falling into the category of 'personality disorder'. When asked about the most likely diagnosis for the individual described, subjects tended to disproportionality feel that personality disorder was the most appropriate diagnosis, despite the fact that it is very rare that this group would be identified as not guilty on such legal grounds. This, it is argued, reflects the use of the representativeness heuristic, leading to an undue focus on the description whilst neglecting the base rates: in this example, the low base rate of those identified as having personality disorder, falling into the relevant legal category. This explanation though holds only if a person is drawn randomly from the reference class from which the base rate is used (Gigernezer, Hell and Blank, 1988).

Availability

This bias refers to the ease with which relevant information can be recalled. This can be due to a variety of factors. These may include recent experiences or the salience of information. For someone who has recently had a patient die by suicide, for example, factors associated with risk in this area are likely to be more available than for a practitioner who has not. This availability in turn has been seen to influence decision-making, being interpreted as demonstrating a confirmation bias, something that has been shown experimentally (Wason and Johnson-Laird, 1972). This has been elaborated on by Kahneman (2011) with reference to the idea of 'What You See Is All There Is' (WYSIATI), which suggests that only those ideas that are activated are processed, with other information therefore being neglected in making decisions.

Anchoring and Adjustment

This bias was reported by Tversky and Kahneman (1974) and in essence it involves the idea that people's judgements tend to fix around a given starting point, with subsequent adjustments to this tending to be insufficient. The phenomena had been experimentally demonstrated with judgements being skewed by providing an arbitrary 'anchor' before judgements were made. This could include a random number followed by participants being asked to estimate an unknown quantity and here the estimates showed a bias towards the random number. The suggested explanation for this was that people were using what was described as an anchoring-and-adjustment heuristic (Nisbett and Ross, 1980). They were seen as first generating a preliminary judgement or 'anchor' and then adjusting this to accommodate further information, with these adjustments usually being too small to correct for the initial anchoring point.

Affect

The affect bias has been more controversial within this tradition and refers to the feelings associated with a given stimulus or the affect it engenders. It has been questioned how far this is distinct and how far it is simply a reflection of availability, experimental artefacts or post hoc explanations (Gigerenzer, 2002). As with availability, it is seen as a rapid and automatic process, that occurs in relation to virtually all thoughts (Murphy and Zajonc, 1993), and there are a range of experimental studies looking at its influence on decision-making. The strength of affect conveyed about a risk has been shown to have marked influences on the way people respond to such information (Slovic, 1987; Slovic, Monahan and MacGregor, 2000). Notably, such effects have been claimed to be quite immediate and to be seen following relatively weak stimuli such as reading a negative story shortly before decision-making (Peters, McCaul, Stefanek and Nelson, 2006).

Heuristics and Judgement

Within forensic practice, it can be said that the term heuristic has often acquired quite negative connotations. They have been inaccurately and somewhat pejoratively described as rules of thumb and have tended to be associated with notions of bias and error. This is of significant concern because there is nothing negative about heuristics, which in fact provide the foundations of decision-making. However persistent, ideas that people typically make decisions using the formal logic of inferential statistics do not reflect reality (Thaler, 2000). This means that in forensic practice, as elsewhere, it is essential to have an accurate sense of what heuristics are, how they work and when they may let us down as a result of cognitive illusions.

In his review of rationality, Gigerenzer (2008) starts by drawing on the original Greek origin of the word heuristic meaning "serving to find out or discover" and noting that Einstein used heuristics in this way, in his 1905 Nobel Prize winning paper (Holton, 1988 *quoted in* Gigerenzer 2008). The nature of heuristics has been well described using concrete examples and a common illustrative example used has been the heuristic for catching a moving object such as a ball. The evolutionary value of being able to do this is evident and is seen across many species, although this may give rise to the problem of creating circular explanations of psychological functions (Holcomb, 1996). It is of course possible to imagine an 'as-if' or optimisation model of how a moving object might be caught. This could involve calculation of all the relevant parameters such as ambient temperature, wind speed, velocity of the ball and many more. These could be input into a model based on Newtonian mechanics, that sought to predict the trajectory of the ball and so direct the individual to intercept it at a given point. Logically, this is similar to many of the algorithmic efforts to predict behaviour using optimisation approaches, although the example of striking a ball is simpler, better understood and so easier to accurately model. Clearly modelling this task, of catching a ball, would involve a potentially large number of complex measurements and analysis of causal information. Using an optimisation approach, it would also require complex computation. In the absence of impressive levels of computing power, this will be a slow process. The ball may have fallen long before the calculations are completed. Given vast computing power, however, it may indeed be possible to develop a model to catch the ball in this way, quickly giving rise to additional problems of robustness and resilience. Having successfully modelled one catch, second and subsequent attempts to catch the ball may not work. The calculations and modelling may not be robust in the face of fresh uncertainty or random factors. The method may not stand up in the face of systemic changes, say a change in air pressure. Of course, people and other species could not deal with the problem of catching a ball in this way. What they need is a method that is swift, robust and resilient and which does not require large amounts of cognitive effort. In reality, people use an apparently simple heuristic to solve the problem in this way. This says that they should first gaze at the ball, second start running towards it and third keep the angle of gaze constant. This is a fast and frugal heuristic that appears to generally work well, although clearly it works better for some than others. It appears to be anchored and evolved in our central nervous system and is shared by other species, many of which can use it as well or rather better than us. By contrast, the optimisation model is one that would quickly be overcome by the number of parameters and demands of calculation. It is a problem that could quickly become computationally intractable even in this simple example given above. Imagine the number of parameters and Newtonian calculations needed for a more complex situation, say playing a game of cricket or baseball on a blustery day.

Proponents of ecological rationality stress that heuristics are evolved within an environmental context and so can only sensibly be judged in that context. The use of content-blind norms, in the manner suggested by cognitive illusions research, is seen as entirely misguided and misleading. This rejection of content-blind norms is far from new. Indeed, the use of such norms was seen as inappropriate and firmly rejected through much of the history of experimental psychology. In the early 20th century, for example, Wilhelm Wundt (1912/1973) argued that the use of content-blind norms had little or nothing to offer in understanding human thought process.

Understanding heuristics then requires an alternative approach and this has been suggested to involve three key aspects:

1   Process rules
2   Capacity that the process rule can exploit to enable it to be simple
3   The types of problems heuristics can solve

A large number of heuristics have been the focus of experimental study and an illustrative example is the recognition heuristic. This involves people weighting information that they recognise when making decisions. This seems to grounded in the anterior frontal medial cortex (FMC) of the brain, and it appears so strong that it needs to be actively overridden (Gigerenzer, 2008). It may, however, be inhibited by low recognition validity, recognition being unrelated to the criterion or direct criterion knowledge. It is most effective when around half a group of objects are recognised and begins to break down as recognition levels become higher. The heuristic is perhaps most easily understood by looking at an experimental example. Asked in a study whether Detroit or Milwaukee is the larger city, only about 60% of U.S. college students got the correct answer. German university students did significantly better on this task. The reason for this apparently odd finding is linked to the recognition heuristic being used. In this example, most people who know little about the size of U.S. cities fall back on the recognition heuristic, guessing that the more familiar city is larger. In this case, they tended to guess Detroit, which was in fact the correct answer. For the U.S. students, however, the recognition heuristic was less available, because they were familiar with both cities. They could not therefore rely on the recognition heuristic, decreasing their accuracy (Gigerenzer and Goldstein, 2011).

Heuristics may also be based on imitation rather than reason. Standard models of decision-making in areas such as economics and decision theory have typically assumed that this is done by trying to optimise or to optimise under constraints. Although this has been increasingly challenged, it has remained a dominant idea in areas such as economics and related areas of management (Thaler, 2000). Failing to optimise in this way, it was assumed, would lead to less optimal strategies dying out through selection, as sub-optimal decision-makers paid the price for their poor decisions. This is not what happens, even within the economic sphere. In the case of making life decisions, such optimisation models (Wald, 1947) suggest a process of sequential analysis and stopping rules, leading to the optimisation of decision-making. The alternative heuristic simply says copy what the majority of the other people do, so where most people get married, copy them. This heuristic tends to work well where people are exposed to similar environments, the environment is stable, the environment is noisy and the consequences immediate. It can, however, also lead people astray in environments that differ significantly from this. It is worth reiterating that the distinction between risk and uncertainty is crucial here. Logic and probability serve as appropriate tools in dealing with risk, whereas heuristics are the appropriate tools for addressing uncertainty.

Critiques of Cognitive Illusions Research

A detailed critique of this area of research was developed by Cohen (1981) in a discussion paper and his response to the peer commentary points that followed. In his review, Cohen made an analogy between the cognitive biases being demonstrated and the earlier demonstration of visual illusions in experimental psychology. The review is an important one, which set out a strong thesis, drawing largely from areas of Cohen's work in philosophy, in which an unfavourable comparison was drawn between visual illusions and cognitive illusions research. Visual illusions research had from its inception made the assumption of an ecological basis to the way perceptual systems solved the considerable challenges involved in vision. As a result, vision was seen to have evolved to meet particular needs in particular environments. The kinds of visual illusions studied by experimental psychologists such as Richard Gregory (1923–2010) or Jean Piaget (1896–1980) were therefore seen as errors occurring for a reason. They are interpreted as consequences of a highly developed visual system that has been memorably described as an intelligent betting machine (Gregory, 1974). The fact that visual perception is not error-free was not seen as evidence of it being ineffective, or in need of replacement but rather as a means of understanding how the system worked normally and under conditions that challenged it. It was seen as a window to the mind for scientific study. Indeed, as anyone who has studied this area of psychology will know, the visual system would in fact work poorly and would not be 'intelligent' if it did not make such errors. An error-free system would extract too much information from the environment, and in doing so, fail to extract the key aspects, producing an overloaded system (Gregory, 1974).

Work in the area of cognitive illusions was criticised by Cohen for taking a very different approach to cognition, arguing that an undue stress has been placed on describing and labelling cognitive biases and using vaguely defined heuristics to account for these. Subsequently, it has been suggested that this has been at the expense of understanding of the function of the heuristics and the contexts in which they produce cognitive illusions (Gigerenzer, 1996; Gigernenzer, 1998; Gigerenzer, Hertwig, Hoffrage and Sedlmeier, 2008). The use of content-blind norms as a means of assessing decision-making has also been strongly challenged. The notion that errors in judgement can be determined in exactly the same way as they are in perception, by replacing physical measurement with logic-based norms, is seen at best to be misleading. Before the development of work on cognitive illusions within experimental psychology, few would have seen such content-blind norms as a useful way to understand judgement and decision-making. Critics have suggested a number of possible reasons for this apparent wrong turn. This has included the suggestion that the approach was in large part the result of the institutionalisation of inferential statistics, with methodology driving theory. Here a revival of Bayesian statistics in cognitive psychology was followed by the emergence of psychological theories that assumed such logical structures to be the basis of psychological processes. Deviations from such norms came increasingly to be seen as evidence of a more fundamental lack of ability to make effective decisions in people.

Findings from cognitive illusions research have been used to support the reduction or removal of human decision-making, to be replaced with what are argued to be more effective methods. This trend can be seen across a number of fields and has been increasingly evident in forensic practice, culminating in suggestions of automating risk assessment through the use of artificial intelligence. Although the evidence for this has been increasingly challenged, this has been slow to impact on forensic practice. It seems a fair summary that the ideas of ecological rationality, suggested by Simon in the 1950s and extensively researched since, have to date had only marginal impacts on forensic practice (Crighton and Towl, 2008; Crighton, 2021). The dominant view of cognitive illusions has increasingly been that these are something to be eliminated as 'noise' and this is an idea that has had wide-ranging impacts (Wason and Johnson-Laird, 1970). These were first evident in cognitive psychology and later on in social psychology (Nisbett and Ross, 1980), behavioural economics (Thaler, 2000) and aspects of law (Starr, 2014) to take a just a few salient examples. In this process, many of the caveats in the original experimental studies have been minimised or lost in the translation to applied settings.

Fundamental problems with the cognitive illusions approach have been highlighted by Gigerenzer (2008) using the example of the logical problem of class inclusion and invariance. In a well-known study in cognitive psychology, Inhelder and Piaget (1958) showed groups of children pictures of 16 flowers. Of these, 8 were pictures of a particular type of flower, primulas. The children were then asked are there more flowers or primulas? Only 47% of children aged 5–7 years old gave an answer in line with class inclusion, that there were more flowers. For the 8 year olds, however, this had risen to 82% giving the correct answer. Unlike much of experimental psychology, this has been a very well-replicated finding. Some cultural and individual differences, in terms of the age at which class inclusion is achieved, have been reported. The central finding, however, has been a robust one. As children get older, they tend to develop the ability to solve this kind of problem as part of a staged development in thinking. Put very briefly this led to a view within developmental psychology that tended to see children as being judicially logical, although this needed to emerge through a process of assimilation and accommodation of new concepts, as they grew up.

This finding obviously conflicted with the emergent findings from cognitive illusions research. For example, a study by Tversky and Kahneman (1983) yielded results that contradicted this finding but did not address the earlier work in developmental psychology. This involved a study that presented college students with what has been called the 'Linda problem'. This has gone on, with some variations, to be a widely used experimental paradigm and it essentially involves presenting a description of a fictional person called 'Linda', which provides information about her in the form of a brief vignette. This describes her interests, educational background and so on. Participants in the experiment are then asked which of two options were more probable:

1   Linda is a bank teller.
2   Linda is a bank teller and an active feminist.

As can be seen, this is a similar class inclusion problem (also sometimes described as a set inclusion problem) to the one involving flowers and primulas, used by Inhelder and Piaget (1958). It can be seen as asking whether Linda is more likely to belong to the larger class (bank tellers) or the presumably smaller class (bank tellers who are also active feminists). By using the logic of class inclusion, it is argued that the first option is the correct one. Using this logic, clearly the set of bank tellers will include the sub-set of active feminist bank tellers. Despite this, most students chose the second option, a finding that has been subsequently replicated using this and other similar experimental paradigms and extended beyond the study of students. This led the researchers to conclude that people were showing an error in judgement, or cognitive illusion. Many similar experiments of this type have been conducted and the findings from these have been used to go further and suggest a more global tendency towards irrational decision-making.

The interpretation of such findings is, however, contested (Gigerenzer, 2008). The irrationality here, it is argued, is not in the reasoning of the participants but in the experimental paradigm itself. The assumption of a content-blind logical norm, based purely on a syntactical definition of rationality, is misplaced. In this problem, it is argued, people take account of the semantic content but also the pragmatic or situational information available to them, in trying to resolve the question posed. This may legitimately differ from a semantic and content-blind logical norm, but it is nonetheless entirely reasonable. Drawing on the analogy with visual illusions, it is suggested that, faced with such a situation, people go on to make intelligent bets rather than conducting any formalised logical analysis. In the Linda problem, this potentially involves different understandings of what the term probable means. When asked about this, people tend to have a range of views about what probable means and only some of these are the same as formal concepts of probability. In line with dictionary definitions, people often see this as more akin to something being plausible. In addition, subjects taking part in such an experiment may look at the additional information and quite reasonably ask themselves why it is there? If all that is required is a simple logical inference, then surely, the experimenter would not have included the additional description, to do so would be pointless. Again, by analogy to visual illusions, people are trying to make an intelligent and context-specific guess. They are reading between the lines. Whether this is what they are doing is of course a question that could be experimentally answered. When this was done, and the question in the Linda problem was changed from asking about how probable, to asking about how many, this cognitive illusion promptly disappeared (Hertwig and Gigerenzer, 1999). This finding also resolved the different findings in the children, where Inhelder and Piaget had asked children about how many flowers, not the vaguer how probable question, so making the triviality of the logic problem clear to the large majority of 8 year olds.

Some Problems while Using Content-Blind Norms

Experimentally derived models of decision-making, based on optimisation, optimisation under constraints and cognitive illusions, all rely on norms based on formal logic. Decision-making by people is then assessed relative to these norms, which are not dependent on the content of question being addressed. Such content-blind norms, it is argued, provide a valid benchmark to assess human judgement and are analogous to the kinds of physical measurements used in experimental research on vision. Ecological rationality approaches question this fundamental assumption, seeing this reliance on content-blind norms as misconceived. Advocates of ecological rationality argue that human decision-making has resulted from a process of evolution that has fitted people to make effective decisions in particular environments. The use of content-blind norms, divorced from the environment is a recent development that is both artificial and unnatural. Using these inappropriate norms, it is argued, often leads to the wrong questions being posed and to confusing and misleading answers to these being generated.

The use of this kind of formal logic, as the benchmark for human rationality, has passed from experimental psychology into applied psychology, in turn becoming increasingly integral to the way forensic practitioners think about risk assessment (Neal and Grisso, 2014). Critics of current practice stress the importance of recognising that this idea has been rejected by many researchers within and outside the field of experimental psychology. These critiques do not appear to have reached much of forensic practice. They are, however, important because they cast doubt on a number of fundamental ideas that have supported the cognitive illusions approach as well as the growing influence of such work in suggesting fundamental irrationality in human decision-making. At a practical level, if people are not flawed judges of risk, or not as flawed as the cognitive illusions research has suggested, the need to constrain and replace them begins to fall away. As indeed does the idea that, given the current state of knowledge, artificial intelligence based on such norms will lead to better decision-making about risk.

Drawing on the views of Goodman (1954) as a starting point, Cohen (1981) argued that formal logic does not, in fact, provide the firm foundation for studying human cognition that has been claimed. Formal mathematical proofs he argued did not offer any better prospects as a firm benchmark of human irrationality. For Cohen, both were ultimately reliant on human intuitions of deductibility as their basis, an idea that he summarised in the following terms

> ...*normative criteria for ordinary human reasoning rely for their substantiation on a procedure analogous to what is called "boot strapping" in artificial intelligence (Dawes and Corrigan, 1974). The intuitions of ordinary people are the basis for constructing a coherent system of rules and principles by which those same people can, if they so choose, reason much more extensively and accurately...*
> (Cohen, 1981: 332)

Philosophical views like this undermine the idea that content-blind formal logic can ever be legitimately seen as equivalent of the physical measurements used in the study of visual illusions.

In commenting on Cohen's review, Wason (1981) seemed to accept that the idea of cognitive illusions as being more helpful than the notion of biases as well as one that may lead to greater insights into the working of the mind. The analogy with visual illusions also suggested that such findings could usefully be seen as aspects of the way cognitive system works, much as visual illusions had done previously for perceptual systems (Gregory, 1973, 1997). Cohen went on, however, to look in greater detail at some of the paradigms used to look at these cognitive illusions, exploring the normative criteria that had been used as the basis for inferring the presence of errors. Looking at the philosophical basis for the mathematical calculus of chance in some detail, he drew attention to the various conceptions of probability in use and the manner in which these had been applied. As has been discussed previously, this was not a new area of study and the differing conceptions of probability have a lengthy history (de

Finetti, 1930; Ramsey, 1931). Based on this analysis, Cohen divided probability judgements into four key types that can be derived building on the ideas of de Finetti and Ramsey:

1. Betting quotients.
2. Logical relations.
3. Relative frequencies.
4. Cause or propensity.

These distinctions are all important to the consideration of risk using notions of probability but they appear absent, or at best poorly applied, in much of current forensic practice. It is therefore perhaps worth spending some time looking at the distinctions Cohen drew out. Both betting quotients and logical relations are described by Cohen as functions of propositions. For example, betting quotients may concern the proposition that a given horse is likely to win a given race. Here, probability is normally treated as a statement about the strength of individual belief in a given outcome. As a subjective fact, this is consistent with other individuals holding different strengths of belief in the same outcome. Two people may, quite legitimately, reach different values for their belief that the horse may win, with one giving a betting quotient of 9 to 1, whilst another may judge this to be 6 to 1. Since both of these are subjective or knowledge-based probabilities, they are not contradictory of one another. The relative frequency form of probability refers to the view most commonly adopted in forensic practice and is a function of sets: to take a simple example, the sub-set of convicted offenders who go on to be reconvicted for a violent offence within 12 months. The notion of propensity probability is a function of problem properties and can be described as being more semantic in nature. Historically, it often appears to have been described more vaguely in terms of *a priori* probability. In many ways, it is the hardest concept to pin down, and its precise interpretation remains open to question and debate. It can, however, be described, at its simplest level, as involving a physical tendency to yield particular outcomes. Taking the example again of tossing a coin, the frequency of it landing as a head will tend to be close to the probability of heads derived from a series of trials. This view of probability, however, relates to the invariant single-case probabilities, here, for a single toss of the coin of ½, or what have also been described as 'generating conditions' (Cohen, 1981). These cannot be empirically determined and the application of this concept goes well beyond the simple example given above including a number of areas of the natural sciences (Popper, 1959).

The use of these different conceptions of probability are significant to an understanding of cognitive illusions and it has been strongly argued that it is entirely legitimate to use different conceptions of probability for different situations or purposes "...just as traders sometimes find it worthwhile to measure quantities of apples by weight and sometimes by number" (Cohen, 1981: 320). These ideas were rejected, in equally strong terms, in some of the commentary articles on Cohen's ideas. This included challenges to the use of statistical examples (Diaconis and Freedman, 1981), challenges based on the difficulty for this view arising out of examples of stubborn and nonsensical intuitions (Kahneman, 1981; Kahneman and Tversky, 1984) and concerns that it created a clearly untestable framework for human judgement (Tversky, 1981).

A flavour of this debate can be given by using one of the paradigms discussed. This is taken from the body of cognitive illusions research and involves the 'taxi problem', which has also become something of a standard paradigm in the area. The experimental paradigm concerns hypothetical jury decision-making, with participants in the study being told that in a given town, blue and green taxis operate in a ratio of 85% to 15% respectively. They are then told that a witness has identified a taxi involved in a crash as being green and that the court has been told that, in such conditions, a witness will be able to distinguish the colour of the taxi in 80% of cases. Subjects were then asked to give the probability that the taxi involved in the crash was blue. The median level given by participants is reported to be around 0.2 (Kahneman and Tversky, 1972). Within the cognitive illusions tradition, this is seen as a serious error, being interpreted as a failure to take into account base rates (blue taxis are much more common than green) and indicative of a bias in people's judgement. This finding appears robust, has been replicated and can be put forward as raising significant concerns about the irrationality of people in making this kind of judgement.

Such an inference of irrationality, however, has been challenged. It has been criticised for depending on the view that the world operates according to Bayes theorem, which does clearly take base rates into account. An alternative view here suggests that the experimental paradigm is either testing a lack of statistical education, or is misconceived at a more fundamental level (Cohen, 1981). The reasoning of the experimenters appears based on an approach that says in the long run:

1. A witness may make 68% correct identifications of a taxi as blue, given by multiplying the fraction of correct identifications 0.8 by the base rate for blue taxis 85%.
2. A witness may make 3% incorrect identifications of a taxi as blue, given by multiplying the fraction of incorrect identifications multiplying 0.2 by the base rate for green taxis 15%.
3. A witness may make 12% correct identifications of a taxi as green, given by the fraction for correct identification 0.8 multiplied by the base rate for green taxis 15%.

4   A witness may make 17% incorrect identifications of a taxi as green, given by the fraction of incorrect identifications 0.2 multiplied by the 85% base rate for blue taxis.

In total, this gives 29% of identifications as being a green taxi. Of these, 17 out of 29 will be incorrect, approximately 59%, which is very different from the 20% estimate that the subjects tend to suggest.

The paradigm itself is strongly criticised as being flawed (Cohen, 1981). Here, it has been argued that the 17/29 fraction is, in fact, the conditional probability for correctly identifying taxi colour. This is not the issue that a jury or court would in fact be faced with. Here, the long run accuracy of identification of taxi colour is simply not a relevant issue. Jurors are being asked in the experimental paradigm to judge a single event: the likelihood that the statement that a green taxi was involved in this accident is incorrect. Participants have been told that around 20% of witnesses are likely to make an error in identifying the colour and so, not unreasonably, they use this as the probability for error. Here, it is proposed that the base rate information is in fact related to an entirely different question. The typical responses seen are therefore not irrational at all; they are in fact in line with Bayes theorem (Cohen, 1979, 1981; Bar-Hillel, 1980). It is worth noting that there is, in fact, no single 'normative' answer to this problem and using signal detection theory yields a different 'normative' answer to the one suggested by Kahneman and Tversky (1972) and which is consistent with what many subjects do (Gigerenzer and Murray, 2015). More generally it has been argued that there is a tendency to see biases where there are none, in turn contributing to a naïve belief that algorithms should replace human judgement (Gigerenzer, 2018).

None of which is to argue that people do not make errors or wrong decisions; we do and no perfect decision-making system exists. Where these errors occur, however, Cohen (1981) suggested, they were often the result of a lack of knowledge, scientific education or the experimental paradigm, rather than any fundamental flaws in human cognition. Taking the example of the resistance to the effects of increasing sample size, commonly reported in studies of cognitive illusions, he noted that it took the mathematical genius of Bernoulli (1954) to discover that the probability of an estimate being correct will vary with the sample size. It is then argued to be hardly a surprise that such ideas do not occur spontaneously to most of us. On applying this idea to another branch of mathematics, he speculated that experiments showing cognitive illusions could probably be developed to show that subjects, without the knowledge of Euclidian geometry, failed to spontaneously apply Pythagoras theorem for right-angled triangles. As a result, the work on cognitive illusions can be seen to have painted an unduly negative and pessimistic picture of people's actual capacities to make such assessments.

Studies of Heuristics

The extent to which the ideas from the work on cognitive illusions has influenced many other areas make the criticisms outlined above all the more important. Other challenges can be illustrated by a brief look at some of the evidence available on heuristic decision-making itself. The representativeness heuristic has been subject to a number of experimental studies concerned with the neglect of base rates and the serious practice implications that might arise from this. A study of faculty, staff and fourth-year medical students at Harvard University in the United States asked participants about a hypothetical scenario, concerning how likely a positive test result was to yield an accurate diagnosis. Here, participants were given a low prevalence of the disease, of 1 in 1000, then told the test's false positive rate was 1 in 20. This is a straightforward problem using Bayesian statistics, which can be easily calculated using a standard formula. The likelihood here that a positive diagnosis will be an accurate one is reported as approximately 2%. Because of the low prevalence, most identified cases will in fact inevitably be false positives. In the study, however, less than one in five of the participants gave a figure close to this. Just under half the groups gave a figure of 95%, suggesting they had neglected base rates entirely (Casscells, Schoenberger and Graboys, 1978). A similar finding in relation to an area of forensic practice is set out by Neal and Grisso (2014), which involved the use of an algorithmic RAI used with sexual offenders, called the Static-99. Here too, the value of the predictive instrument was compromised by the low base rates for reoffending. Using a Bayesian approach, the most accurate prediction here would always be one of not reoffending. Using the assessment instrument actually reduced accuracy below this level. Again, as with the green and blue taxis paradigm discussed earlier, practitioners appear to neglect base rate information, seeing this as irrelevant to the question of concern.

The interpretation of the anchoring-and-adjustment heuristic has also been questioned on the basis of a number of studies. These have suggested that the use of this heuristic can in fact be seen as an entirely reasonable compromise between errors and the costs of processing information. Here, experimental studies have reported that when subjects are not provided with an anchor, they generate one themselves. These generated values tend to be reasonable and quick approximations to the correct value (Epley and Gilovich, 2006). A clear ecological basis for anchoring in this way, outside the context of psychology experiments, has also been suggested. In real-world settings, with clear exceptions, people will typically provide relevant information rather than randomly generated information. Treating such information as a useful clue and not moving too quickly and too far from it, would therefore be a rational strategy

(Lieder, Griffiths, Huys and Goodman, 2018). The relevance of this apparent bias to forensic practice is also open to question. It is influenced by various relevant factors. The anchoring bias is larger where people are more uncertain about the quantity being estimated. People with high levels of knowledge about the quantity concerned appeared immune to this bias, whilst less knowledgeable subjects were not (Wilson, Houston, Etling and Brekke, 1996). Familiarity and expertise also appear to reduce but not eliminate anchoring effects (Lieder, Griffiths, Huys and Goodman, 2018).

There has been debate around the extent that availability and affect heuristics can be distinguished. Both have been studied experimentally and this has yielded significant insights into the way these heuristics operate, suggesting a potential ecological basis. A study by Pachur, Hertwig and Steinmann (2012) found the estimated frequency of a risk was strongly related to the average number of instances that participants could recall and less strongly related to affect. The researchers noted that this was not explained by limited variability in this respect between the risks. Significantly, they observed that, when judging risks, people were more likely to rely on direct experiences over indirect ones or affective information. None of which suggests an irrational approach lacking an ecological basis. Although a somewhat artificial experimental study, the potential implications for forensic practice are not hard to discern, most obviously perhaps where practitioners and decision-makers have direct experience of the kinds of risk they are assessing.

Are Cognitive Illusions and Ecological Rationality Essentially Similar?

It has sometimes been suggested that cognitive illusions research and ecological rationality are essentially similar, or even that they are simply two faces of the same coin. This is not the case and has been firmly rejected by researchers in the ecological rationality tradition (Gigerenzer, 2008). Confusion between the two approaches may, in part, be the result of the common terminology around heuristics but they in fact represent two very different, incompatible schools of thought. The cognitive illusions approach has stressed biases and errors in seeking to understand human thinking, taking as its starting point the use of formal logic to provide baselines for comparison. Human decision-making is compared with this to identify systematic errors. The heuristics used by people are seen as sub-optimal and sometimes self-serving approximations, which lead us astray in making judgements. Heuristics are therefore seen as being generally suited to less important, less complex decision-making, useful where the costs of gathering large amounts of information may be disproportionately high. At a practical level, this has been used to support the idea that people's role in such decision-making needs to be corrected, constrained or replaced.

Ecological rationality would reject such views, seeing heuristics as a powerful, robust but not infallible means of making judgements. Heuristics are not seen as second best or certainly not as simple 'rules of thumb' but rather, as powerful characteristics evolved to fit particular environments. Heuristics in fact are seen as better in some situations, than approaches based on various types of formal logic. Advocates of ecological rationality stress that many real-world situations involve problems that can quickly become computationally intractable, where methods based on formal logic are used. Approaches based on optimisation (with or without constraints) it is argued, will also tend to lack robustness and resilience, tending to be slow where speed of action may be important. By contrast, it is argued that heuristics can provide the best solution available to make decisions in these kinds of conditions, regardless whether these are of high or low importance (Gigerenzer, 2008).

The development of this view of human decision-making in psychology is traced back to the work of Simon (1953, 1955). Notably, this took a very different view of human cognition from his contemporary Piaget, who had stressed the role of formal logic, seeing the process of cognitive development being, in essence, a progressive unfolding of this (Piaget, 1972). In rejecting this view, Simon used the analogy of a pair of scissors to describe his view of human cognition. He saw this as involving two 'blades': the structure of the task environment and the computational capabilities of the individual. Based on this analogy, he noted that it impossible to explain how scissors cut, simply by looking at one blade in isolation. At best this would only give partial insights. It was, however, more likely to seriously mislead. Any adequate understanding of human decision-making therefore required a study of both human cognition and the environment in which it operated. This approach has led on to the subsequent development of two key concepts: the 'ecological rationality' itself and the 'adaptive toolbox'.

The Adaptive Toolbox

This can be summarised as the collection of heuristics able to find solutions to problems quickly and using limited information. It has been described as a view of bounded rationality that is based on three premises (Gigerenzer and Todd, 1999):

1   Psychological plausibility. Essentially how decisions are actually made given the behavioural repertoire that a species has.

2   Domain specificity. Essentially, the heuristics that are used in specific contexts, as opposed to the general methods used in optimisation approaches.
3   Ecological rationality. Essentially, how well heuristics are adapted to the structure of environments both physical and social.

This has led to a focus on experimental studies of real-world decisions and these have suggested that people do not normally use approaches based on optimisation or formal logic. Rather they use heuristics that are very different from such content-blind norms and that may yield different results. These heuristics can be seen to operate quickly and are less demanding in terms of time and effort. More surprisingly perhaps, they have also been shown, when used in their ecological context, to be able to produce better results, directly conflicting with many of the findings suggested from cognitive illusions research. Researchers from this tradition have been critical of the cognitive illusions approach on multiple grounds. Most fundamentally perhaps, it has been criticised as involving labelling, rather than explaining, the observed errors and deviations from logic-based norms (Gigerenzer, 1998).

Ecological rationality views support the idea that effective decision-making under conditions of uncertainty requires an ability to ignore information, to effectively perform complex estimates. Ignoring some information in this manner is seen as a positive in many situations, yielding more robust solutions. A concrete example of this is given in relation to the work of Markowitz (1990), an economist who researched asset allocation in finance. In the real world of financial markets, however, he reported not using his own optimised models, preferring a simple 1 divided by N (1/N) heuristic (Gigerenzer, 2008). This is a technique familiar from children's birthday parties and it can be shorthanded to cutting the cake equally between all. In financial settings, it means allocating the total sum equally across a number of different assets, a practice that accords with what people naturally tend to prefer. It can be seen as a way of spreading risks. On the face of it, however, it looks unduly simple, certainly when compared with the kind of sophisticated economic modelling that exists. It looks like the kind of simple 'rule of thumb' described critically in the cognitive illusions school of thought. Yet studies of various optimisation strategies, when compared with this simple heuristic, have shown that none consistently outperformed it (Pflug, Pichler and Wozabal, 2012). The main issue here is not computational intractability, with the computing power available in economic and financial settings a great deal of analysis of this type can be done. Rather, it is the robustness of the optimised models. These turn out to be better at fitting the historical data than the 1/N heuristic but to be worse at predicting the future outcomes. This lack of robustness seems to be a product of overfitting the historical data to produce the most accurate prediction. By contrast, the 1/N heuristic does not estimate any parameters to begin with, so it cannot overfit the data in this way.

The question of whether optimisation or heuristics work better is therefore an empirical one. Assumptions that heuristics will generally perform better or worse are unfounded. In some cases, optimisation models perform better and in others, more poorly. It is argued from the ecological rationality perspective that understanding where this might be the case is of central importance. Taking the example above, it has been found that the larger the uncertainty and number of assets and the smaller and learning sample, the greater the advantage the 1/N heuristic has. It is not the case that optimised models cannot outperform the heuristic but the conditions in which they can do so are significant. In a case of a relatively modest assumption of 50 assets to allocate wealth to, optimisation strategies have been found to need a time window of around 500 years to outperform the heuristic approach (DeMiguel, Garlappi and Uppal, 2006). It is not hard to see the limitations of optimised models in light of such findings, or why the simpler heuristic would be preferable.

Of the four models outlined above, optimisation approaches are perhaps the most antithetical to psychological approaches, with their stress on formal logic as the best basis for decision-making when faced with uncertainty. Here the way that people think about such problems becomes at best of marginal interest and at worst a nuisance. There is indeed something of a tradition of such thinking, deriving largely from economics, where human decision-making has been modelled on the basis of people as perfectly rational agents. This persisted despite the concerns that were raised by some economists (Keynes, 1921; Thaler, 2000). Analogies can be drawn here between such approaches and the radical behaviourism theories that dominated psychology in North America from the 1920s to the 1950s. Similar to optimisation theories, this school of thought completely rejected the study of cognitive psychology as irrelevant, seeing what happens between stimuli and responses as a 'black box'. Many other areas of the social sciences have been strongly influenced by views of this kind, that have rejected or downplayed the role of cognition, most obviously in the area of economic risks with people's decisions-making being modelled on the basis of formal logic within uncertain marketplaces. Indeed, the term *homo economicus* was coined to describe and gently mock this rather strange character and their operation in the real world (Thaler, 2000). The area of experimental psychology concerned with cognitive illusions served a key role here in challenging these kinds of ideas, demonstrating that people often were not the kind of formal logic-based actors, supposed in economic models of risk. The cognitive illusions shown were a demonstration of this divergence and so the invalidity of models based on such false assumptions. Critics, however, might suggest that in retaining formal logic as a benchmark, they were falling into similar error to economic theorists who believed so much in *homo economicus*.

Conclusion

The aim of this chapter has been to take a necessarily brief look at critiques of the current approaches to risk in forensic practice from, what has broadly been described as a psychological perspective. Essentially, these revolve around the question of whether people are equipped to make effective decisions about risk. The dominant view in much of forensic practice has come to be that people's decision-making is subject to a range of systematic biases or cognitive illusions, attributable in turn to the use of various simple heuristics to make decisions. As a result, it has typically been assumed that people are generally not very good at assessing risks and when compared with various types of formal logic they can fail badly. These fundamental weaknesses in human cognition have been used to support constraints on decision-making around risk or the replacement of people in such processes altogether. Within forensic practice, such views have become increasingly dominant, and this has been associated with a growth in ever more structured RAIs, either to replace or constrain expert decision-making.

Critiques of this perspective have drawn largely but not exclusively on notions of ecological rationality and have challenged many of these assumptions, developing fundamentally different theoretical approaches. These have seen people's decision-making as largely the product of evolutionary pressures, in given environments. Accordingly, the use of content-blind norms based on formal logic are seen as an invalid and generally unhelpful approach. The results of this work have suggested that viewing human cognition as fundamentally flawed is itself a serious error, with the accuracy of people's decision-making being strongly dependent on context and the presentation of information. Heuristics when used in their ecological context, can perform better than apparently more sophisticated approaches. This critique suggests that constraining or removing human judgements from decisions around risk is a serious error. Adapting environments to better suit natural ways of thinking is seen as a better way to improve complex decision-making around questions of risk and probability than replacing expert decision-making.

Dealing with Risk Better 8
Analysis and Treatment of Risks

The focus of the chapters that follow is the very practical question of how, in light of the various critiques, current forensic practice might be improved. There are no easy answers to this and some of the solutions proposed will necessarily be more speculative than the criticisms. Whether current practice needs improvement and the ways in which this might be done are open questions that are likely to be contentious. At this point, it is perhaps worth reiterating that this text forms part of a series about forensic practice, with two key aims. The first of these is to bring out critical perspectives on existing practice: the second is to introduce new thinking.

Both are important, since contention and differences of view are a fundamental part of the scientific method. Processes of systematic challenge and theory development have acted, across a wide range of areas, to improve understanding and applied practice. Science itself can be seen as reducing to nothing more or less than a process of using critical common sense to test and develop ideas, leading to better explanatory models. This rests on a motivating process of creating plausible theories, then testing these in ways that put them at risk of being refuted. This method has proved to be tremendously successful in advancing our understanding of our world. Historically, the main alternative has involved appeals to authority and status, an approach that is wholly rejected here. Suggestions for dealing with risk more effectively in forensic practice are motivated by a desire to arrest the deterioration in this area.

Much of the existing literature on risk assessment in forensic practice might be taken to suggest that this is unnecessary and that the field is not deteriorating but flourishing. Such views would suggest that current methods do not need to be reformed at all. The use of grandiose terms such as 'state of the art' and

DOI: 10.4324/9781003108665-9

'gold standard' are often heard in this area: Typically to describe checklist-based Risk Assessment Instruments (RAIs). The preceding critiques of current practice have hopefully provided a counter to such hubris. Efforts to deal with risk in forensic practice has increasingly come to be dominated by methodologically simple approaches, often applied in questionable ways. Risk assessment has often been reduced to lists of correlates of general outcomes, drawing on weak evidence (Silva, 2020; Crighton, 2021). Performance of the approaches that have come to dominate the field is, at best, sub-optimal. At times, it appears actively harmful of efforts to deal with risks more effectively. Given the importance of some of these areas of risk involved in forensic practice, this must surely be a grave concern, one that is in need of urgent attention. Many of the critiques outlined earlier are substantive and, as such, require response. Most cannot be lightly dismissed and many of the criticisms raised have serious practical implications, which do not suggest easy answers.

The Scale of the Problem

It is worth pausing to think for a moment about the shear breadth of risks that are addressed across forensic practice. Efforts to predict, treat and manage these is by no means a trivial intellectual problem and not one that is likely amenable to any quick and easy fixes. A striking aspect of current forensic practice is, however, its increasingly narrow focus, both in terms of risks and methodology. This is striking and many forms of risk that clearly fall within the realm of forensic practice, appear to have been largely or wholly neglected. Strong interest has been evident in assessing risk in areas such as predicting anti-social behaviour and violence in detained patients and released prisoners. Apparent blind spots, however, are often hard to account for and defend. Only recently has there been much interest in areas of risk such as politically motivated violence, hostage taking or arson. There has been an overwhelming focus of interest in assessing risk for convicted sexual offenders detained in hospital or correctional settings; interest in areas such as the risks of sexual violence in a range of community, social and professional settings have been almost entirely absent, although with some exceptions (Towl and Walker, 2019). Interest in the risks associated with so called 'white collar' crimes, such as fraud, corruption and tax evasion have received little interest, whilst considerable efforts have been expended on predictive policing of socially deprived areas, with the same behaviours in more privileged settings being neglected. Undertaking probabilistic risk assessments of detected, convicted, imprisoned and socially excluded groups appears to have taken priority over analysis and development of effective risk treatment and management.

This perhaps reflects the growing 'class privilege' of the professions involved. Current forensic practice may often be amplifying, rather than reducing, social and economic injustices. The focus of interest and direction of travel can be criticised as increasingly taking on an increasingly narrow mantle of social control, which medical and social work professions previously wore but often now appear keen to let go (Conrad, 1992; Richards, Coulter and Wicks, 2015). It is argued here that such a focus is not the best or most productive role for forensic practitioners, if the aim is to contribute most effectively to better public health and public protection.

Narrowness in current practice is also striking in the way that methodology has developed and diverged from other areas of risk. Sexual violence provides an illustration of this where, within forensic practice, it has become common to see this assessed using single RAIs, typically marketed to assess broadly defined risks of 'sexual violence' or 'sexual offending'. This necessarily covers an astonishingly broad range of risks. It can reasonably be suggested that, even based on cursory analysis, much of what is captured under this breadth will have fundamental differences. Varied forms of 'sexual violence' may share little in common, other than inferred motive, making it reasonable to question both the validity and utility of such generic assessments. Distinct risks are likely to benefit from, indeed to require, detailed analysis to understand their nature. In the absence of this, any effort to adequately assess likelihood and direct risk treatment, evaluation and manage risk is likely to be wholly inadequate.

Checklist RAIs and generic algorithms have increasingly dominated forensic practice. These approach risk using broad criteria to give probabilistic estimates and do this based on a modest number of correlates. These have tended to be unduly general, although some checklist instruments have been modified to include scope to add additional risk factors or indicators, felt to be associated with risk. Individual characteristics and framing conditions of the assessment where considered, have involved some history taking and brief 'formulations' of behaviour. Risk of 'sexual violence', however, might, in practice, mean a series of sadistically motivated rapes, familial sexual abuse, cases of necrophilia or non-contact sexual offences. A series of sadistic rapes might involve same sex victims, opposite sex victims or both. It may, of course, involve more than one type of sexual violence. It might involve violence towards strangers or the abuse of formal power relationships. It may involve high-frequency and acute risk in some settings and cases; in others, it may present a low-frequency chronic risk. Forensic practice needs to be able to address various forms of risk that change, dealing effectively with areas of low-frequency chronic risk, such as those presented by some older previously convicted sexual offenders as well as high-frequency acute risks that might be presented by young people in settings such as universities. The idea that such a variety of risks can be effectively addressed, with little in the way of further analysis, using generic checklist RAIs or simple algorithms seems implausible.

Adding to this is the serious and now well-known concern that the vast majority of sexual violence goes unreported and undetected, with even that small proportion, which is detected, being unlikely to result in prosecutions or convictions (Towl and Walker, 2019). This suggests that RAIs based on reconviction data for prisoners and detained patients may, in reality, be of little or no relevance to the vast majority of risks of sexual violence. Indeed, they may be actively misleading. Individual characteristics such as race, sex, age, social class and other individual characteristics may be systematically unrepresentative, when the focus is on the tiny fraction of those who have been in custody. Linked to this, the framing conditions involved in assessing those in correctional, hospital or community settings as well as previously detected and undetected individuals engaging in sexual violence, seem likely to be fundamentally different.

Analysing Risks

The use of risk assessment within forensic practice can be seen as a small part of a much wider historical trend, which saw the expansion of risk-based thinking across many areas of human activity. The roots of this were touched on earlier and detailed consideration of this is largely the province of economic and scientific historians (Covello and Mumpower, 1985). A major facet of risk-based approaches certainly appears to have been a need to address negative effects arising from rapid scientific, technological and social change. Recent trends can be seen as mirroring changes that followed the industrial revolutions of the 18th and 19th centuries. Then as now, issues of risk became pressing in light of rapid change that presented new dangers. More recently, areas within the social and natural sciences have been very quickly reshaped by scientific and technical developments. The life sciences provide a vivid example of this with clear relevance to forensic practice. Here, notions of risk have become increasingly central, with the use of probabilistic information coming to form an increasing part of practice. It is now common to talk about risk of heart disease, risk of mental disorder or risk of ecological or climate damage and, in turn, to identify risk treatments. Concepts of risk have come to influence forensic practice in a similar way. Notions of risk in forensic practice, however, have been complicated by its close interface with law and here issues of risk have been tied up with issues of punishment and social control. Risk has become increasingly central to areas as diverse as policing, mental health, family life, corrections and the courts, with questions of retribution, deterrence, protection and punishment often being central. Although these are often neglected in practice, they are quite different from questions concerning risk-based treatment and management.

Recent development of risk-based thinking within forensic practice has also been notable in other respects. Strikingly, routine practice has appeared to become increasingly isolated from its own independent research base, as well as the research base and current practice in other areas. A parallel body of commercially driven research has developed with a focus on specific RAIs. This trend, it can be argued, has been associated with a deterioration in methodological sophistication. The language and terminology used by forensic practitioners has become increasingly idiosyncratic, in turn hampering the exchange of ideas. A better shared understanding of historical developments might have helped here but instead there has been a curiously ahistorical approach in forensic practice. Key foundational issues and history surrounding risk often appear to be poorly understood. This is in stark contrast to many other areas and can be seen as cutting directly across scientific method, which stresses the central role of theory building and testing over time (Meehl, 1978). To draw a contrast, it is genuinely difficult to imagine any natural scientist looking at the area of electromagnetism now, without first understanding the work of Michael Faraday (1791–1867) and James Clerk Maxwell (1831–1879) (Faraday, 1839; Maxwell, 1873). It should be equally incomprehensible for forensic practitioners to think about risk, without an understanding of key historic developments and theories.

Questions of risk are complex and it is argued here, often highly specific, so any effective consideration of risk will require a high degree of analysis. This suggests an important shift of focus. A stress on detailed analysis of the nature of the risks presented and the ways in which these might be changed is needed. For example, terms such as 'anti-social behaviour' or 'sexual violence' need to be the starting point for analysis, not its end point. In this respect, current practice can be legitimately criticised for its growing adoption of simplistic and mechanistic approaches. This is not a new or original observation but rather one where concerns have been repeatedly identified (Wald and Woolverton, 1990; Steadman, Silver, Monahan et al., 2000; Monahan, Steadman, Silver et al., 2001).

In thinking about the analysis of risks, it is perhaps worth stressing that probability itself is not straightforward but is in fact a very active area of research and scholarship. There is no single concept of probability, no single theory of probability. If the way that risk is dealt with in practice is to progress, the complex nature and limited understanding of probability needs to be recognised. This is not evident in many areas of forensic practice, where probabilities have increasingly been treated in ways that appear both surprising and concerning (Meehl, 1978; Imrey and Dawid, 2015; Gigerenzer, 2018). Probability theory in fact remains an area of very active research, although in forensic practice, it often appears that all development in the area ended with the work of Kolmogorov (2018). Remarkable as this work undoubtedly was, it did not end thinking about and development of probability theory, any more than Piaget's work ended work on cognitive development. The central point here for developing forensic practice is that the differing conceptions of probability are important; they have differing implications and contributions to make efforts to deal with complex risks and uncertainty.

One of the broad theoretical distinctions in probability has been discussed extensively in earlier chapters and this seems central to many questions about risk in forensic practice. This is the distinction between groupings that are often called 'objective', frequentist or relative frequency probability and those termed 'subjective', 'knowledge-based' or sometimes 'Bayesian' probability. Both can be seen as having the common aim of describing a degree of belief but they do this in different ways. These two broad views of probability have played a key role in understanding risks, in many different settings. As such, they are clearly relevant to efforts to improve practice. A progressive decline in efforts to use of knowledge-based probabilities has been evident and where these might have been applied, vague and undefined qualitative descriptions such as 'high', 'medium' and 'low' have been used instead. Only comparatively recently has there been a rediscovery of interest in knowledge-based probabilities in forensic practice (Towl and Crighton, 1996; Hodges, 2019; Crighton, 2021). The contrast with many other areas concerned with risk is stark, where the use of knowledge-based probabilities has become a key tool in analysing many areas of risk.

Minimally, efforts to improve practice require a better understanding of these kinds of key statistical concepts as well as a much greater willingness to work with other experts, at the point that the limits of understanding and competence are reached. The rediscovery of knowledge-based conceptions of probability has a great deal of potential, in the development of more meaningful and useful descriptions of many of the risks seen in forensic practice. The use of vague and undefined terms such as 'high' or 'moderate to high' risk seems to be a very lazy alternative to developing and working with knowledge-based probabilities: one that falls well short of being a scientifically credible approach to risk and uncertainty.

Barriers to Change

There is an apparent resistance, in some quarters at least, to taking on board many of the criticisms of current practice. Given the growth in risk-based thinking and the modern development of scientific risk-based approaches, which forensic practice generally claims to be part of, this requires some attempt at explanation. One view is that there has been a gradual but progressive decoupling of large areas of forensic practice from the academic evidence base on risk. This has been paralleled by the growth of a body of largely commercially driven research and practice. Both trends have occurred alongside a worrying growth in the use algorithmic methods to address, amongst other areas, questions of risk. Various possible reasons for these trends have been suggested over recent decades (Wald and Woolverton, 1990; Starr, 2014; Skeem and Monahan, 2020) and one key driver seems to have been an increasing marketisation of practice. Addressing issues of risk has increasingly relied on commercially developed RAIs, strongly influencing practice. Development of algorithms and checklists has increasingly been undertaken on this basis, as have related areas such as training and accreditation. This trend was extensively criticised by Wald and Woolverton (1990) who looked in detail at the area of child protection in North America, although the arguments made seem every bit as relevant to current forensic practice more broadly. In looking at the area, they noted that commercial imperatives meant that many RAIs were developed in haste and for profit. Once developed, RAIs come to be seen as 'products' to be actively marketed in an effort to gain and increase market share. There is a clear tension here between looking at precisely specified and individualised risks and the use of RAIs that address an economically viable market.

Marketisation, in general, and issues of commercial interest and confidentiality, in particular, may also act in opposition to traditional scientific methods, reducing independent scrutiny of this technology. Those who have commercially developed RAIs are generally not incentivised to open their products to academic scrutiny. Nor are they incentivised to make fundamental and expensive changes as risks change, as opposed to undertaking regular rebranding and superficial updates. Given the nature of forensic practice, this surely cannot be acceptable and practice development in the area of risk will need to tackle such serious market failures.

Linked to this is the use of parochial and unhelpful terminology that has recently developed in forensic practice. This has little merit beyond the marketing sphere, serving to create unnecessary barriers to the exchange of ideas and development of practice. As such, this should be promptly dispensed with. The term risk assessment in forensic practice is now rarely seen as part of a wider and more complex process of risk analysis. It typically refers to some form of probabilistic risk assessment, conducted largely in isolation from any wider process of analysis and evaluation. This is likely to become increasingly damaging, associated as it is with narrowing of approach. The use of this technical language in the marketing of RAIs also raises serious ethical issues, with statistical claims of 'reliability' often being misunderstood as demonstrating accuracy or utility. Adopting terminology that is seen across the broader field of risk has the potential to start breaking down the isolation of thinking in forensic practice and challenge and reverse current bad practices. It also has the potential to clarify for practitioners that the generation of probabilistic risk assessments forms only a small part of a much wider process of expert analysis, intervention and communication.

Critiques from outside forensic practice show just how narrowly focused much of it has become, with often remarkably limited aspects of any given case being considered. It has been suggested that this trend may serve managerial purposes that have little to do with effectively addressing risk, such as exercising greater control over professional staff. Here the use of currently dominant methods of risk assessment can be seen primarily as a means of increasing control and standardising costs. The growing reliance on RAIs have also been suggested as a means to provide greater legal certainty, providing a defence of practice and also for the denial of services to those who may need them (Wald and Woolverton, 1990). The growth of such managerial control seems evident in many areas of current forensic practice, possibly emerging as a result of the growth in what has been termed new public management (Towl, 2021). There has been a slowness in recognising this trend and important aspects of risk have, as a result, been increasingly neglected, misunderstood or treated superficially. At the same time, resistance to positive change in some quarters has become more powerful and entrenched. Some of the critiques discussed earlier show the problems that may result.

As well as these failures in seeing risk assessment in its context as part of broader processes, forensic practice can be criticised for progressively reducing attention on the psychology of decision-making. This has been associated with an increasingly simplistic view of this area, with poorly founded assumptions being routinely made. Ideas that people suffer from serious flaws in respect of making judgements about risk have become received wisdom, leading to the view that irrational and poor judgements are inevitable, for both experts and non-experts alike. This has driven approaches to risk assessment in different ways, leading some to advocate removing human judgements from the process and working towards replacing this with automated artificial intelligence systems based on formal logic. Others have advocated retaining expert judgement but placing ever greater constraints on this. Work largely from experimental cognitive psychology has increasingly challenged the validity of the fundamental assumptions these views rest on. People can and do make errors in judgement when compared with more formal approaches, such as using inferential statistics. The interpretation and implications of this have, however, been strongly challenged almost since the inception of ideas about cognitive illusions (Cohen, 1981; Gigerenzer and Selten, 2002). Concerns about the way such errors in judgement have been demonstrated and evaluated have been raised, with many being the result of experimental paradigms, rather than any fundamental deficits. Human decision-making is seen as being highly effective within its evolutionary context and much of the work showing cognitive illusions is seen as simply demonstrating that people do not perform well outside this context (Simon, 1955; Gigerenzer, 2008). Here, experimental paradigms can be criticised as focusing on demonstration of failings, rather than experimental investigations of how cognition works and how performance might be improved. The relevance and meaning of this have been the subject of robust and ongoing debates and ideas that cognition, just like perception, needs to be judged in context is far from new. This has clear and continuing relevance to the current topic in that it stresses the need people have always had to deal competently with a variety of risks and uncertainty. The fact that humans and other species have survived, testifies to the fact that they have often done so effectively throughout evolutionary history, suggesting that a capacity to do this well exists within us. How effectively people deal with such questions will, however, tend to be heavily reliant on environmental factors such as context and framing. These may act to impede or improve performance. This experimental evidence is somewhat reassuring, given that human judgement is an inevitable part of dealing with risk and uncertainty. Even for risk analyses that draw most heavily on sophisticated quantitative methods, it is people who developed these techniques, who will determine the questions asked and what to do with the answers (Cohen, 1981).

In considering risk, it seems increasingly clear that people do not naturally default to formal methods such as inferential statistics to make judgements. People do not normally rely on Bayesian networks, logistic regression equations or any similar formal methods. Rather, they use heuristics that can operate quickly and that do not place excessive demands on capacity. Again, this has often been seen as a failing, which explains the errors or cognitive illusions that can be demonstrated in human judgements of risk. Such assumptions have not been generally supported. When used within their ecological context, heuristics can outperform apparently more complex formal approaches and are often more robust in the face of changing conditions. The implications of this suggests that adapting environments to better suit the ways people naturally approach problems may be central to performance, which can be greatly improved in this manner.

Substantial experimental evidence supports the view that this seems to apply equally to highly expert and numerate groups (Gigerenzer and Selten, 2002; Gigerenzer, 2018). This has serious ramifications for improving risk assessment in forensic practice and perhaps the most important of these is that efforts to remove or greatly constrain the role of people in the decision-making processes may be seriously misguided. Under the wrong conditions, whether created by circumstance or deliberately, people can clearly be misled in making judgements about risk. Many forms of gambling or advertising clearly illustrate this vulnerability. This is, however, an argument for the power of environmental effects on judgement rather than one that supports the hypothesis of fundamental flaws in cognition. In fact, modifying environments to suit people's natural capacities, rather than seeking to replace them or straightjacketing them seems a promising way to improve risk assessment.

Doing Better

The lack of drive to improve current forensic practice, or indeed to arrest recent decline, may be linked to the commercial and managerial drivers outlined above. Arguably though, it is clearly possible to improve significantly on currently dominant RAIs and current levels of performance do not present a fixed ceiling. A first step towards this and one advocated here is the development of more broad-based understanding and analysis of risk and uncertainty, that aims to getter better understanding of specific questions. This presupposes a willingness to draw on research and practice from other areas and specialisms, particularly those that have proved most effective across the social and natural sciences. These have typically started with the common scientific practice of using language in careful ways that precisely specify terms, aiding the exchange of ideas. Building on this, they commonly describe related stages, phases or processes. Probabilistic risk assessment usually forms a small part of this, whether in the form of relative frequency or knowledge-based probabilities. It is not, however, seen as something that can sensibly happen in isolation from analysing and understanding risks. A possible model of this is set out in Figure 8.1 for illustrative purposes.

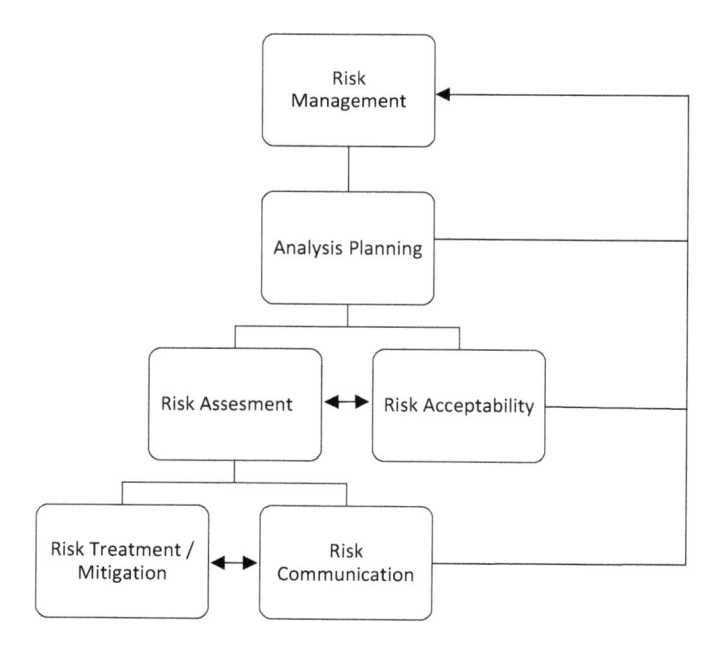

Figure 8.1 A simple model of risk.

Within this model, risk analysis can be seen as a critical part of the process and this is very different from most current forensic practice, with its general adoption of broadly defined behaviours or legal categories. Analysis can itself be further broken down into separate parts or stages of analysis and all of this is captured within a wider process of risk management. For present purposes, this is set out in a very simple diagram, showing risk management as an overarching and controlling process. Probabilistic risk assessment can be seen as part of this framework but is seen as resting fundamentally on the quality of analysis.

Risk analysis and risk evaluation have both been increasingly lost as concepts in forensic practice, perhaps explaining this trend to jump directly to some form of generic probabilistic assessment. Where these concepts are considered at all, they have tended to be increasingly conflated. As a result, risk assessments have increasingly come to be done without adequately detailed analysis or evaluation of the acceptability and tolerability of risk. In day-to-day practice, consideration of risk is often now reduced to a choice between the often-questionable application of simple algorithms or, more commonly, applying one of a number of commercially supplied checklist RAIs. The assumptions that underpin these and the levels of uncertainty and knowledge associated with them are rarely made explicit. Any sense of what levels of risk are acceptable and as a result what kinds of risk treatment might be indicated or justified is almost always left unaddressed. All of which means that those relying on such assessments are presented with, at best, a very limited picture of risk and, at worst, a misleading one.

Risk Analysis: Planning

Risk analysis can itself be logically broken down further as an aid to practice and here it has been simply divided into planning, methods, assessment and evaluation. The planning phase of risk analysis is important because it allows formal consideration of alternatives as well as the selection of the preferred ways forward. Systematic consideration of alternatives can ensure that the approaches chosen are sufficiently accurate and robust to address the questions posed. Various solutions can then be considered in terms of how well they meet given needs, allowing these to be set out, along with potential measures of performance and costs.

Importantly, the planning aspect of risk analysis is one that can be applied and reapplied at any point. The way that this part of analysis is conducted may differ at various points and may be undertaken, for example, in relation to systems that are being planned, constructed, that are operational or need decommissioning and replacement. The planning part of risk analysis can itself also be broken down further and here an approach based on two main divisions is used to illustrate this (Aven, 2010). One division is focused on problem definition, the gathering of relevant information and consideration of how the work will be organised. The second involves the selection of the methods of analysis. Both of these aspects of planning have been neglected in current forensic practice, being largely displaced by generic commercial RAIs. Adequate planning, however, allows the objectives of the assessment to be explicitly set out and additionally provides for identification of the boundaries of the assessment and consideration of changes to risk. The nature and extent of planning will depend on the issue involved and it need not, in practice, always be a very resource-intensive process. Taking the analogy of building, architects are likely to be able to plan a house extension with very modest effort, drawing in large part on many previous examples. Building a new teaching hospital by contrast, is likely to involve very extensive planning work. The selection of the methods used in planning are similarly likely to draw on experience and common methods can legitimately be applied to different cases. This should not, however, be assumed. It will not always be possible or appropriate and indeed all cases are likely to differ to some extent, meaning that unthinking application of a few standard methods to all cases is likely to be less effective.

Risk Analysis: Methods

There are a wide variety of methods for the analysis of risk and all have relative strengths and weaknesses. Some examples of analytic methods are outlined here and these are illustrative, rather than being an attempt to provide an exhaustive list. They are suggestive of some of the methods that forensic practitioners might usefully draw on, to improve the quality of analysis of risks across a range of practice. Probably the simplest of the analytic methods available involves the use of simple diagrams and pictorial representations.

The simplest example of this kind of approach is probably the use of 'bow tie' diagrams, which show possible initiating events summarised on one side of the diagram and the potential consequences listed on the other, with the event itself forming the knot of the tie (ASEMS, 2017). These simple diagrams can serve a valuable function in terms of clarifying the questions being addressed, but they can also be useful as an aid to communication of risk information. This type of diagram can be elaborated on with the addition of other aspects of risks, such as the expected consequences, the uncertainties involved and the framing conditions. Uncertainties here referring to deviations that may be associated with either lack of knowledge or random variation, whilst framing conditions concern the limitations associated with practical aspects of a risk analysis that need to be planned for, such as time, costs and information availability. The use of pictorial aids to analysis may also provide useful insights into risk treatment, identifying multiple points at which barriers or interventions might be used to break causal chains of events. Pictures may aid risk treatment and management by identifying those likely to be most effective but also by identifying less obvious alternatives.

The selection of methods for risk analysis can be broken down into 'forward' or 'backward' approaches, with forward approaches involving the identification of initiating events and the working through of these in terms of likely consequences. Depending on the risks being analysed, this can be an extensive process, covering a large number of imagined relevant events and scenarios. It may, however, be a much more circumscribed analysis, focused on a small number of initiating events judged to be likely. Backwards approaches by contrast tend to be less resource-intensive and are typically applied to areas that are better understood. These involve working backwards from an event (normally an adverse event) and setting out likely causal factors, risk factors and indicators. Both methods serve as an important guide to the resources likely to be involved in adequate assessment, treatment and management as well as the potential costs involved.

More formal methods have also been developed as aids to risk analysis and these include relatively simple and informal approaches, through to highly structured analytic techniques. The simpler end of this spectrum would include informal generation or 'brainstorming' of ideas, either singly or in collaboration with others. More formal and structured methods are, however, typically needed when faced with complex problems. Areas such as terrorism or large-scale corporate fraud provide the most obvious examples likely to require structured and detailed methodologies. At present, this kind of analysis is increasingly rare in forensic practice and this trend has continued, despite it becoming increasingly clear that adequate analysis is fundamental to effectively dealing with risk (Slovic, 2002). The down side of such approaches is that they do require high levels of professional training and expertise, along with an in-depth knowledge of the area or system being studied. Risk analysis methods do not provide the kind of standardised and automated templates that currently dominate forensic practice. In turn, the absence of this level of professional expertise may in part be due to the growing reliance on generic RAIs, compounded by the de-skilling and manualisation of many areas of risk treatment (Thomas-Peter, 2006; Towl, 2021).

The development of some form of probabilistic assessment of risk builds on the processes of risk analysis and it is suggested here that this can only ever be as good as the quality of analysis that provides its foundations. Importantly, what has not been identified through analysis will not form part of any probabilistic risk assessment, and this makes a lot of current forensic practice particularly troubling. In jumping directly to probabilistic assessments, in the absence of adequate analysis, it seems likely that initiating events and outcomes may be inadequately considered or missed entirely. Adequate identification of threats and hazards is fundamental to accurate risk assessment and forms a critical basis for effective risk treatment and management. Work in other fields often stresses the need to ensure that analysis does not deteriorate into a routine or mechanistic activity. Rather, the process of analysis is seen as a creative process, drawing on evidence and expertise, where efforts are made to actively try to identify the unusual and feed this into the other aspects of the process. This involves both systematic and creative thinking around the issue being addressed, with the suggestion here that an eighty-twenty rule can be a useful guide. This rule of thumb suggests that it takes around 20% of the time and effort involved to identify 80% of the threats or hazards, with 80% of the time being needed to identify the remaining less obvious 20% (Aven, 2010).

Analysis can, depending on the complexity of the questions being addressed, involve both causal and consequence analysis. Causal analysis is a 'backward'-looking methodology that involves looking at what is needed for a particular event to occur, then trying to determine those aspects that may be causal. Consequence analysis is a 'forward'-looking method and involves looking at multiple events to consider the possible consequences and interactions arising from these.

At a more developed level, such analyses might use formal methods to elicit initiating events, consequences and adverse outcomes. These may in turn be linked to consideration of individual differences from other cases, identifying specific conditions that may influence risk and how these are rated in terms of impact. Conditions with minimal impacts might be included here through to those requiring immediate or urgent action. In forensic practice, the nature of the risks associated with individuals varies significantly and it is also not uncommon to see deviations from typically seen scenarios, based on things such as individual attitudes, patterns of substance use, history of weapons use, involvement with peer groups and many more uncertainties. There may in turn be constraints that impact on risk, such as accommodation issues or family dynamics, and there will normally be more than one way in which these pathways' links to adverse events might be addressed. Inevitably, such analysis will be framed by practical constraints around what can realistically be done to deal with risks. This does not, however, reduce the importance of making these explicit.

Cause and Effect Analysis (CEA) or Ishikawa Diagrams

Starting with the simpler methods, CEA or Ishikawa diagrams (NHS and NHS Improvement, 2021) were developed from the area of industrial quality control but have much wider application. It is an informal and qualitative method, not amenable to quantitative analysis. In essence, it involves specifying an event and then drawing a main line from this. Other lines are then drawn diverging from this. These diverging lines can represent the contributors to the event in terms of any number of what are judged to be major factors. For example, the risk event line might be patients failing to attend for supervision or treatment appointments and the contributors to this might be defined as people, procedures, materials and equipment. In turn, further lines may be drawn to these major contributors, so that a contributor to procedures might be the absence of a system of appointment reminders. In turn, this might be broken down into the provision of appointment cards, text message reminders the day prior to appointments and telephone reminders on the day of the appointment. This analysis leads to a pictorial representation of all the factors that seem to contribute to the main event and they are often called fishbone diagrams, because of the visual resemblance between the pattern of lines and the skeletal structure of fish. The method can provide a useful and indeed powerful means of visualising what is contributing to any given risk, with the diagram acting as a qualitative process map.

Structured What If Technique (SWIFT)

SWIFT is a popular framework for conducting a systematic analysis of risks and is a step up in terms of formality compared with CEA diagrams (Card, Ward and Clarkson, 2012). It has been widely applied in health settings although it has a much wider application. SWIFT is a derivation of more complex but less flexible methods and advocates of the method see it as striking a balance between thorough analysis and avoiding excessive bureaucracy and formality. As the name suggests, the method draws on asking a series of leading questions, to identify deviations from normal conditions. In essence, asking a series of 'what if?' questions. These may involve looking at elements such as human error, technical failure, system failures and any areas deemed relevant. The structured approach can be seen in many ways as an enhanced form of brainstorming and it allows for more detailed identification of hazardous situations, initiating events and adverse events. As an analytic method, it may also make it easier to see potential combinations of events in more complex situations or systems as well as risk treatment measures that might impact on these. The technique has been widely used to address questions in areas such as patient safety and it can be used individually or in groups, depending on the complexity of the risks being addressed. The method can involve both qualitative and quantitative analyses.

Fault Tree Analysis (FTA)

Fault Tree Analysis (Abecassis, McElroy, Patel et al., 2015) is one of a number of 'tree-based' approaches to risk analysis and was developed in the 1960s by Bell Labs, initially to look at faults and the risk of faults in telecommunications systems that were at the time becoming increasingly complex. The method has come to be widely used where complex risks are involved and the method draws on a logical tree-like structure. This illustrates the relationship between an adverse event and the failures leading to it. In using this method, an undesirable outcome is specified as a 'top event' and the 'component' failures leading to this form a branching structure below this. A variety of symbols have been used to draw these diagrams, with no universally agreed symbolic representation.

In common with other tree-based methods, this is an iterative process of analysis. At its simplest, this will involve gates representing AND decisions as well as OR decisions, at each step. This kind of thinking will be familiar from computer program or coding but even if unfamiliar, the logic is straightforward. FTA can be useful for understanding complex risk problems better since it can show failure combinations that can result in adverse outcomes. These may not be obvious when using less structured approaches. Taking the example of the 9/11 terror attacks in the United States, or similar attacks in London and Spain, these involved a variety of complex and interacting factors coming together in a particular way. Diagrammatic representation of these kinds of problems can be of value in identifying the basic events that lead to the top event happening, often called cut sets or minimal cut sets. This method can also be described using mathematical set notation; although in forensic practice examples, it can often be identified visually. More complex situations may, however, require analysis using some form of algorithm.

Event Tree Analyses (ETA)

Event Tree Analyses (Despotou, Jones and Arvanitis, 2016) are used as a means of looking at the consequences of an initiating event, or put another way what type of scenarios may emerge from an initiating event. The method can be used qualitatively or quantitatively, and as with FTA, it involves posing multiple questions or recursive partitions with yes/no answers. Here, the convention is that yes answers branch upwards, and no answers branch downwards, and within this type of analysis, the branch structure may often duplicate. This can itself be useful information about risks, showing multiple paths to given outcomes.

The branching of questions can be divided in many ways depending on the nature and complexity of the problem. For example, it might be divided into those relating to physical phenomena and those relating to risk barriers within a system. Where the aim is one of risk reduction, then the focus of the ETA is likely to be on the later. It may also be useful to apply either relative frequency or knowledge-based probability values to the branches of such analyses, or in other cases, they may be more useful as a qualitative analysis.

Bayesian Networks

Bayesian networks consist of specifying events as nodes of a network (Zoullouti, Amghar and Nawal, 2019). This can be shown in tabular form or pictorially, using arrows to indicate dependencies between these nodes. Each node in such a network may be in various states and the number of these is selected by the analyst. A simple example showing one node of such an analysis is given in Figure 8.2, and this can be expanded to show multiple nodes of analysis for more complex examples.

Networks of this kind allow for the calculation of conditional knowledge-based probabilities, which may be tabulated. In this example, these are hypothetical but in practice, they may be defined by one or more experts. The use of such Bayesian networks has proved very popular within a range of social and natural sciences, and here, medicine is a clear example from applied biology,

	Meth amphetamine dependent abuse/ Anger Scale score > 85 Present %	Meth amphetamine dependent abuse/ Anger Scale score not > 85 Present %	Not Meth amphetamine dependent abuse/ Anger Scale score > 85 Present %	Not Meth amphetamine dependent abuse/ Anger Scale score not > 85 Present %
Violence to peer's present	95	85	90	2
Violence to peers absent	5	15	10	98

Figure 8.2 A hypothetical Bayesian network with two conditions.

where they have been used to look at areas including diagnosis and treatment (Arora, Boyne, Slater et al., 2019). Curiously, the method has been sparingly used in forensic practice.

Risk Analysis: Probabilistic Assessment

The process of analysis to this point should provide firm foundations for a probabilistic risk assessment, providing an appropriately detailed picture of the risks being considered and the evidence this draws on. It also provides a sense of the uncertainties involved and the framing of the risks. In turn, this allows for the estimation of likelihood, which may be in the form of knowledge-based or relative frequency probability statements as well as evaluation of outcomes. In current forensic practice, this tends to involve giving a numeric value for an adverse event or more commonly, an undefined probabilistic label for it, such as a 'high', 'low' or 'moderate to high'. The outcomes associated with these tend to be in the form of descriptive labels, such as 'serious physical harm'. It is rarely the case that descriptive labels are specified in a meaningful way or that methods such as cost–benefit analysis or cost–utility analysis are used.

Probabilistic estimates of risk are conditional on background knowledge, and it is essential to consider this if the level of uncertainty involved in any assessment is to be dealt with appropriately. In other fields, this is often summarised in the form of a risk matrix that describes this, but does not analyse it. Such matrices focus on the analysis in terms of how reasonable the assumptions used are, how much data there is, how reliable and relevant this is to the question and so on. Where there is broad agreement amongst experts, then the background knowledge is likely to be stronger than where there are widespread disagreements. Finally, where the phenomena are well understood, the knowledge base is likely to be stronger. To take examples from forensic practice, the knowledge base in relation to violence is likely to be stronger than that for sexual violence, with the knowledge base for areas such as terrorism being weaker still, suggesting much greater uncertainty. In thinking about this, Flage and Aven (2009) suggest that evidence can be considered systematically in a number of ways, yielding estimates of its strength as measured against operational criteria.

In relation to some problems, it may be appropriate to use additional techniques to improve the quality of both analysis and the probabilistic risk assessments deriving from it. A clear example of this would be major terrorism incidents, which may involve low-frequency adverse events with severe impacts. Here, analysis and probabilistic assessment will involve a high degree of irreducible uncertainty, making such risks particularly challenging. Simple algorithmic approaches are of little use, with the most accurate prediction from these being the non-occurrence of these rare events. Predicting that it will not happen will nearly always be correct but here the false negatives may be catastrophic. The kind of checklist RAIs that have come to dominate current forensic practice have surprisingly been extended to this area (Herzog-Evans, 2018). Yet, these are likely to fare even worse than simple algorithmic approaches, with the suggestion that this is a challenge that these methods fail to meet (Gudjonsson, West and McKee, 2015; Fischbacher-Smith, 2016). It also seems likely, given the extent of uncertainty present, that these assessments will rest assumptions based on weak knowledge. Given the high expected costs from incidents and perceived threats, false negatives are of grave concern and missing a quarter or more cases is not something that can be easily accepted. Equally, the very high rate of false positives is likely to have costs, both visible and hidden, with, for example, large numbers of citizens with no involvement in terrorism being identified and subject to unwarranted attention (Fischbacher-Smith, 2016; Sageman, 2021). Very different approaches to risk analysis, assessment and treatment are warranted and indeed needed here compared with the generic RAIs seen in much forensic practice. Effective responses are likely to rest here on formal methods to test and refine the quality of risk analysis and, in turn, the use of heuristics to assess likelihood, risk treatment and risk management options. An example of this would be the use of a method sometimes called 'red team–blue team' analysis. This involves the development of two independent and opposing expert teams that are diverse in terms of skills, background and outlook. Typically, a 'red' team takes on the role of providing detailed forensic and expert challenge to the 'blue' team analyses based on:

1 Areas of ignorance.
2 Arguing for events thought to have negligible probability.
3 Checking that relevant signals or warnings are properly reflected.

The use of such resource-intensive methods is likely to be limited to areas such as terrorism or large-scale financial fraud, where the costs of false negative assessments may be critical. Whether complex or simple, however, work to this point should have painted a broad-based picture of risk that sets out how the analysis was planned, the key assumptions that underpin it, an analysis of causes and consequences leading to estimates of likelihood and costs. The reference to painting a picture here is deliberate, stressing the idea that effective analysis needs to be a creative process, rather than the unthinking application of weak generic methods. Within this, pictorial analyses can provide a powerful aid to thinking, one that plays to the strengths of human cognition. A marked and unhelpful reticence in using pictures in this way has been evident in much of forensic practice. Explanation of this is speculative given the lack of study but it may be associated with concerns that such methods lack scientific credibility. Such views about using pictorial representation of complex ideas to aid understanding do not appear to have afflicted other more advanced scientific fields (Luisi and Thomas, 1990; Meynell, 2018).

No such picture is complete, however, without a consideration of how sensitive it is to the assumptions made and the limitations of what is known. How robust analyses are depends on these and will be sensitive to changes in both. This applies to even the most rigorous methods and the probabilities calculated for an event tree are likely to change in the face of changing information. Reluctance in sharing this is misplaced, short-sighted and potentially harmful (Edwards, 1968; Fischoff, 1995; Edwards, Elwyn, Covey et al., 2001; Edwards, Elwyn and Mulley, 2002; Adekola, Fischbacher-Smith and Fischbacher-Smith, 2018).

Risk Evaluation

The importance of openness in communication is central to the area of risk evaluation, which concerns the kinds and levels of risks that are judged acceptable and the range of risk tolerability. Of course, these are not simply empirical questions but involve value judgements, inevitably bringing conflicting perspectives and interest that will need to be balanced. As a result, it is essential if this is to be done well, that the risk picture developed should be as accurate as possible and that this should also be clearly and honestly communicated. The importance of this was elegantly described by Fischoff (1995) in a review that set out the developmental steps in risk communication. Starting from the dysfunctional approach of issuing expert edicts, the approach to this area of risk is seen as progressing through stages of development. When appeals to authority and status failed, the next response can be seen as a form of blinding the audience with science, providing detailed statistical values, tables and equations. Such approaches can at best be seen as ineffectual but often they appeared counterproductive, leading to suspicion about the process and dismissal of expertise. The essence of dealing with this area of risk, it is argued, involves active efforts to make the processes involved as clear and transparent as possible, treating decision-makers and stakeholders as partners in the risk process (Fischoff, 1995). This requires the sharing of detail around assumptions and uncertainties as well as open consideration of how risks have been evaluated. Expert assessors may, for example, have very different views of tolerability of risk, compared with those who have to face the risks considered. Reticence and discomfort around this aspect of risk can be marked in forensic practice, a growing trend that is likely to be linked to increasingly dysfunctional politics impacting on practice (Barkow, 2019). Such aversion, however, seems misplaced and lacking in professional courage if risk is to be dealt with rationally. Presenting very limited risk pictures to decision-makers and stakeholders, through many currently dominant RAIs that largely or wholly neglect such considerations, seems likely to enable rather than challenge this growing dysfunction. There is a need for clarity about how strong or how weak the foundations of risk analyses are and openness in risk evaluation. Being explicit in this way is likely to lead to better decision-making and is certainly likely to lead to better informed discussions of risk-based approaches. This is an area of forensic practice that has in recent years visibly deteriorated, despite its significance and repeated identification as an area of concern (Monahan, 1981; Fishchoff, 1995; Towl and Crighton, 1996; Fischbacher-Smith, Irwin and Fischbacher-Smith, 2010). As a practical illustration of this from the United Kingdom, it was as recently as the 1980s a common part of the work of correctional staff to engage with the public. Prisons managers, psychologists, probation officers and others would frequently engage with civic groups, schools and public events to explain their roles in this area. Work of this kind has become increasingly marginalised with the growth of New Public Management approaches (Towl, 2021).

Risk Treatment

Surprisingly perhaps the term risk treatment is not widely used in forensic practice. Issues of risk treatment where they are considered, tend to be unhelpfully conflated with risk management (Aven, Baraldi, Flage and Zio, 2014). There are clear disadvantages to this and the two areas are treated here as being distinct. Risk treatment itself can be usefully broken down and here is seen as comprising two parts:

1   The comparison of alternatives for risk treatment and the identification and assessment of relevant measures within this.
2   A process of reviewing and judging these from a risk management perspective.

There are a variety of ways in which risk treatment alternatives might be compared. Most obviously perhaps, this might involve looking at the extent of change to the likelihood of adverse events that can be achieved. It may, however, also involve considering ways of reducing the nature or impact of adverse events. Other things being equal, the use of barriers or interventions that reduce the chances of adverse events happening are likely to be preferable. Rather oddly, this has been largely neglected in many areas of forensic practice, with clinical custom and practice often appearing predominant. Interventions are often advocated, even where the effects may be marginal, or, in some cases, have been shown to increase risk. Barriers are typically given little consideration as a form of risk treatment. A stark example of this is the frequent recommendation for sexually violent individuals to complete psycho-social groupwork treatments in prison or secure mental hospital settings. The evidence on this form of risk treatment suggests it has been associated with an increased probability of further sexual violence (Towl and Crighton, 2016). Yet, it is rare that other types of risk treatment are given similar consideration, most obviously, here the scope for investment in higher levels of prevention work with undetected offenders or the use of higher levels of skilled supervision with and monitoring with identified offenders, where evidence of impacts on risk is more encouraging (Romero and Williams, 1983; Beier, Grundmann, Kuhle et al., 2015). Having identified approaches that have the largest effects on reducing the likelihood of adverse events, other considerations are likely to be relevant. These may include efforts to reduce the impacts of such events, should they occur. Other considerations here include efforts to assess the robustness and resilience of risk treatments as well as their strategic value.

Other considerations also emerge from this and again these have been largely but not wholly neglected in forensic practice. The costs associated with risk treatment itself, both in terms of financial costs but also in terms of other risks that may emerge, are significant. The most striking neglect in this respect is perhaps the growing resort to incarceration based on risk as a form of risk treatment. The costs associated with this are rarely made explicit to stakeholders and are seldom compared with alternatives. Because such costs are not transparent, the use of this barrier method of risk treatment is often resorted to easily and as if it were a free good. It is a view of risk management that has perhaps reached its zenith in the United States, where historically unprecedented policies of mass incarceration first developed, before spreading internationally. Indeed, the sheer scale of this has made it increasingly difficult to continue to ignore the escalating financial costs associated with this form of risk treatment even for wealthy nations, even if other costs can still be largely ignored.

To be explicit about this, taking the use of a typical placement in a correctional setting for a child under 18 years of age in the United Kingdom as an example, placement in custody is expensive. Costing far more than a place at an expensive boarding school, with individual outcomes that tend to be vastly different. In 2016, it was reported to the UK Parliament that accommodation cost averaged £75,000 per year to keep a child or young person in prison custody. Accommodation in a secure children's home was even more expensive, averaging an eye-watering £204,000 per year (UK Parliament, 2016). How this compares with the cost of alternative forms of risk treatment is seldom if ever made transparent to decision-makers and stakeholders. The question of whether spending taxation in this way is of good value is therefore never asked or answered, nor are comparisons made with other ways to spend limited resources, such as education or health services. These issues have received surprisingly little attention at a practice level, perhaps as a result of an ever-growing concentration of forensic practitioners in these settings.

The idea of discussing the relationship between risk treatment and risk tolerability limits has also been generally absent in forensic practice. The use of structured approaches to this, such as the As Low as Reasonably Possible (ALARP) principle (Nesticò, He, De Mare et al., 2018) are very rarely seen. One way of approaching this principle involves looking at the existing situation or 'base case' and then identifying measures that might reduce risk by fixed amounts: say 10%, 50% and 90%. With the example of suicides in prison settings, the base case would be the current approach to suicide prevention and the aim would be to develop a picture of risk treatment measures that could achieve reductions of 10%, 50% and 90%. This formal approach has a number of advantages for both risk treatment and management as it makes areas such as cost, implications and uncertainly explicit and open to rational consideration.

As well as considering issues such as cost and feasibility, the process of reviewing and judging risk treatment should necessarily include consideration of unintended effects. Any actions intended to reduce risk are likely in practice to have various effects. In rare cases, these may be entirely positive but more typically, they will involve a mix of positive and negative or adverse effects. The way in which suggested measures are likely to act and interact is therefore an important consideration within the risk treatment part of any risk analysis. This can range for a relatively crude and qualitative approach through to more detailed and quantitative analyses, depending on the specific issue. The significant point here, however, is that the various impacts and costs of risk treatment should always be actively and openly considered.

Risk Management

The term risk management is used here to capture an overarching process of dealing with risk (Smith and Fischbacher, 2009). As such, all of the other aspects of dealing with risk will feed into and inform risk management. An adequately developed risk picture should provide a sound basis for informing judgements and making decisions and this will form a key input to risk management. Approaches such as ALARP can also be used here, where agreed guidance or standards around what is acceptable and what is tolerable has been developed. As highlighted already, it is actively harmful if such processes become mechanical and unthinking. There are several reasons for this, which go back to the way risk is conceptualised, with such approaches tending to rely on fixed combinations of probability and expected values. As outlined earlier, this is generally a wholly inadequate way to address risk, failing to address key areas. Simple arithmetic of probability and costs, of this kind, may of course, form a part of any risk picture and so inform risk management, it will not, however, be adequate on its own. Effective risk management depends on a more adequate picture of risk than this and as part of the process needs to specify and require this.

Conclusion

In dealing better with risk, there is a pressing need to halt and reverse a number of recent trends in forensic practice. Moves towards using generic RAIs, often developed commercially, have detracted from more promising approaches as well as decoupling from the academic evidence base on risk. A key casualty here has been risk analysis, which has suffered increasing neglect and replacement with token or superficial approaches.

Thankfully, there is a great deal that can be taken from the evidence base on risk and uncertainty to address these concerns. Directly applicable methods that can aid analysis exist and the application of probability has greatly developed across the social and natural sciences. Forensic practice can draw on these to quickly improve current practice, improving the quality of risk analysis: in turn driving better evaluation, treatment and management. Effective analysis in turn clarifies the nature of the problem. In particular, the extent to which the state space and probabilities are known or may be estimated.

Dealing with Risk Better   9
Probabilistic Risk Assessment

Current forensic practice, with its focus primarily on giving probabilistic assessments of risk, might be defended in the face of many of the criticisms raised earlier if it were, nevertheless, highly effective. Indeed, a cursory review of the field might appear to support such a sanguine view with various Risk Assessment Instruments (RAIs) often supported by large amounts of research and data, along with an extensive industry of training, accreditation and support services. All of this might understandably lead to the conclusion that all is well, that we can be confident in relying on current practices, which are highly effective. If true, it could be argued there is scant need to focus on the much more extensive analysis, outlined in the previous chapter, where assessments are already doing such a good job. Issues of risk evaluation and management here fall away, becoming a problem for others to address, with allocation to risk treatments becoming highly mechanistic. In light of many of the critiques outlined earlier, such views appear seriously, even dangerously, misjudged.

Academic research has tended to suggest a high degree of interchangeability between current widely used RAIs. This has led to suggestions that they are in fact working by drawing on a small pool of common risk factors and indicators (Kroner, Mills and Reddon, 2005). The ceiling values for these RAIs, using the Area Under the Curve (AUC) statistic, have been reported to generally fall around the 0.7 level (Coid, Yang, Ullrich et al., 2009; Yang, Wong, Coid et al., 2011). This is significantly better than random chance, which perhaps accounts for the continued use of these RAIs. It is, however, hardly an impressive level of performance. Comparison with other areas where efforts have been made to develop probabilistic assessments, illustrate just how poorly forensic practice is doing. Drawing on the example of breast cancer screening, undoubtedly a

DOI: 10.4324/9781003108665-10

complex problem, one large-scale study across the United Kingdom and United States looked at the use of an assessment system, supported by Artificial Intelligence (AI) analysis to improve accuracy. Here an AUC statistic of 0.889 was reported, with 95% confidence interval for the AUC being reported as 0.871–0.907. The ability to meaningfully report this statistic to three decimal places is notable and the study was based on a large group of patients (25,856) meaning that the results could be determined with greater accuracy and confidence (McKinney, Sieniek, Godbole et al., 2020).

The importance of improving the performance of assessments can be clarified by looking at the result in terms of natural frequencies. Taking the relatively straightforward situation of a risk with a high prevalence rate, the effects are clear. The simplified example given in Figure 9.1 shows the results of using an assessment with 0.7 accuracy and Figure 9.2 shows the effects of increasing this to 0.9. Here a hypothetical base rate of 50% has been used, which might in this example represent levels of broadly defined sexual violence, in a particular community setting. Incidentally, this also gives the hypothetical assessment its best chance to perform well. In both cases, the predictions are clearly better than chance. Both inevitably yield false positives and false negatives. If this were not the case, the problem ceases to be one concerned with risk. The differences between the two analyses are, however, striking from a practical point of view. Simply from a visual inspection, the 0.7 level of accuracy can be seen to lead to results that are unimpressive, with a large number of individuals being misallocated. In this example, 3,000 of those assessed end up being wrongly characterised. The gains from the more accurate assessment reduces this to a much more convincing and indeed useful level of 1 in 10, correctly allocating 2,000 more cases. The key point here is not to provide any detailed statistical analysis, rather

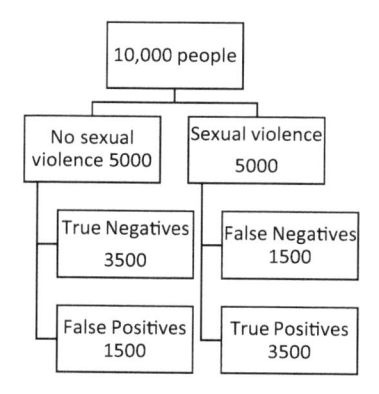

Figure 9.1 Natural frequency results for a hypothetical risk assessment of a specified sexually violent act with 0.7 accuracy and 50% prevalence.

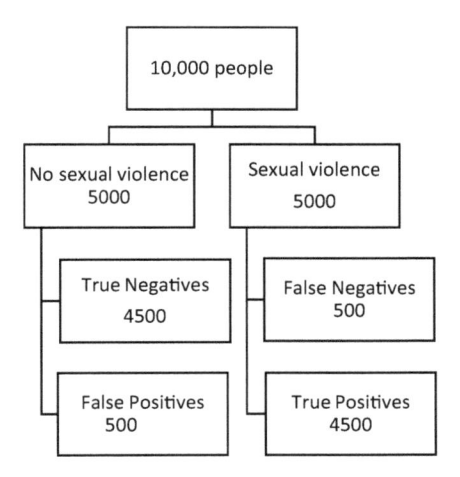

```
                    ┌─────────────────┐
                    │  10,000 people  │
                    └────────┬────────┘
                 ┌───────────┴───────────┐
        ┌────────┴────────┐     ┌────────┴────────┐
        │ No sexual violence│   │ Sexual violence │
        │       5000       │    │       5000      │
        └────────┬────────┘     └────────┬────────┘
        ┌────────┴────────┐     ┌────────┴────────┐
        │  True Negatives │     │ False Negatives │
        │       4500      │     │       500       │
        └────────┬────────┘     └────────┬────────┘
        ┌────────┴────────┐     ┌────────┴────────┐
        │  False Positives│     │  True Positives │
        │       500       │     │       4500      │
        └─────────────────┘     └─────────────────┘
```

Figure 9.2 Natural frequency results for a hypothetical risk assessment of a specified sexually violent act with 0.9 accuracy and 50% prevalence.

it is to draw out the importance of making gains, even apparently small gains, in the accuracy of probabilistic risk assessment. In practice, even what might appear to be incremental gains have serious effects. The willingness to accept poorly performing assessments in forensic practice is troubling and has not been accepted in many other fields of risk.

The costs associated with accepting such low ceilings for accuracy often remain hidden in forensic practice. The costs are, however, considerable in both human and economic terms. High levels of false negatives in this hypothetical case of sexual violence result in many sexually violent individuals being misidentified, as not presenting a risk and so not being allocated to risk treatments. Many others who would not have engaged in sexual violence are misclassified as presenting a risk and allocated to unnecessary and potentially harmful risk treatment. Gains in the accuracy of assessment will have major effects on many of these individuals. Current forensic practice needs to be improved in the way that other fields have done by refusing to accept current poor performance and demanding better.

The current low levels of accuracy seen in forensic RAIs also raises broader policy questions, about whether continued use of these is ethical or defensible. The considerable expense associated with these might be better used in other ways. An implicit or explicit acceptance of low ceilings of accuracy in forensic practice is unlikely to be tolerated indefinitely. The contrast with many other areas across the social and natural sciences, where similarly disappointing initial findings have acted as major drivers for research and development, is not a positive one. This may well be something that decision-makers and stakeholders might reflect on, with a view to driving improvements in practice.

Changing Practice

A fundamental question to be addressed here is whether the use of probabilistic estimates of risk is appropriate to the various contexts of forensic practice. Critics have suggested that risk assessments have increasingly been used in inappropriate ways, in practice. The use of probabilistic estimates of risk to inform punishment and to direct policing have been a particular focus of criticism here. At a fundamental level, these examples raise important questions about whether people should ever be punished, or policed, for what they might do, rather than what they have done. The questions raised here are perhaps more difficult and intractable than in situations where risk assessment has been used to inform, or direct, various forms of treatment. The idea that it is appropriate to offer different treatment to people based on probabilistic information is not without ethical issues of its own, but where the state space is well understood, this has generally received high levels of support. To take a specific example, risk-based screening for breast cancers has been widely implemented in many countries. Individuals may subsequently be offered treatment, as a result of analysis and risk assessment of how likely they are to develop life-threatening cancers. This process has a known element of misclassification. Some people will be wrongly identified as being at high risk and may go on to receive unnecessary, possibly harmful or life-threatening, risk-based treatments. Some will die prematurely who would otherwise have lived. Others will be wrongly identified as low risk and be inappropriately reassured, missing the opportunity for treatment that may have extended their life. These outcomes present difficult ethical issues, resting as they do on probabilistic information. They can, however, be discussed and debated, with what are felt to be acceptable balances struck (Wilson, Purdon and Wallston, 1988). Crucially, however, the people involved in these assessments have considerable agency. They are informed about these balances transparently and they are then free to make informed decisions about their own treatment.

The conditions that apply to many forms of risk assessment in forensic settings are fundamentally different to a patient deciding whether or not to consent to a particular screening programme. For those subject to probabilistic assessments in forensic contexts, the choices tend to be far more limited or non-existent. Where facial recognition software is used to produce estimates of risk of anti-social behaviour, or algorithms are used to flag a call to emergency services as risky, the person may know nothing of the process and have no opportunity to give or withhold consent. There may be little or no transparency. This despite the fact that such assessments may have direct impacts on them. Here, understanding and agreement about the areas where risk assessment has spread to has often been absent. Accuracy of assessment, levels of true and false positives may not be known, or may be kept from public view even if they are. Even then, they may not have been subject to independent scrutiny, public discussion or evaluation. Questions of consent and agreement are clearly less straightforward within such systems.

The extension of RAIs to policing and corrections raise obvious ethical concerns as RAIs have been applied here with minimal public discussion and debate, often under a dubious cloak of improved public protection. Here, the use of risk has been justified and the implementation of technology-based methods put in place, relying on often strong but poorly founded claims of efficacy. In both contexts, it can be argued that the implementation of the technology has run well ahead of the legal and social policy controls over it, and as a result, many of the effects have received inadequate scrutiny. This has begun to change recently, with the emergence of more thoughtful and considered debate. These have involved fundamental concerns around basing punishment on the likelihood that someone might do something through to individual biases, where RAIs are tapping directly or through proxy measures into legally protected characteristics such as sex, sexual orientation, race, social class and age. Here, the change in context very much matters and the transition from health-based uses to policing and correctional use seems critical. Going back to the example of screening for breast cancer, it would be entirely appropriate to consider sex in assessing risk to guide risk treatment. Not to do so would in fact be clinically and ethically inappropriate (Merz, Fischoff, Mazur and Fishbeck, 1993; Nyström, Larsson, Wall et al., 1996). Similarly, in looking at the risk of something like sickle cell anaemia, ignoring race would generally be accepted to be quite wrong. Age and wealth are clearly risk indicators for many health problems and are routinely included in determining public health risk treatments (Andrews, 2001; Baum, 2005). In such cases, however, the focus is on providing something positive, that is likely to be of benefit to those with protected characteristics. Where such characteristics have been included in RAIs used in mental health contexts, to direct risk treatment, a similar argument can be made to support this use. Extension of this to areas such as policing, sentencing and corrections, however, raises different and increasingly difficult questions around the legality and ethics of using such information. Some have sought to defend this on the narrow empirical grounds that these protected characteristics are valid predictors. Such a response is not remotely persuasive and appears to miss the fundamental point of the criticisms.

Not least of the concerns from a forensic practice viewpoint is the level of inaccuracy of predictions at an individual level. This seems particularly acute in uses such as policing and corrections, where the individual has little or no control. Drives to increase the automation of these kinds of assessment, significantly reducing the extent of human control over these RAIs, risk making a bad situation much worse. The need for consent in other settings can of course be overridden, in some instances. In most jurisdictions, however, these circumstances are closely circumscribed and controlled by law. There are very good reasons for having these checks and balances and instances where consent can be overridden tend to have strong protections in place. Taking the example of civil mental health law in the United Kingdom, compulsion to undertake risk-based treatment work is under the control of a small number of mental health professions, who are overseen by, admittedly inadequate legal frameworks, limiting and controlling their powers. Even these checks and balances have often been absent in developing applications of risk in areas such as policing and corrections. The central point here being that much greater care and thought is needed in forensic practice in the use of RAIs. Arguably, the primary focus should have remained on risk treatment rather than other, more controversial, applications of a limited technology. Even in this more restricted use of RAIs, the use of protected characteristics to inform risk needs to be considered much more carefully than it has been. Any use of these needs very clear and strong justification that is open to independent scrutiny, not simply bland appeals to actuarial utility. Worryingly, this does not appear to be the case in much current practice with recent trends being, if anything, in the opposite direction. Here practice can be criticised as falling behind other areas of the social and natural sciences in how risk is thought about and how probabilistic risk assessments are arrived at.

Algorithms have routinely been used to give apparently precise estimates of likelihood for poorly analysed and defined risks, resting on legally protected characteristics or proxies for them. These have been used for algorithms that try to actuarially predict vaguely defined outcomes. These might reasonably be expected to yield poor and unfair results. Additionally, the expansion of RAIs developed for one population to application with very different populations is clearly inappropriate. Inevitably, such predictors will not function as effectively and may indeed, not be predictive at all, or provide inaccurate and misleading results. Yet, this is what has been seen in some areas of forensic practice in recent years (Barnett, Wakeling and Howard, 2010; Monahan and Skeem, 2013; Monahan, 2017a).

How to Develop More Accurate Assessments

The implications of the modest ceiling for accuracy seen in most current RAIs and the application of these to poorly analysed and vague questions about risk have already been set out in some detail. The types of probabilistic risk assessments used in forensic practice have generally relied on the application of notably simple methods such as forms of linear regression analysis to poorly analysed problems. It is perhaps not surprising that the results of this have been so disappointing. All of which might logically give rise to questions of whether this is a function of the problems addressed or the methodological inadequacy of the approaches adopted. Is the complexity of the problem so marked that this is simply the best we can do? Or is the current low ceiling of probabilistic risk assessments a function of poor practice? It is argued here that the latter explanation accounts for much of the current weakness in practice, where there has been an apparent willingness to accept thinking and methods that simply look scientific, rather than being scientific.

It can of course be convincingly suggested that the kinds of questions of risk faced in forensic practice are often highly complex and challenging. As a result, the analysis and probabilistic risk assessment that follows from this is, in no way, a trivial intellectual problem. Equally, however, it is not evidently the case that these problems are intractable, or that they are any more complex than those faced in other better developed areas of the social and natural sciences that have concerned themselves with risk. This view of the situation receives significant support from existing, highly successful, efforts to improve the analysis and assessment of risk within forensic practice. This research is important in trying to answer the question posed above, so for that reason, it is set out in some detail, sufficient to understand its main findings.

The MacArthur Study

The MacArthur risk assessment study was a large-scale multi-site and multi-disciplinary research project conducted in North America, at around the turn of the 21st century. It is illustrative of how approaches to risk analysis and probabilistic risk assessment can be dealt with far better than is currently the case in most forensic practice (Monahan, Steadman, Silver et al., 2001). The study concerned the risk of various forms of violent behaviours in a large group of people, across multiple sites, who were in contact with mental health services. In planning and developing this study, researchers clearly undertook extensive analyses of the risks prior to developing assessment methods. As a result, important methodological gaps and weak assumptions used in routine practice were identified and addressed. Lamentably, the kinds of gaps and weak assumptions identified appear every bit as relevant and applicable to much of forensic practice now, as they did 20 years ago. They included the following:

1   The use of a constricted range of risk factors
2   Reliance on weak criterion measures of violence

3   The narrowness of the segment of the patient population studied
4   The stress on single site studies

The research set about trying to actively address all of these concerns within the study, first by using multiple sites with different characteristics. Additionally, a broad sample of patients was involved, going beyond the typical practice of studying those, primarily men, who had been convicted for violent offences. The study also involved developing and using stronger criterion variables for violence and setting out the assumptions on which these were based. The researchers used the analytical process of triangulation (Denzin, 1970, 2012) to inform this: In essence, involving the use of three sources of information to assess individual levels of violence by looking at official reports of violence, collateral reports of violence from others and self-report by the individuals being assessed. Active efforts were made to ensure greater accuracy of self-report and a broad sampling of participants in the study was used, which included both men and women. Crucially, the researcher's analysis led them to question some of the conventional assumptions around the assessment of risk of violence. These included the distinctly odd convention of, implicitly or explicitly, treating violence as a unitary phenomenon. Violence was instead divided into more serious incidents, which involved injury or credible threat and other aggressive acts, which were less serious and included verbal aggression. Additionally, these incidents were considered across three different units of analysis relating to the incidents, the individual patients and patterns over time.

As part of the study, a pool of potential risk factors was generated and the best of these were chosen, based on the current knowledge base. This was taken forward on the explicit assumption that any model based on a small number of factors would not be adequate and as a result, 134 items were retained for analysis. This data was then analysed, using the still dominant approach of regression, where a line is fitted to the data. The authors reported that this did not work significantly better than cheaper and simpler methods and the statistical model derived from this regression analysis was reported to not capture the richness of the information, apparently relying on a relatively small number of variables. This view is consistent with reviews of the use of regression analyses, which have identified this and several other significant weaknesses in this method of formal analysis (Berk, 2004).

To address this, the researchers moved on to use a tree-based approach, drawing on Classification Tree Analysis (Lewis, 2000). As with some other tree-based methods, this involves starting with a 'top' characteristic and then conducting a series of partitions (Gardner et al., 1996), leading to the identification of subgroups or categories, based on different sets of characteristics. This has the advantage that it can describe multiple high- and low-risk groups. There is an obvious value to this from a clinical or practice viewpoint, as unlike regression-based approaches, it means that every patient does not need to be assessed on every item to conduct the assessment. They could instead be assessed only on relevant items by working through the branching structure. Arguably, it is also much more intuitive when used in practice, as well as more usefully informing questions of risk evaluation, treatment and management. By providing more closely defined groups of those engaging in different forms of violence, the method often suggests an obvious focus on risk treatment.

The accuracy of a simple classification tree analysis, however, was reported to be no better than for the linear regression approach. Here, the AUC statistic was reported to be 0.81 for the logistic regression method and 0.79 for the classification tree approach, suggesting almost identical performance in terms of predicting risk. The researchers therefore went on to look at the convention, then prevalent, of allocating people into two groups based on qualitative descriptors of 'high' and 'low' risk. Instead, they decided to divide risk into three groups, high risk, low risk and a third undifferentiated risk group. In turn, they adopted the approach of quantitatively specifying the levels for each of these categories and did this on the basis of operational definitions. Noting that qualitative descriptions can mean very different things to different observers, the researchers used the base rate for violence in the group studied to construct these operational definitions. The high-risk group was therefore defined as those showing twice the base rate for violence or more. The low-risk group was defined as those showing half the base rate for violence or less. These are of course arbitrary divisions for the different levels of violent behaviour but they have the major advantage of being transparent and consistent.

Repeating both analytic methods, using these operational definitions, led to an important finding that both methods were in fact leaving a large number in the undifferentiated category; essentially where the analysis was not distinguishing individuals from the base rate for violence. This was reported to be 42.9% of those studied for logistic regression and 49.2% for the classification tree approach. This kind of finding is often hidden in current practice, where RAIs may in fact be yielding a large number of assessments that do not distinguish people from the population base rate. In this case, both statistical analyses used had only been able to classify just over half of those assessed. The MacArthur researchers addressed this by looking again at this undifferentiated group of patients, where the assessment had not added anything useful, in terms of distinguishing the level of risk from the base rate. This was done by re-analysing this undifferentiated group, to see if further analysis could be used to distinguish them from the base rate. This was done again by use of a tree-based approach, which was repeated, a method described as iterative classification tree (ICT) analysis. The classification tree approach was repeated for a second time for the group of patients who had not been differentiated from the base rate for violence, and this further analysis was able to allocate 119 out of 462 (26%) to either high- or low-risk groups. A third iteration in turn allocated 63 out of the remaining 343 (18%) and a fourth iteration reallocated 60 out of the 280 remaining (21%) at which point, further iterations were judged by the researchers to be inappropriate. For comparison purposes, the researchers also conducted a comparable process of repeated regression analysis. Both methods in fact improved the identification of high- and low-risk groups, with the repeated regression analyses managing to allocate 62% to either high- or low-risk groups. The tree-based method performed better, however, with 77% being reallocated in this way. Repetition of a tree-based analysis had therefore resulted in the better allocation and better fitting of the data. Given this, the fact that patients did not need to be assessed on every item as well as the ability of the ICT method to identify potentially useful categories of high- and low-risk individuals, the method was seen as being preferable to the alternative regression method.

The analysis used did of course raise concerns of overfitting and the prospect that the model might show shrinkage or lower predictive accuracy when used with other populations. The researchers set out this concern explicitly and went on to test this statistically by combining multiple models, each containing different combinations of risk factors. The purpose in doing this was described as providing more chances for an individual to be allocated to high- or low-risk groups. Where individuals tended to be allocated to high- or low-risk groups more often, using these different models, it was suggested confidence in the allocation would be higher. The results of this analysis were reported for 'optimal' and 'clinically feasible' ICT approaches, and here, the reported AUC values were given as 0.82 and 0.80 respectively.

Importantly, the fact that this led to differential allocations was also made clear. In this study, 38% were allocated to the low-risk group twice, 12% to the high-risk group twice and 8.0% to the average risk group twice. This meant that 57% showed the same group allocation using different models, which was felt by researchers to suggest that the combination of the two models was able to identify more extreme groupings. Such differential allocation is of course a characteristic of risk classification but one that, even now, is seldom made explicit in forensic practice. To be otherwise, the different models used would need to be perfectly correlated, and in practice, this will never be likely. In the MacArthur study, the two models above were reported to correlate at a level of 0.52, suggesting that they correlated reasonably well with the criterion of violence but only moderately with each other. Here, the researchers argued that there was clear value in combining ICT analyses. Of those who were twice classified as low risk, the rate of subsequent violence was 3% within 20 weeks of discharge; for those twice allocated as high risk, the rate of subsequent violence was 64%.

This range was much wider than seen for any single ICT model. In fact, a combination of five ICT models was reported to yield the best predictive accuracy with the rates of violence ranging from 1% to 76% and an AUC statistic of 0.88.

The MacArthur study outlined above is put forward here to stress some key points about dealing more effectively with risk and ambiguity. The first of these is to stress the key role of careful risk analysis. Any efforts to develop probabilistic assessments forms part of this broader process of analysis and is founded on it. Weak and flawed analysis will invariably undermine the quality of risk assessment. This is stressed here as part of a scientific approach to dealing with risk. A process that necessarily involves the testing and revision of ideas, which will often also extend to questions of risk evaluation and risk treatment. Crucially, the MacArthur study showed clearly what was possible by significantly improving the quality analysis and probabilistic assessment, achieving an AUC value much better than the typical ceiling of around 0.7 reported for the RAIs that continue to dominate forensic practice. Indeed, the level achieved approached that reported in the example of screening for breast cancer, outlined above. As stressed earlier, the importance of such gains in forensic practice are often enormous in both human and other terms.

Conclusion

An obvious question that occurs from this is why this key research has not been seminal in changing forensic practice. It is possible to speculate at various levels about the reasons for this sustained lack of uptake in practice over two decades. Most obviously, perhaps the MacArthur study was a costly endeavour, involving a large and highly expert team. The idea of applying such methods to routine practice might be resisted on cost grounds alone. Yet, as seen in discussing the effects of accuracy of assessments earlier, this would be a serious error of judgement. The costs of misallocating large numbers of people based on poor-quality risk assessments are very high in human and economic terms. The financial costs of this alone are certainly orders of magnitude higher than the costs of dealing with risk more effectively in the first instance. They are, however, often not transparent, with the links to failures in methodology being opaque. For example, those unnecessarily detained, at considerable expense, are hidden. A second linked barrier to change here may, as already discussed, be the increased and increasing marketisation of this area of forensic practice. With many RAIs being developed for profit and in a commercialised system, there are few drivers for the kinds of careful analysis and methodological sophistication seen in the MacArthur study. The drivers here of course need to be at political and policy levels. Where customers are not attentive to the need for change, however, it is unlikely to happen. Many of those concerned with the difficult challenge of risk management in forensic contexts appear, at present, to be content with poor levels of accuracy, as long as the processes used look at a superficial level scientific. Faced with often aggressive marketing of current RAIs, they could, however, legitimately feel they have been misled. The reality is that the methods that currently dominate forensic practice are not very good, levels of accuracy can be greatly improved on and that the hidden costs of failing to do so are enormous but largely hidden.

Dealing with Risk Better
Changing the Environment

10

Some events appear unsuitable for the use of algorithmic methods, no matter how careful and sophisticated the analysis and assessment. Specifically, algorithmic methods have long been known to deal poorly with low-frequency events, and this becomes particularly critical where these have high impacts. An example of this, drawn from forensic practice, is the risk of self-inflicted deaths in prisons. Although the rates in prisons are shockingly high when compared with the community, they are still in statistical terms low-frequency events. They are also an example of uncertainty, with a state space that appears unknown and unknowable (Gigerenzer, 2021). This makes actuarial predictions about risk impractical, as can clearly be seen using efforts to screen for this risk as an illustration. The idea of using various forms of risk assessment instrument (RAI) to screen for suicide in prison settings is one that can be seen to have been used repeatedly. The suggestion from proponents of this approach is that those at high risk can be identified and directed to risk treatments.

Assuming that an assessment could be developed to perform at similar levels to the RAIs that currently dominate the market in forensic practice, around a 0.7 level of accuracy using the area under the curve statistic, what would this mean in practice? Using natural frequencies clarifies the nature of the challenge here. Taking a sample of 10,000, chosen partly as an arithmetic convenience and partly with a sense of how many people might actually pass through a busy prison in a year, the results can be worked through. Of these 10,000 prisoners, a small proportion will end their own life in custody. The reasons for this will be many, complex and highly uncertain. The distress and pain in each case, dreadful.

In thinking about how risk assessment might function here, an arbitrary and entirely hypothetical rate for self-inflicted deaths of 1% has been used to

DOI: 10.4324/9781003108665-11

166 Changing the Environment

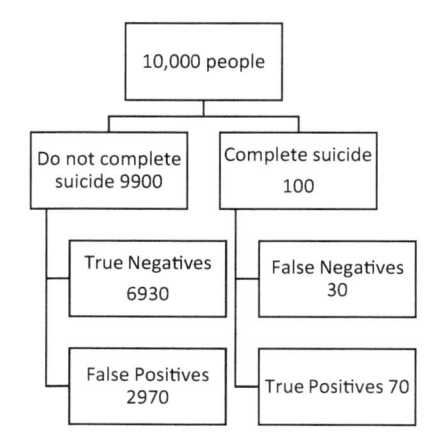

Figure 10.1 Natural frequencies for a hypothetical screening assessment for self-inflicted deaths in prisons based on 0.7 accuracy level and 1% prevalence.

think about this group, although in fact the true rates are typically lower than this. Figure 10.1 gives a simple picture of the results. From visual inspection alone, the results are not encouraging of such efforts to screen for risk. Actuarially, the most accurate prediction will inevitably be that someone will not kill themselves.

This hypothetical situation is not atypical of the one's forensic practitioners face on a daily basis, in that it involves trying to estimate the likelihood of a rare and uncertain event. Here, it is one that presents a chronic risk at the institutional level and acute risks at the individual level. It makes clear that using assessments with such a modest ceiling will result in large inaccuracies. In this example, it suggests around 42 false positives for each true positive case identified. Meanwhile, just under one in three self-inflicted deaths will have been missed as false negatives. Given the low base rate, efforts to increase the accuracy of prediction do not help much, at least not within the realms of what is likely to be achievable. Mental health staff in any prison engaged in such an activity are likely to quickly become disenchanted with it, not least because the false negative cases are likely to be highly salient for them. Those managing the process of risk could also be forgiven for becoming disillusioned. Charitably assuming each of the screening assessments by mental health staff cost £50, the RAI process alone would cost £500,000 per annum to provide for a population of 10,000. This is before thinking about the considerable treatment costs for the large number of false positive cases identified, or opportunity costs associated with staff undertaking more productive work. It seems reasonable to suppose most prison managers, charged with dealing with this kind of risk, would be able to think of other better ways to spend such a sum to reduce suicides, rather than this weak risk assessment process, for example, by investing in risk reduction during the early days of imprisonment as a better use of resources to save lives.

Getting Rid of the 'Cargo Cult' Science

The main alternative to the algorithm-based RAIs are those based on checklists: often also described as structured clinical judgement or protocol-based RAIs. These have seen progressive growth in popularity and arguably have become the predominant methodology in many areas of forensic practice. A significant industry and strong professional interests appear to have developed around this form of RAI. The basis for this approach to risk assessment is, however, strikingly weak in terms of outcomes. These RAIs are often marketed as a way of spreading 'good' clinical practice, by imposing structure or protocols for risk assessment and treatment. Yet, as with generic actuarial RAIs, they are typically based on vague and broadly defined risks, such as 'sexual violence' or 'antisocial behaviour'. Efforts at risk analysis tend to be superficial and rarely extend beyond some history taking and efforts at problem 'formulation'. Yet as discussed in previous chapters, it is clear that in using weak criteria, a great deal of additional complexity is simply ignored and lost from consideration. Checklist RAIs have often been commercially developed, and here market pressures may conflict with good practice in risk assessment. More generic RAIs will have a much larger market, thereby creating an incentive to use broad criteria or categories of risk.

Checklist RAIs typically involve the assessment of individuals on the basis of standard lists of risk factors and risk indicators. Some may involve protective and promotive factors, although this is less common. All tend to use weakly defined criteria, often involving quite circular definitions. Some allow for the inclusion of additional items and omission of items that cannot be assessed, or appear irrelevant to individuals. The analyses of these checklist items, statistical and otherwise, are generally elementary in nature. For example, few seek to put values on the contribution of individual factors or indicators, or to put meaningful values on risk. In place of this, general verbal descriptions of likelihood are used such as 'high' or 'moderate' risk. These, of course, may hold very different meanings to different assessors, decision-makers and stakeholders.

As discussed earlier, this method of risk assessment consistently shows a relatively low ceiling of data fitting or predictive accuracy. Most perform at above chance levels when this is measured but the performance appears to cluster around modest levels of accuracy (Yang, Wong and Coid, 2010). Such limitations are now well known to practitioners and researchers, raising questions about the growth in popularity and dominance of this risk assessment approach as well as the apparent acceptance of such modest levels of predictive accuracy. An important study by Kroner, Mills and Reddon (2005) perhaps gives an important clue to this. Looking at a range of RAIs, they found that they were largely interchangeable and in fact remarkably cheap and easy to create. They found that RAIs of this type could be produced by taking randomly drawn items from other checklists: memorably described by the researchers as 'coffee can' instruments, after the receptacle used to randomly draw checklist items. These randomly generated checklist RAIs performed similarly to the originals. This led to the suggestion that this type of RAI was in fact drawing on a small pool of well-known correlates to achieve the modest levels of performance seen. Given how easy RAIs of this kind are to make, it is perhaps unsurprising that the method has grown so quickly, within an increasingly commercial system of development.

Given the obvious empirical limitations, however, it is harder to understand why they have been so successful in displacing alternative methods of assessment of risk and uncertainty, such as clinical and algorithmic assessments. Here two possible drivers present themselves. One is that the use of checklist RAIs might have been welcomed by those managing services. The use of checklists here shows activity and suggests efforts to manage risk. Less positively, they have acted as a means of controlling and limiting the work of professional groups. They have facilitated efforts to quantify work of this kind, converting complex analysis into unduly simple metrics. Taking corrections as an example, the complex process of dealing with risk and uncertainty might be reduced to the number of checklist completions in a given time frame.

A second, linked, driver is the possibility that checklist RAIs of this kind are an archetypal example of 'cargo cult' science (Feynman, 1974). This can be described as a method with the surface appearance of science, mimicking its methods but, in reality, meeting none of its fundamental requirements. Commercially produced RAIs have been very actively marketed as technical products, often mimicking the appearance of genuinely scientific methods. They are often sold on the basis of technical presentations and this seems to have been a clear driver in terms of the growth in popularity.

Although checklist RAIs do not work particularly well, they do appear to perform consistently at above chance levels. The ability of checklists to do this, including those generated by random selections of risk items from other checklists, warrants some thought. The primary explanation, suggested here, is that checklist RAIs may appear to be effective by drawing on inbuilt decision-making heuristics. Typically, this might involve the use of the tallying heuristic with counting of the cues in favour of one alternative over another.

These heuristics can be accurate, robust and resilient in dealing with the kinds of uncertainty and risks people typically face or have faced in natural environments (Simon, 1955; Gigerenzer and Selten, 2002). Such heuristics can in fact be shown, when used in context, to often perform rather better than any available alternatives.

These are of course questions that can themselves be answered using scientific method. It would be relatively straightforward to unpick how checklist RAIs work at the level of individual decision-making. Here, there is a wealth of high-quality evidence from experimental psychology and, it is suggested, this provides very little encouragement for the methodology of checklist RAIs. Answering this question may not, however, be essential at this point. The empirical question of interest here, for forensic practitioners, is not so much how checklist RAIs work but whether they can significantly outperform the use of alternative methods. For given outcomes, as part of a process of assessment, do checklist RAIs outperform heuristics in decision-making? If they cannot do so, this suggests that the whole panoply and expense of checklist RAIs may be adding nothing useful to practice. The argument put forward here is that in fact, by introducing an additional layer between heuristics and decision-making, such checklists may be reducing accuracy. By placing an additional layer over the process of using natural heuristics, such RAIs may, in fact, be having adverse impacts. In many cases, forensic practitioners might do better to simply draw directly on the heuristics. At best, the use of checklist RAIs seems to be an unnecessary cost, detracting from more productive activity. These might include putting greater effort into analysing and understanding areas of risk, as discussed in some detail earlier. Or at a more prosaic level, this might involve efforts to calibrate expert judgements to achieve better accuracy: something that is routine in many areas of risk but almost entirely absent in forensic practice (International Organisation for Standardization, 2018; Dressel and Farid, 2018). Additionally, as indicated above, sometimes a focus directly on risk treatment may be a better investment in saving lives than efforts to fit data to historic samples or predict outcomes.

Changing Environments to Make Better Decisions

Within forensic practice, natural decision-making processes about risk and uncertainty have, in recent years, been largely neglected. These draw on simple but robust methods such as 'take the best', 'tallying' or 'minimalist' heuristics. The working of these heuristics, however, is strongly influenced by the environment. They appear to work best where conditions can be made to closely mimic those in which the heuristics evolved. Conversely, they can fail where the environment significantly differs from this, through deliberate manipulation or otherwise.

Experimental work in developmental psychology by Inhelder and Piaget (1958) and others subsequently, suggested that even very young children can deal with complex information in a logical and rational manner. In contrast, drawing on cognitive illusions research, it has become commonplace in forensic practice to assume a fundamental irrationality and fixed tendency to make errors even in highly trained adults. This later view is not well supported by the evidence, which in fact suggests people find it difficult to deal with information presented in certain ways. We can also be fooled, in ways that have been suggested to be analogous to the way our visual system can be fooled by certain presentations of visual information. In discussing this, it is probably worth again stressing how late ideas of mathematical probability emerged in the history of human thought with the foundations emerging largely from the 17th century (Daston, 1988). Development in this area is by no means complete but this late emergence does seem to suggest that thinking in this way does not come naturally. For most of human existence, information has been dealt with in the form of natural frequencies in the environment, not as conditional probabilities. Difficulty in dealing with these context-free problems about the likelihood of events might then be seen as unsurprising. In solving real world problems of this kind, multiple logical strategies often seem to be used, and these are based on natural frequencies and a switching between different strategies, to reach a solution. Understanding what is going on here and how this might be used to improve performance, requires studying this interaction between the tasks and individuals. In turn, these need to be tested against multiple hypotheses and not simply against a null hypothesis as has become common (Meehl, 1978; Gigerenzer, 2008).

Work in developmental psychology suggests that the way we deal with these kinds of problems emerges, with an overlapping model of development suggested (Siegler, 1999). This proposes that competence changes over time, in the form of overlapping waves or stages of development. Four waves of development have been suggested: guessing, counting, pre-Bayesian and Bayesian solutions. A significant level of methodological sophistication is needed to address this complexity. Given the right structure, however, children, at the appropriate developmental stage, do indeed show the ability to solve complex problems involving probability. For example, they can solve Bayesian conditional probability tasks when presented with natural frequencies, rather than conditional probabilities. In one such study, when tasks were presented as conditional probabilities, only 47% of adults and none of the children were able to solve these kinds of problems (Siegler, 1999). The contrast with the performance using natural frequencies is both striking and informative, with significant improvements seen. Indeed, it was reported that one fourth grade child solved all ten conditional probability questions correctly and three of the group achieved eight or more correct answers, outperforming adult MBA students. Even where children and adults were getting answers wrong, the researchers observed that most were following clear strategies and not simply guessing. Although the strategies used tended to be non-Bayesian, there was nothing irrational about them. For example, they used a representative thinking approach that looked at the frequency of two events co-occurring, ignoring base rates and false positive rates. Interestingly, it has been observed that this closely corresponded to the null hypothesis significance testing method that has come to be so widely used, so harmfully, in many areas of psychology (Meehl, 1978; Gigerenzer, 2004).

The main relevance of such findings, from this and similar research studies, is twofold. First, it illustrates the critical importance of how information is presented. Second, it suggests the emergence of more effective strategies as part of a developmental sequence and that this, in turn, might be systematically taught. Both ideas have great importance for improving forensic practice. This view sees people as having evolved to deal with information in the form of natural frequencies. As a result, presenting information in this familiar way, seems likely to greatly improve the ability to deal effectively with it. This is a finding that has been shown repeatedly across groups, from young children through to the most highly trained adult clinicians. Similarly, the importance of a developmental sequence in the approach used in solving such problems has been highlighted as of practical importance. What is clear from these kinds of experimental studies is that, from an early age, most develop the ability to reason in a Bayesian manner but that they do so on the basis of context-dependent natural frequencies. This reflects the kinds of problems that our ancestors had to deal with in natural environments. Teaching practitioners to do this and communicating risks and uncertainties to others in this manner is likely to contribute significantly to more effective practice.

As discussed earlier, the ideas deriving from cognitive illusions and ecological rationality approaches to understanding human cognition have very different practical implications. The former approach stresses fundamental weaknesses in human cognition that need to be constrained and ideally eliminated. Setting aside for the moment whether such biases have been overstated, such a viewpoint suggests a need, in relation to complex problems, to replace or constrain natural decision-making. Advocates of this can point to a number of systematic errors that people make, when faced with particular types of problems. Taking an example from forensic practice, when faced with types of violence that we have personal experience of, our judgements, it is suggested, are liable to be systematically influenced. Structured approaches based on inferential statistics do not suffer from this, whilst checklists are suggested to reduce such effects.

Advocates of ecological rationality reject much of this, stressing the adaptive value of the interaction between environments and cognition. Here, it is noted that apparent biases tend to disappear or be minimised, for example, as a result of high levels of knowledge and training. This also happens in response to changes to the presentation of information (Dressel and Farid, 2018; Gigerenzer, 2021). Where this is not effective, the idea that environmental conditions can be actively shaped to improve people's ability to assess risk is advocated, where this can make it easier to draw on effective inbuilt skills and heuristics. Here, stress is placed on the need to shape tasks to suit the way we think, rather than efforts at constraining human decision-making as far as possible.

One of the major strengths of heuristics appears to be their robustness in dealing with uncertainty. They continue to work in the face of challenges that other methods struggle to deal with, such as coping with low-frequency high-impact events. Heuristics also often do not suffer from the kind of shrinkage seen in many algorithmic RAIs. This is not a new finding and an early study of the comparative efficacy of optimising and heuristic approaches was undertaken in the 1970s. This involved a paradigm where people were asked to try to predict educational outcomes based on a range of data. Specifically, the researchers looked at predicting which Chicago high school would have the highest dropout rates (Dawes and Corrigan, 1974). This is analogous to many of the questions faced in forensic practice and the study looked at a number of cues likely to be of relevance, including attendance rates, social and economic makeup of the schools, the ethnic makeup of the school, class sizes and standardised test scores. This data was assessed using regression analysis, and this was compared with three heuristics: the 'take the best', 'minimalist' and 'tallying' heuristics.

Here, the tallying heuristic used all the cues, as did the multiple regression algorithm. People using the take the best heuristic to predict school dropout rates used an average of 2.4 cues and for the minimalist heuristic averaged 2.2 cues, so both of these heuristics neglected some information (Czerlinski, Gigerenzer and Goldstein, 1999). The regression analysis achieved the best fit to the historic data, but it was not the best in terms of prediction. Here, it was outperformed by both the take the best and tallying heuristics. It did, however, perform slightly better than the minimalist heuristic. The researchers concluded that by extracting too much information from a data set, a better fit to historic data could be achieved, accounting for more of the variance. This appeared to be achieved by overfitting the data and would suffer regression to the mean when used prospectively. In simple terms, more of the random variation had incorrectly been treated as being predictive, however, since this would no longer be present in another sample, a substantial loss of predictive power would be seen. The two heuristics that outperformed multiple regression appeared more robust, as a result of ignoring and not trying to fit much of this random variation or 'noise'. As such, the heuristics were able to focus on information that was more likely to be genuinely predictive.

This finding links to research looking at expert decision-making, which has shown that this is often based on surprisingly narrow samples of information and the use of take the best heuristics. This has often been portrayed as evidence of the poor quality of unaided decision-making, even by the most highly trained of experts. This view, however, is largely based on the assumption that this heuristic will be less effective. In reality, this focused approach to problems, drawing on knowledge-based probabilities, may often lead to quicker and better decisions. As noted by Gigerenzer (2008, 2021), this is an empirical question and not one of belief. Where and when heuristics are effective and how the environment might serve to improve accuracy are all questions that may be answered experimentally. This point was well illustrated in a study of clinical decision-making, which concerned risk-based allocations to cardiology treatment in North America (Green and Maher, 1997). This study involved decision-making at a Michigan hospital in the United States, where the problem was that 90% of presenting patients were being seen as high risk and being sent to the specialist coronary care unit (CCU). This had led to serious overcrowding and poor quality of care for those patients who were genuinely high risk and in clinical need of the CCU. To stop the initial response of admitting so many patients to CCU, possibly as a result of defensive professional practices, an expert system based on a sophisticated algorithm was introduced. This had been developed for use in a university teaching hospital elsewhere in the United States, to address a similar issue: it was based on logistic regression using multiple cues to assess each patient. This algorithmic RAI worked in reducing the allocations to CCU. It was also reported to be widely disliked and poorly adopted by clinicians: It had a limited impact in practice. Similar reactions in forensic settings are not uncommon, where the results of algorithmic predictors of risk often appear to be routinely ignored in practice.

As a result of this experience in Michigan, the researchers developed an alternative approach, using what was described as a 'fast and frugal' decision tree. This was designed to mirror the take the best heuristic and was based on knowledge-based probabilities around risk. Importantly, it was also an open tree approach, meaning that clinicians could see each of the branched decisions as they worked through them. Here, the first branch of the tree related to the presence of the S and T wave segment changes on an ECG. If present, then the patient was admitted to the CCU on that basis alone as being at high risk. If not, then the clinicians moved to the next question, whether the chief complaint was chest pain. If the answer was no, then they were admitted to regular nursing care. If the answer was yes, and they were reporting chest pain, then the question asked was if there were any other factors such as NTG (nitro-glycerine mediated vasodilation) or other detailed ECG changes. If present, then the patient was admitted to the CCU and if not to regular nursing care (Green and Mehr, 1997). This can be seen as a process that accords with the way skilled clinicians naturally tend to work and use this heuristic. Here, being comfortable using the method and the open nature of the tree-based model seem important. The branching structure provided an easily intelligible aid to decision-making about risk, both to expert assessors and those managing risk more widely. The method may in turn also have been particularly helpful to inexperienced or less competent clinicians.

This open decision tree method was reported to be more accurate in predicting myocardial infarction than clinicians as a group, also having better sensitivity and lower false positive rates. Strikingly, however, it was also more accurate than the regression-based approach, despite clearly using much less information. This fast and frugal tree can be seen to use the building blocks from the take the best heuristic. It provides an ordered search and a one-reason stopping rule, with a one-reason decision-making. It also orders these cues in the same frugal way that people naturally tend to do, by ignoring dependencies. Perhaps because of this, the method was reported to have proved more acceptable to clinicians, with better uptake than the regression-based method. It was transparent, unlike the closed algorithm predictor, so the experts making the assessment could clearly see the basis for decisions being made and retained the scope to overrule where they felt it was warranted.

A similar approach to risk has been illustrated in studies of decision-making in Magistrates' Courts in the UK. Here, a fast and frugal tree showed a predictive accuracy of 92% in relation to decisions about risk: here, determining whether someone presented an unacceptable risk for being given bail. It is worth noting that in the UK, unlike in some other states, there is generally a presumption in favour of granting bail. This tree involved just three questions. The first being whether the prosecution opposed bail or requested conditional bail. If so, then some form of punitive action was taken, such as bail being denied, if not the Magistrates moved on to the second question, whether a previous court had imposed conditions on bail or remanded the person into custody. If so, then some form of punitive action was taken. If not, then the third question was addressed, whether the police had asked for imposed conditions or remand in custody. If not, then the person was given bail. If they had, then some punitive action was applied. As with the health example mentioned earlier, this approach to risk can be seen to draw on the take the best heuristic. It involved three yes/no questions from an ordered search, based on knowledge about predictors, with a one-reason stopping rule and one-reason decision-making. This was compared with a linear unit weighting model based on 25 cues. This more complex model did not perform as well as the open decision tree, yielding 85% accuracy and clearly involving much more data gathering and analysis (Dhami, 2003).

In other areas, heuristics can perform less well in the environments that people are faced with. This appears to be especially true of what have been called 'dread' risks, a common example of this being air crashes. This has resulted in great emphasis being placed on reducing the risks associated with flying, with remarkable success. In reality, however, many more people are killed and injured as a result of errors in healthcare than air travel, yet this has traditionally received far less attention and effort to reduce deaths and serious injury. A number of explanations have been suggested for this, none of which is fully satisfactory. The finding does, however, have serious consequences and suggests that our heuristic decision-making is fallible and that an accurate understanding of knowledge-based probabilities may be very important. Following the terror attacks in the United States on 11 September 2001, for example, many people switched from flying to driving. Since driving is considerably more dangerous than flying, in terms of deaths and injuries per mile travelled, this was associated with many more subsequent deaths and serious injuries than would otherwise have been likely. Indeed, it was estimated that around 1,600 additional deaths resulted from this change of means of travel, more people than those who were killed in the initial terror attacks (Gigerenzer, 2006a; Gigerenzer, 2006b; Gaissmaier and Gigerenzer, 2012).

The role of environmental factors in the estimation of risks has also been extensively studied in the context of healthcare. Such characteristics appear to be very significant even for highly trained staff and may serve to make already difficult tasks of risk assessment even more challenging than they need to be. For example, the chances of tests detecting diseases are normally conveyed as conditional probabilities. In practice, even highly trained practitioners have difficulty integrating this and distinguishing between concepts such as sensitivity, specificity and positive predictive power. All of these are conditional probabilities and using information in this form does not come easily to most. Likewise, concepts of relative and absolute risk are often important in forensic practice and more widely but may be poorly understood. Such concepts tend to become more transparent and easily understood when they are given as natural frequencies, rather than as conditional probabilities (Gigerenzer and Hoffrage, 1995). Taking a clinical example as illustrative of this, a patient following tests might be told that a treatment for breast cancer reduces the risk of death by 25%. Without knowing the type of risk, it is easy to misinterpret this information in a number of ways. Here, the information might refer to the relative risk, meaning that the risk of death reduces from that seen in similar patients, say from 4 in

1,000 down to 3 in 1,000. By simple calculation, this is of course a 25% reduction but in terms of absolute risk, it represents a reduction of 1 death in 1,000 (Nyström, Larsson, Wall et al., 1996).

Similarly, prophylactic mastectomy (surgical breast removal) in high-risk groups may legitimately be described as reducing deaths by 80%. This can refer to the Relative Risk Reduction (RRR), where 5 out of 100 who do not have a mastectomy go on to die from breast cancer, compared to 1 in 100 of the group who have the operation. The Absolute Risk Reduction (ARR), however, is a much less impressive 4 out of 100. Following from this is the Number Needed to Treat (NNT) statistic, simply the reciprocal of the ARR. Staying with the example of prophylactic mastectomy, the ARR of 4/100 and the NNT is given by dividing 1 by the ARR. This gives a value of 25, meaning that you would need to treat 25 patients for each positive outcome. This is stressed here to draw attention to the importance of how information is presented and how this can improve practice and decision-making about risk. Presentation of information determines, to a very large extent, how people process information and, for most of human existence, this has involved natural frequencies and not conditional probability. Confusions between relative and absolute risk is common even in experienced forensic practitioners but may be greatly reduced simply by reference to natural frequencies.

The Attractions of Simplicity

Most of the developments in forensic practice over recent decades have involved the use of apparently more complex methods, deployed to aid in risk assessment increasingly at the expense of risk analysis and evaluation. This is evidenced by the growth and diversification of RAIs, based largely on the assumption that these methods can invariably yield more accurate estimates of risk than expert judgements. This trend also appears to have been driven, in part, by ideas of optimisation similar to those that historically dominated areas such as economics and management. As seen earlier, such assumptions are at best oversimplistic and, it is argued here, have resulted in increasingly poor practices. Across a range of practical settings involving uncertainty, ranging from military checkpoints to legal decision making the use of heuristics, often aided by use of fast-and-frugal trees (FFT's) have been shown to be highly effective. They can be so by drawing on fundamental strengths that exist in human decision making, rather than seeking to replace it (Katsikopoulos, Şimşek, Buckman and Gigernenzer, 2020).

Psychological research suggests that complex methods do not always lead to the desired results. In addition, simplicity in the form of 'clinical' decision-making drawing on inbuilt heuristics often have their own largely hidden attractions, including being more robust, more accurate, faster and less demanding of resources. Heuristics can be simple because they can draw on highly evolved or highly trained abilities. These may in fact involve highly complex forms of data processing (Körding and Wolpert, 2004), but this is largely automatic and hidden in terms of conscious effort. Using such heuristics in the right contexts, or shaping decision-making environments to draw on these heuristics, may avoid problems of overfitting and a lack of resilience and robustness that often afflict other methods.

Conclusion

In introducing this text, the aim was to provide a critical review of risk assessment in forensic practice and in doing this, a number of questions were raised. What are the foundations of this work? How is it done now? What is wrong with how it is done now? How might it be done better? Hopefully, a start has been made in trying to address or at least promote discussion and debate about these questions. A number of themes have emerged from this process and not everyone will agree with the view taken of these. Disagreement, however, is an important and positive aspect of any scientific endeavour, providing the motivation for further thought, experimentation and discussion around an area that presents major challenges. There is a need to avoid inhabiting echo chambers of current forensic practice and to critically review policy and practice.

A central theme that emerges here is that current forensic practice, in relation to risk assessment, is not in a good place. It has arguably seen a general deterioration, certainly in the first two decades of this century. This contrasts with some of the more grandiloquent claims for current methods. Current practice has shown an increasing tendency to drift away from the broader academic evidence bases in the field, resulting in approaches that often appear idiosyncratic and parochial. Research and thinking from other disciplines, which have grappled, often more successfully, with comparable problems, has been largely ignored. More worryingly still, much of the evidence from research within, or close to, forensic practice, has been similarly neglected. In part, this may reflect a peculiarly ahistorical approach within forensic practice. Foundational ideas around risk have often gone unrecognised or, where recognised, have been misapplied. This compares poorly to many other areas of the social and natural sciences.

Another factor involved in the current poor state of risk assessment, it is suggested, has been the growing commercialisation of the area. Increasingly, approaches to risk and assessment have been subject to commercial drivers and pressures. These have not always been compatible with the traditions of scientific good practice and independent scrutiny. Certainly, they have created pressures for approaches to risk based on very broad and weak criteria, which will be associated with large markets. The development of a detailed analysis and an ever-greater differentiation aimed at, in science, cuts directly across this.

Growing commercial influences on risk assessment also seem to have interacted with a growing managerialism in many areas of forensic practice. Here, the use of standardised checklists and generic algorithms seems to have a few obvious appeals. Such methods are relatively easy to quantify into managerial metrics. Less obviously perhaps, they also increase managerial control over forensic practice, specifying what is measured and assessed. In turn, this is likely to control and limit what is identified in terms of risk treatment: fitting individuals to what is available rather than what is needed. Questions of risk analysis and evaluation largely disappear from the control of forensic practitioners. Whilst not inevitable, this often appears to have resulted in rationing of services in ways that are not transparent. Finally, perhaps least plausibly, current practice has been seen from a managerial viewpoint as a check against litigation. This may indeed have worked in the short term, with the ability to fall back on claims that risk has been objectively determined, with high levels of accuracy directing risk treatments. As these claims have been explored in depth, this has quickly crumbled away (Towl and Podmore, 2019). Indeed, it can reasonably be suggested that much current practice has served to drive, not reduce, litigation.

A further concern about current forensic practice is the focus on risk assessment, at the expense of analysis. The components of analysis appear largely absent in many areas of practice. Since analysis forms much of the foundation of scientific approaches, this is rather alarming. The view stressed here is that there is an increasingly pressing need to reverse this. Much greater effort needs to be put back into the analysis of risk and uncertainty, developing more detailed pictures of what is being assessed, developing knowledge and theory of the areas involved. From a risk perspective, giving apparently precise answers to wrong or weakly formed questions will, at best, be of little value. At worst, this may be deeply harmful. Risk analysis therefore needs to take a central place in improving risk assessment. Equally, the idea of risk treatment has clear value and relevance, and needs to become more of a distinct focus, separated more clearly from notions of management. This conflicts directly with the ever-greater stress on pre-packaged methods in forensic practice which have often reduced professional control and discretion, and contributed to the direction and rationing of services, without making the basis for these decisions transparent. In some cases, this may systematically further disadvantage already disadvantaged groups.

Improving the quality of risk assessment in forensic practice is likely to involve a reversal or many of the dominant trends of recent decades. These include the idea that risk can be assessed well using broad criteria and quick and simple templates, or generic algorithms based on simple inferential statistics. Accurate assessment rests on careful analysis and broad criteria are an anathema to this. Equally, the notion that expert assessment is inevitably and fundamentally flawed, requiring its control by means of checklists, or replacement by means of algorithm and artificial intelligence, is not supported by the evidence. In the area of risk, research in what was called 'heuristics and biases' has had long-term and negative effects, contributing to a sense that expert judgements and decision-making cannot be relied on, in view of inherent biases. In turn, this may have contributed to further legitimating the use of 'objective tools'. Within economics, this work may once have served a valuable function, correcting models of human decision-making that often neglected psychology, or indeed appeared anti-psychological. In the area of risk, it has, paradoxically, often been used to support just this kind of thinking. Approaches based on the ecological rationality of cognition start from a very different place, seeing human judgements of risk as being effective in the right context as, in fact, the product of extended selection in dealing with just the kind of risks and uncertainties presenting in much of forensic practice. Demonstrations of cognitive illusions, it is stressed, do not negate the value of these often-powerful heuristics that we naturally possess as human beings. Any more than demonstrating visual illusions tells us that this system is hopelessly flawed and in need of replacement with artificial intelligence. The implications of this are important and diametrically opposed to the heuristics and biases viewpoint, suggesting two things. Firstly, that environments can be adapted to get the best from those making such assessments. Secondly, that far from being hopelessly flawed, the use of expert clinical judgments based on heuristics may be the best we have when faced with uncertainty (Katsikopoulos, Şimşek, Buckman and Gigerenzer, 2020).

The growing commercial influence and managerial constraints on professional practice that have flowed from recent developments in forensic practice, have had, in relation to risk, overwhelmingly negative effects. This seems in large part responsible for driving the uptake of currently dominant methods, the managerial attractions of which are not hard to discern. Easily quantified, apparently defensible and providing a means of rationing scarce services, all have an appeal. Add to this at times aggressive and often highly technical marketing, to audiences that could not reasonably be expected to evaluate it, giving a heady and dangerous mix. The alternative, of providing better training in risk for experts, managers and decision-makers alike, has less immediate appeal. Such a view would, however, be a short-term and misplaced one. Currently, dominant methods of risk assessment are often far from convincing and are liable to increasingly unravel when challenged.

There has often been an apparent sense that current practice is the best that can be done. Dealing with complex, interacting risks and uncertainties that are often poorly understood, frequently with a lack of theoretical models to explain many of the behaviours of concern. The risks themselves are often dynamic and certainly non-linear in nature. Faced with this, so the argument goes, the current low ceiling of risk assessment may indeed be the best that can be achieved. This counsel of despair, however, is evidently wrong. By using different methods, it is demonstrably possible to improve on current levels of performance. This needs an approach to risk assessment that sees it as part of a more extensive process of thinking about risk and uncertainty, with greater stress on analysis, evaluation and treatment: bound together under the umbrella of risk management. It also requires a focus on better training and support of experts, decision-makers and stakeholders in the area of risk. All of which can most usefully be seen as an iterative and interactive process, going well beyond the current focus on generating probabilistic risk assessments and limited, largely mechanistic, risk management responses.

As a final observation, one emerging theme from the critiques of current practice has been that there is no 'one size fits all', or even 'one size fits most', template for the kinds of risks seen in forensic practice. Such an approach is likely to perform poorly. Forensic practitioners need not be afraid of adopting a range of analytic techniques and methods, in an effort to deal more effectively with the challenges they face. External bodies and risk managers also need to be challenged where they have contributed to the growth of poor practices, as indeed do those who have oversold the quality of currently dominant models. It is perhaps worth echoing, at this point, views that were eloquently expressed by Wald and Woolverton (1990) in relation to complex and demanding area of risk in child protection. They lamented the development of many template RAIs, making claims of accuracy and cost-effectiveness, which had been, to use their memorable phrasing produced in haste and for profit. They concluded that if the aim were to deliver the best approach to risk, protecting vulnerable children as best we can from serious harm, there really was no alternative to high levels of training, development of skills and provision of services to support children and families. It is argued that this applies equally to the wider field of forensic practice and if risks are to be dealt with effectively, such a view holds as true today as it did then.

References

Abecassis, Z. A., McElroy, L. M., Patel, R. M., Khorzad, R., Carroll IV, C., and Mehrotra, S. (2015). Applying fault tree analysis to the prevention of wrong-site surgery. *Journal of Surgical Research*, *193*(1), 88–94.

Abel, G. G., Becker, J. V., Mittelman, M., Cunningham-Rathner, J., Rouleau, J. L., and Murphy, W. D. (1987). Self-reported sex crimes of nonincarcerated paraphiliacs. *Journal of Interpersonal Violence*, *2*(1), 3–25.

Adekola, J., Fischbacher-Smith, D., and Fischbacher-Smith, M. (2018). Light me up: Power and expertise in risk communication and policy-making in the e-cigarette health debates. *Journal of Risk Research*, 1–15.

Agan, A., and Starr, S. (2017). The effect of criminal records on access to employment. *American Economic Review*, *107*(5), 560–564.

Andrews, G. R. (2001). Promoting health and function in an ageing population. *BMJ*, *322* (7288), 728–729.

Andrews, D.A. and Bonta, J. (2007). *The psychology of criminal conduct (4th edition)*. Cincinnati: Anderson Publishing.

Andrews, D. A., Bonta, J., and Wormith, J. S. (2006). The recent past and near future of risk and/or need assessment. *Crime and Delinquency*, *52*(1), 7–27.

Angelino, E., Larus-Stone, N., Alabi, D., Seltzer, M. and Rudin, D. (2018). Learning certifiably optimal rule lists for categorical data. *Journal of Machine Learning Research*, *18*, 1–78.

Arbuthnot, J. (1710). An argument for devine providence, taken from the constant regularity observ'd in the births of both sexes. *Philosophical Transactions*, *27*, 186–190.

Arora, P., Boyne, D., Slater, J. J., Gupta, A., Brenner, D. R., and Druzdzel, M. J. (2019). Bayesian networks for risk prediction using real-world data: A tool for precision medicine. *Value in Health*, *22*(4), 439–445.

ASEMS. (2017). *ASEMS Toolkit*. London: Ministry of Defence. Available from: asems.mod.uk/toolkit

Austin, J., Coleman, D., Peyton, J., and Johnson, K. D. (2003). *Reliability and validity study of the LSI-R risk assessment instrument*. Washington, DC: The Institute on Crime, Justice, and Corrections, George Washington University.

Aven, T. (2010). *Misconceptions of risk*. Chichester, UK: John Wiley and Sons.

References

Aven, T. (2012). The risk concept—Historical and recent development trends. *Reliability Engineering and System Safety, 99,* 33–44.

Aven, T. (2013). Practical implications of the new risk perspectives. *Reliability Engineering and System Safety, 115,* 136–145.

Aven, T. (2015). *Risk analysis.* Chichester, UK: John Wiley.

Aven, T. (2016). Risk assessment and risk management: Review of recent advances on their foundation. *European Journal of Operational Research, 253*(1), 1–13.

Aven, T., Baraldi, P., Flage, R., and Zio, E. (2014). *Uncertainty in risk assessment.* Chichester, UK: John Wiley.

Aven, T., and Renn, O. (2009a). On risk defined as an event where the outcome is uncertain. *Journal of Risk Research, 12*(1), 1–11.

Aven, T., and Renn, O. (2009b). The role of quantitative risk assessments for characterizing risk and uncertainty and delineating appropriate risk management options, with special emphasis on terrorism risk. *Risk Analysis: An International Journal, 29*(4), 587–600.

Aven, T., Vinnem, J. E., and Wiencke, H. S. (2007). A decision framework for risk management, with application to the offshore oil and gas industry. *Reliability Engineering and System Safety, 92*(4), 433–448.

Ayers, S. (1997). The application of chaos theory to psychology. *Theory and Psychology, 7*(3), 373–398.

Bar-Hillel, M. (1980). The base rate fallacy in probability judgements. *Acta Psychologica, 44,* 211–233.

Barkow, R. E. (2019). *Prisoners of politics.* Cambridge, MA: Harvard University Press.

Barnett, G. D., Wakeling, H. C., and Howard, P. D. (2010). An examination of the predictive validity of the Risk Matrix 2000 in England and Wales. *Sexual Abuse, 22*(4), 443–470.

Baum, F. (2005). Wealth and health: The need for more strategic public health research. *Journal of Epidemiology and Community Health, 59*(7), 542–545.

Beck, A. T., and Steer, R. A. (1984). Internal consistencies of the original and revised beck depression inventory. *Journal of Clinical Psychology, 40*(6), 1365–1367.

Bedford, T., and Cooke, R. (2001). *Probabilistic risk analysis: Foundations and methods.* Cambridge: Cambridge University Press.

Beier, K. M., Grundmann, D., Kuhle, L. F., Scherner, G., Konrad, A., and Amelung, T. (2015). The German Dunkelfeld Project: A pilot study to prevent child sexual abuse and the use of child abusive images. *The Journal of Sexual Medicine, 12*(2), 529–542.

Belfrage, H., and Douglas, K. (2012). *Interrater reliability and concurrent validity of HCR-20 (version 3).* Unpublished data analyses. Mid Sweden University, Sundsvall, Sweden. Quoted in Douglas, K. S., Hart, S. D., Webster, C. D., and Belfrage, H. (2013). *HCR-20 V3 assessing risk for violence.* Burnaby, CA: Simon Fraser University.

Bentham, J. (1827). *Rationale of judicial evidence, specially applied to English practice.* London: Hunt and Clark.

Berk, R. A. (2004). *Regression analysis: A constructive critique* (Vol. 11). Thousand Oaks, CA: Sage.

Bernoulli, D. (1954). Exposition of a new theory on the measurement of risk. *Econometrica, 22*(1), 23–36. (Translation of Bernoulli D 1738 Specimen theoriae novae de mensura sortis; Papers Imp. Acad. Sci. St. Petersburg, 5, 175–192).

Bettinson, V., and Dingwall, G. (2013). Challenging the ongoing injustice of imprisonment for public protection: James, Wells and Lee v The United Kingdom. *The Modern Law Review, 76*(6), 1094–1105.

Braverman, D. W., Doernberg, S. N., Runge, C. P., and Howard, D. S. (2016). OxRec model for assessing risk of recidivism: Ethics. *Lancet Psychiatry, 3*(9), 808–809.

Brennan, T., Dieterich, W., and Ehret, B. (2009). Evaluating the predictive validity of the COMPAS risk and needs assessment system. *Criminal Justice and Behavior*, 36(1), 21–40.

Budd, J., Miller, B. S., Manning, E. M., Lampos, V., Zhuang, M., Edelstein, M., et al. (2020). Digital technologies in the public-health response to COVID-19. *Nature Medicine*, 26(8), 1183–1192.

Burgess, E. W. (1928). Factors determining success or failure on parole. In A. A. Bruce (Ed.), *The workings of the indeterminate sentence law and the parole system in Illinois*. Springfield: Illinois State Board of Parole.

Byrne, J. M., Pattavina, A., and Taxman, F. S. (2015). International trends in prison upsizing and downsizing: In search of evidence of a global rehabilitation revolution. *Victims and Offenders*, 10(4), 420–451.

Cabinet Office. (2002). *Risk: Improving Government's capability to handle risk and uncertainty. Strategy Unit Report*. London: Cabinet Office.

Card, A., Ward, J., and Clarkson, P. (2012). Beyond FMEA: The structured what-if technique (SWIFT). *Journal of Healthcare Risk Management: The Journal of the American Society for Healthcare Risk Management*, 31(4), 23–29.

Casey, P. M., Warren, R. K., and Elek, J. K. (2011). *Using offender risk and needs assessment information at sentencing: Guidance for courts from a national working group*. Nappa, CA: National Center for State Courts.

Casscells, W., Schoenberger, A., and Graboys, T. B. (1978). Interpretation by physicians of clinical laboratory results. *New England Journal of Medicine*, 299(18), 999–1001.

Clemen, R. T., and Winkler, R. L. (1999). Combining probability distributions from experts in risk analysis. *Risk Analysis*, 19(2), 187–203.

Cocozza, J. J., and Steadman, H. J. (1978). Prediction in psychiatry: An example of misplaced confidence in experts. *Social Problems*, 25(3), 265–276.

Cohen, L. J. (1979). On the psychology of prediction: Whose is the fallacy? *Cognition*, 7, 385–407.

Cohen, L. J. (1981). Can human irrationality be experimentally demonstrated?. *Behavioral and Brain Sciences*, 4(3), 317–331.

Coid, J. W., Yang, M., Ullrich, S., Zhang, T., Sizmur, S., Farrington, D., and Rogers, R. (2011). Most items in structured risk assessment instruments do not predict violence. *The Journal of Forensic Psychiatry and Psychology*, 22(1), 3–21.

Coid, J., Yang, M., Ullrich, S., Zhang, T., Sizmur, S., Roberts, C., Farrington, D. P., and Rogers, R. D. (2009). Gender differences in structured risk assessment: Comparing the accuracy of five instruments. *Journal of Consulting and Clinical Psychology*, 77(2), 337–348.

Conrad, P. (1992). Medicalization and social control. *Annual Review of Sociology*, 18(1), 209–232.

Cooke, R. (1991). *Experts in uncertainty: Opinion and subjective probability in science*. Oxford: Oxford University Press.

Cooke, R. M., Marti, D., and Mazzuchi, T. (2021). Expert forecasting with and without uncertainty quantification and weighting: What do the data say? *International Journal of Forecasting*, 37(1), 378–387.

Cournot, A. A. (1843). *Exposition de la théorie des chances et des probabilités*. Paris: Hach.Livre-BNF.

Couzens, R. (2011). *Evidence-based practices: Reducing recidivism to increase public safety; A cooperative effort by courts and probation 10*. Available at: http://www.courts.ca.gov/documents/EVIDENCE-BASED-PRACTICES-Summary-6-27-11.pdf

Covello, V. T., and Mumpower, J. (1985). Risk analysis and risk management: An historical perspective. *Risk Analysis*, 5(2), 103–120.

Crighton, D. A. (2004). Risk assessment. In A. Needs and G. Towl (Eds.), *Applying psychology to forensic practice*. Oxford: BPS Blackwell.

Crighton, D. A. (2021). Risk assessment. In D.A. Crighton and G.J. Towl (Eds.), *Forensic psychology (3rd edition)*. Chichester, UK: John Wiley.

Crighton, D. A., and Towl, G. J. (2008). Principles of risk assessment. In D.A. Crighton and G.J. Towl (Eds.), *Psychology in prisons*. Oxford: Blackwell.

Czerlinski, J., Gigerenzer, G. and Goldstein, D.G. (1999). How good are simple heuristics? In G. Gigernezer, P.M. Todd and the ABC Research Group. *Simple heuristics that make us smart* (97–118). New York: Oxford University press.

Darjee, R., Russel, K., Forrest, L., Milton, L., Savoie, V., Baron, E., and Stobie, S. (2016). *Risk for sexual violence protocol: A real world study of the reliability, validity and utility of a structured professional judgment instrument in the assessment and management of sexual offenders in South East Scotland*. Retrieved from: http://www.rmascotland.gov.uk/news-and-information/latest-news/risk-sexual-violence-protocol-rsvp-publication-real-world-study-reliability-validity-and-utility-rsvp/

Daston, L. (1988). *Classical probability in the enlightenment*. Princeton, NJ: Princeton University press.

Dawes, R. M., and Corrigan, B. (1974). Linear models in decision making. *Psychological Bulletin*, 81(2), 95–106.

Dawes, R. M., Faust, D., and Meehl, P. E. (1989). Clinical versus actuarial judgement. *Science*, 243, 1668–1774.

Dawid, A. P., Musio, M., and Murtas, R. (2017). The probability of causation. *Law, Probability and Risk*, 16(4), 163–179.

Debidin, M. (Ed.) (2009). *A compendium of research and analysis on the Offender Assessment System (OASys) 2006–2009*, Ministry of Justice Research Series 16/09. London: Ministry of Justice.

de Finetti, B. (1930). Fondamenti logici del ragionamento probabilistico. *Bollettino dell'Unione Matematica Italiana*, 5, 1–3.

de Finetti, B. (1974). *Theory of probability* (Vol. 1). New York: John Wiley and Sons.

DeMiguel, V., Garlappi, L., and Uppal, R. (2006). Implementation details and robustness checks appendix to "optimal versus naive diversification: How inefficient is the 1/N portfolio strategy?". London Business School, working paper. Available online at: https://citeseerx.ist.psu.edu/viewdoc/download?doi=10.1.1.508.6796andrep=rep1andtype=pdf

Denzin, N. K. (1970). *The research act in sociology*. Chicago, IL: Aldine.

Denzin, N. K. (2012). Triangulation 2.0. *Journal of Mixed Methods Research*, 6(2), 80–88.

Descartes, R. (1644). *Principia philosophiae (Principles of philosophy)*. Amstelodami: Apud Ludovicum Elzevirium.

Despotou, G., Jones, R. W., and Arvanitis, T. N. (2016). Using event trees to inform quantitative analysis of healthcare services (119–122). In J. Mantas, A. Hasman, G. Galloset, A. Kolokathi and M. Househ (Eds.), *Unifying the applications and foundations of biomedical and health informatics*. Amsterdam: IOS Press.

de Vries Robbé, M., and de Vogel, V. (2010). *Pilot study of the HCR-20 (version 3)*. Unpublished data analyses. Van der Hoeven Kliniek, Netherlands. Quoted in Douglas, K. S., Hart, S. D., Webster, C. D., and Belfrage, H. (2013). *HCR-20 V3 assessing risk for violence* (24–26). Burnaby, CA: Simon Fraser University.

de Vries Robbé, M., de Vogel, V., and de Spa, E. (2011). Protective factors for violence risk in forensic psychiatric patients: A retrospective validation study of the SAPROF. *International Journal of Forensic Mental Health*, 10(3), 178–186.

Dhami, M. K. (2003). Psychological models of professional decision making. *Psychological Science*, 14(2), 175–180.

Diaconis, P., and Freedman, D. (1981). The persistence of cognitive illusions. *Behavioral and Brain Sciences*, 4(3), 333–334.

Douglas, K. S., Guy, L. S., Reeves, K. A., and Weir, J. (2005). *HCR-20 violence risk assessment scheme: Overview and annotated bibliography.* Implementation Science and Practice Advances Research Center Publications. Retrieved from: https://escholarship.umassmed.edu/psych_cmhsr/335

Douglas, K.S., Hart, S. D., Webster, C. D., and Belfrage, H. (2013). *HCR-20^{V3} assessing risk for violence user guide.* Burnaby, CA: Simon Fraser University.

Doyle, M., Shaw, J., and Coid, J. (2013). *Validation of risk assessments in medium secure services (VORAMSS): Preliminary HCR-20 (version 3) analyses.* Unpublished data analyses University of Manchester, UK and Queen Mary University London. Quoted in Douglas, K. S., Hart, S. D., Webster, C. D., and Belfrage, H. (2013). *HCR-20^{V3} assessing risk for violence user guide.* Burnaby, CA: Simon Fraser University.

Dressel, J., and Farid, H. (2018). The accuracy, fairness, and limits of predicting recidivism. *Science Advances*, 4(1), eaao5580.

Ducro, C., and Pham, T. (2006). Evaluation of the SORAG and the Static-99 on Belgian sex offenders committed to a forensic facility. *Sexual Abuse: A Journal of Research and Treatment*, 18, 15–25.

Dunn, A. L., Trivedi, M. H., Kampert, J. B., Clark, C. G., and Chambliss, H. O. (2005). Exercise treatment for depression: Efficacy and dose response. *American Journal of Preventive Medicine*, 28(1), 1–8.

Edens, J. F., Penson, B. N., Ruchensky, J. R., Cox, J., and Smith, S. T. (2016). Interrater reliability of violence risk appraisal guide scores provided in Canadian criminal proceedings. *Psychological Assessment*, 28(12), 1543–1550.

Edwards, W. (1968). Conservatism in human information processing. In B. Kleinmuntz (Ed.), *Formal representation of human judgement.* New York: Wiley.

Edwards, A., Elwyn, G., Covey, J., Mathews, E., and Pill, R. (2001). Presenting risk information – A review of the effects of framing and other manipulations on patient outcomes. *Journal of Health Communication*, 6, 61–82.

Edwards, A., Elwyn, G., and Mulley, A. (2002). Explaining risks: Turning numerical data into meaningful pictures. *BMJ*, 324(7341), 827–830.

Ellis, R. L. (1844). On the foundations of the theory of probabilities. Read February 14, 1842, *Transactions of the Cambridge Philosophical Society*, 8, Part I, 1–6.

Epley, N., and Gilovich, T. (2006). The anchoring-and-adjustment heuristic: Why the adjustments are insufficient. *Psychological Science*, 17(4), 311–318.

Epstein, R. A. (1989). The utilitarian foundations of natural law. *Harvard Journal of Law and Public Policy*, 12, 711–751.

Faraday, M. (1839). I. Experimental researches in electricity. Fifteenth series. *Philosophical Transactions of the Royal Society of London*, 129, 1–12.

Farmer, A., and Tiefenthaler, J. (1997). An economic analysis of domestic violence. *Review of Social Economy*, 55(3), 337–358.

Farrington, D. P. (Ed.). (2017). *Integrated developmental and life-course theories of offending.* London: Routledge.

Farrington, D. P. (2021). New findings in the Cambridge study in delinquent development. *The Encyclopedia of Research Methods in Criminology and Criminal Justice*, 1, 96–103.

Fass, T. L., Heilbrun, K., DeMatteo, D., and Fretz, R. (2008). The LSI-R and the COMPAS: Validation data on two risk-needs tools. *Criminal Justice and Behavior*, 35(9), 1095–1108.

Ferson, S. (2005). *Bayesian methods in risk assessment.* Unpublished Report Prepared for the Bureau de Recherches Geologiques et Minieres (BRGM). New York. Available at: http://citeseerx.ist.psu.edu/viewdoc/download?doi=10.1.1.87.4577andrep=rep1andtype=pdf

Feynman, R. P. (1974). Cargo cult science. *Engineering and Science, 37*(7), 10–13.

Fine, T. L. (2014). *Theories of probability: An examination of foundations.* New York: Academic Press.

Fiorentini, L., and Marmo, L. (2019). *Principles of forensic engineering applied to industrial accidents.* Chichester, UK: John Wiley and Sons.

Fischbacher-Smith, D. (2010). Beyond the worst case scenario: 'Managing' the risks of extreme events. *Risk Management, 12*(1), 1–8.

Fischbacher-Smith, D. (2016). Framing the UK's counter-terrorism policy within the context of a wicked problem. *Public Money and Management, 36*(6), 399–408.

Fischbacher-Smith, D., Irwin, G.A. and Fischbacher-Smith, M. (2010). Bringing light to the shadows: risk, risk management and risk communication. In P. Bennett, K. Calman, S. Curtis and D. Fischbacher-Smith (Eds.), *Risk Communication and Public Health* (23–38). Oxford: Oxford University press.

Fischoff, B. (1995). Risk perception and communication unplugged: Twenty Years of Process. *Risk Analysis, 15*(2), 137–145.

Fishburn, P. C. (1988). Expected utility: An anniversary and a new era. *Journal of Risk and Uncertainty, 1*(3), 267–283.

Fisher, R. (1955). Statistical methods and scientific induction. *Journal of the Royal Statistical Society, 17*(1), 69–78.

Flage, R., and Aven, T. (2009). Expressing and communicating uncertainty in relation to quantitative risk analysis. *Reliability: Theory & Applications, 4*(2–1 (13)), 9–18.

Fox, B. H., and Farrington, D. P. (2016). Behavioral consistency among serial burglars: Evaluating offense style specialization using three analytical approaches. *Crime and Delinquency, 62*(9), 1123–1158.

Fox, B. H., and Farrington, D. P. (2018). What have we learned from offender profiling? A systematic review and meta-analysis of 40 years of research. *Psychological Bulletin, 144*, 1247–1274.

Gaissmaier, W., and Gigerenzer, G. (2012). 9/11, Act II: A fine-grained analysis of regional variations in traffic fatalities in the aftermath of the terrorist attacks. *Psychological Science, 23*(12), 1449–1454.

Gambino, M. (2019). Risk assessment in an age of neoliberalism: John Monahan's The Clinical Prediction of Violent Behavior (1981). In D. Kritsotaki, V. Long, M. Smith, et al. (Eds.), *Preventing mental illness* (171–186). Cham, Switzerland: Palgrave Macmillan.

Gardner, W., Lidz, C. W., Mulvey, E. P., and Shaw, E. C. (1996). A comparison of actuarial methods for identifying repetitively violent patients with mental illnesses. *Law and Human Behavior, 20*(1), 35–48.

Garrett, B. L., and Monahan, J. (2020). Judging risk. *California Law Review, 108*, 439–493.

Gigerenzer, G. (1996). On narrow norms and vague heuristics: A reply to Kahneman and Tversky. *Psychological Review, 103*(3), 592–596.

Gigerenzer, G. (1998). Surrogates for theories. *Theory & Psychology, 8*(2), 195–204.

Gigerenzer, G. (2002). *Reckoning with risk: learning to live with uncertainty.* London: Penguin.

Gigerenzer, G. (2004). Mindless statistics. *The Journal of Socio-Economics, 33*(5), 587–606.

Gigerenzer, G. (2006a). Bounded and rational. In R. J. Stainton (Ed.). *Contemporary debates in cognitive science* (115–133). Oxford, UK: Blackwell.

Gigerenzer, G. (2006b). Out of the frying pan into the fire: Behavioral reactions to terrorist attacks. *Risk Analysis, 26*, 347–351.

Gigerenzer, G. (2008). *Rationality for mortals: How people cope with uncertainty*. New York: Oxford University Press.
Gigerenzer, G. (2018). The bias bias in behavioral economics. *Review of Behavioral Economics*, 5, 303–336.
Gigerenzer, G. (2021). What is bounded rationality? In R. Viale (Ed.), *Routledge Handbook of Bounded Rationality* (55–69). London: Routledge.
Gigerenzer, G. and Engel, C. (Eds.). (2006). *Heuristics and the law*. Cambridge, MA: MIT Press.
Gigerenzer, G. and Gaissmaier, W. (2011). Heuristic decision-making. *Annual Review of Psychology*, 62, 451–482.
Gigerenzer, G., and Goldstein, D. G. (2011). The recognition heuristic: A decade of research. *Judgment and Decision Making*, 6(1), 100–121.
Gigerenzer, G., Hell, W. and Blank, H. (1988). Presentation and content: The use of base rates as a continuous variable. *Journal of Experimental psychology: Learning, Memory, and Cognition*, 24, 754–770.
Gigerenzer, G., Hertwig, R., Hoffrage, U., and Sedlmeier, P. (2008). Cognitive illusions reconsidered. In C.R. Plott and V.R. Smith (Eds.), *Handbook of experimental economics results* (Vol. 1, pp. 1018–1034).
Gigerenzer, G., and Hoffrage, U. (1995). How to improve Bayesian reasoning without instruction: Frequency formats. *Psychological Review*, 102(4), 684–704.
Gigerenzer, G., and Murray, D.J. (2015). *Cognition as intuitive statistics*. New York: Psychology Press.
Gigerenzer, G., and Selten, R. (Eds.). (2002). *Bounded rationality: The adaptive toolbox*. Cambridge, MA: MIT Press.
Gigerenzer, G., and Todd, P. M. (1999). *Simple heuristics that make us smart*. New York: Oxford University Press.
Goel, S., Shroff, R., Skeem, J., and Slobogin, C. (2021). The accuracy, equity, and jurisprudence of criminal risk assessment. In R. Vogl (Ed.), *Research handbook on big data law* (9–28). Northampton, MA: Edward Elgar Publishing.
Goodman, N. (1954). *Fact, fiction and forecast*. London: Athlone.
Gould, C., McGeorge, T., and Slade, K. (2018). Suicide screening tools for use in incarcerated offenders: A systematic review. *Archives of Suicide Research*, 22(3), 345–364.
Grann, M., and Wedin, I. (2002). Risk factors for recidivism among spousal assault and spousal homicide offenders. *Psychology, Crime and Law*, 8(1), 5–23.
Green, L., and Mehr, D. R. (1997). What alters physicians' decisions to admit to the coronary care unit?. *Journal of Family Practice*, 45(3), 219–226.
Greenspan, A. (2004). Risk and uncertainty in monetary policy. In *Remarks at the meetings of the American Economic Association, San Diego, California*.
Gregory, R. L. (1973). *Eye and brain: The psychology of seeing*. New York: McGraw-Hill.
Gregory, R. L. (1974). *Concepts and mechanisms of perception*. New York: Charles Scribner's Sons.
Gregory, R. L. (1997). Knowledge in perception and illusion. *Philosophical Transactions of the Royal Society of London. Series B: Biological Sciences*, 352(1358), 1121–1127.
Grêt-Regamey, A., and Straub, D. (2006). Spatially explicit avalanche risk assessment linking Bayesian networks to a GIS. *Natural Hazards and Earth System Sciences*, 6(6), 911–926.
Grove, W. M. (2005). Clinical versus statistical prediction: The contribution of Paul E. Meehl. *Journal of Clinical Psychology*, 61(10), 1233–1243.
Grove, W. M., Zald, D. H., Lebow, B. S., Snitz, B. E., and Nelson, C. (2000). Clinical versus mechanical prediction: A meta-analysis. *Psychological Assessment*, 12(1), 19–30.

Gudjonsson, G. H., West, A., and McKee, A. (2015). Risk assessment of terrorist offenders: A challenge too far? In J. Pearse (Ed.), *Investigating terrorism current political, legal and psychological issues* (123–143). Chichester, UK: John Wiley.

Gurol-Urganci, I., de Jongh, T., Vodopivec-Jamsek, V., Atun, R., and Car, J. (2013). Mobile phone messaging reminders for attendance at healthcare appointments. *Cochrane Database of Systematic Reviews, 2013*(12), CD007458. https://doi.org/10.1002/14651858.CD007458.pub3

Halley, E. (1693). An estimate of the degrees of the mortality of mankind, drawn from curious tables of the births and funerals at the city of Breslaw; with an attempt to ascertain the price of annuities upon lives. *Philosophical Transactions of the Royal Society A, 17,* 596–610.

Hamilton, M. (1960). The Hamilton depression scale—Accelerator or break on antidepressant drug discovery. *Psychiatry, 23,* 56–62.

Hansen, N. B., Lambert, M. J., and Forman, E. M. (2002). The psychotherapy dose-response effect and its implications for treatment delivery services. *Clinical Psychology: Science and Practice, 9*(3), 329–343.

Hanson, R. K. (2001). *Note on the reliability of STATIC-99 as used by the California Department of Mental Health evaluators.* Unpublished Report. Sacramento: California Department of Mental Health.

Harcourt, B. E. (2015). Risk as a proxy for race: The dangers of risk assessment. *Federal Sentencing Reporter, 27*(4), 237–243.

Harris, A., Phenix, A., Hanson, R. K., and Thornton, D. (2003). *Static 99: Coding rules revised 2003.* Ottawa, ON: Solicitor General Canada.

Harris, G. T., Rice, M. E., and Quinsey, V. L. (1993). Violent recidivism of mentally disordered offenders: The development of a statistical prediction instrument. *Criminal Justice and Behavior, 20*(4), 315–335.

Hart, S. D., and Boer, D. P. (2014). Structured professional judgment guidelines for sexual violence risk assessment: The Sexual Violence Risk-20 (SVR-20) and Risk for Sexual Violence Protocol (RSVP). In R. K. Otto and K. S. Douglas (Eds.), *Handbook of violence risk assessment* (269–294). New York: Routledge.

Hern, A. (2020). Ofqual's A-level algorithm: Why did it fail to make the grade? *Guardian,* Friday 25th August.

Hertwig, R., and Gigerenzer, G. (1999). The 'conjunction fallacy' revisited: How intelligent inferences look like reasoning errors. *Journal of Behavioral Decision Making, 12*(4), 275–305.

Herzog-Evans, M. (2018). A comparison of two structured professional judgment tools for violent extremism and their relevance in the French context. *European Journal of Probation, 10*(1), 3–27.

HM Treasury. (2004). *The orange book: Management of risk-principles and concepts.* London: HM Treasury.

Hodges, H. R. (2019). *Towards a Bayesian approach in criminology: A case study of risk assessment in youth justice.* Unpublished Doctoral thesis, Swansea University. http://cronfa.swan.ac.uk/Record/cronfa48027

Holcomb, H. R. (1996). Just so stories and inference to the best explanation in evolutionary psychology. *Minds and Machines, 6*(4), 525–540.

Holton, G. (1988). *Thematic origins of scientific thoughts (2nd edition).* Cambridge, MA: Harvard University Press.

Hopkin, P. (2018). *Fundamentals of risk management: Understanding, evaluating and implementing effective risk management.* London: Kogan Page.

Howard, P. (2009). OGP2 and OVP2: The revised OASys predictors. In *Ministry of Justice Analytical Series: A compendium of research and analysis on the Offender Assessment System (OASys).* London: Ministry of Justice.

Howard, P., Francis, B., Soothill, K., and Humphreys, L. (2009). *OGRS 3: The revised offender group reconviction scale*. London: Ministry of Justice.

Imrey, P. B., and Dawid, A. P. (2015). A commentary on statistical assessment of violence recidivism risk. *Statistics and Public Policy*, 2(1), 1–18.

Inhelder, B., and Piaget, J. (1958). *The growth of logical thinking from childhood to adolescence: An essay on the construction of formal operational structures*. London: Routledge.

International Organisation for Standardization (ISO). (2009). *Risk management principles and guidelines*. Geneva: International Organisation for Standardization.

International Organisation for Standardization (ISO). (2018). *Risk management guidelines*. Geneva: International Organisation for Standardization.

International Risk Governance Council. (2005). *Risk governance towards an integrative approach*. Geneva: International Risk Governance Council.

Irwin, G. A., Smith, D., and Griffiths, R. F. (1982). Risk analysis and public policy for major hazards. *Physics in Technology*, 13(6), 258–265.

Jackson, K. J. (2016). *Validation of the risk for sexual violence protocol in adult sexual offenders*. Unpublished PhD dissertation, Simon Fraser University.

Kahneman, D. (1981). Who shall be the arbiter of our intuitions? *Behavioral and Brain Sciences*, 4(3), 339–340.

Kahneman, D. (2011). *Thinking, fast and slow*. New York: Macmillan.

Kahneman, D., Slovic, P., and Tversky, A. (Eds.) (1982). *Judgements under uncertainty: Heuristics and biases*. Cambridge: Cambridge University Press.

Kahneman, D., and Tversky, A. (1972). Subjective probability: A judgment of representativeness. *Cognitive Psychology*, 3(3), 430–454.

Kahneman, D., and Tversky, A. (1984). Choices, values, and frames. *American Psychologist*, 39, 341–350.

Kao, Y. F., and Velupillai, K. V. (2015). Behavioural economics: Classical and modern. *The European Journal of the History of Economic Thought*, 22(2), 236–271.

Katsikopoulos, K., Şimşek, Ö., Buckman, M. and Gigerenzer, G. (2020). *Classification in the wild*. Cambridge, MA: MIT Press.

Keynes, J. M. (1921). *A treatise on probability*. London: MacMillan and Co.

Knight, F. H. (1921). *Risk, uncertainty and profit*. Boston, MA: Houghton Mifflin Company.

Kolmogorov, A. N. (2018). *Foundations of the theory of probability (2nd English edition)*. New York: Dover Publications.

Körding, K. P., and Wolpert, D. M. (2004). Bayesian integration in sensorimotor learning. *Nature*, 427(6971), 244–247.

Kraemer, H., Kazdin, A., Offord, D., Kessler, R., Jensen, P., and Kupfer, D. (1997). Coming to terms with the terms of risk. *Archives of General Psychiatry*, 54, 337–343.

Kraemer, H. C., Stice, E., Kazdin, A., Offord, D., and Kupfer, D. (2001). How do risk factors work together? Mediators, moderators, and independent, overlapping, and proxy risk factors. *American Journal of Psychiatry*, 158(6), 848–856.

Kroner, D. G., Mills, J. F., and Reddon, J. R. (2005). A coffee can, factor analysis, and prediction of antisocial behavior: The structure of criminal risk. *International Journal of Law and Psychiatry*, 28(4), 360–374.

Kropp, P. R., and Hart, S. D. (2000). The Spousal Assault Risk Assessment (SARA) guide: Reliability and validity in adult male offenders. *Law and Human Behavior*, 24(1), 101–118.

Kropp, P. R., and Hart, S. D. (2015). *SARA-V3 user manual for version 3 of the spousal assault risk assessment guide*. Vancouver, Canada: PRI.

Kropp, P. R., Hart, S. D., and Belfrage, H. (2020). *Brief spousal assault form for the evaluation of risk (B-SAFER). User manual*. Vancouver, Canada: PRI.

Långström, N. (2004). Accuracy of actuarial procedures for assessment of sexual offender recidivism risk may vary across ethnicity. *Sexual Abuse: A Journal of Research and Treatment*, 16(2), 107–120.

Laplace, Marquis de, P. S. (1820). *Théorie analytique de probabilités (edition troisième)*. Paris: Courcier. English translation *A Philosophical Essay on Probabilities* (1951). New York: Dover Publications.

Laplace, P. -S. (1825). *Essai Philosophique sur les Probabilités (5th edition)*. New York: Springer. Translated by A. I. Dale (1995).

Lejarraga, T., and Hertwig, R. (2021). How experimental methods shaped views on human competence and rationality. *Psychological Bulletin*, 147, 525–564.

Lewis, R. J. (2000, May). An introduction to classification and regression tree (CART) analysis. In *Annual meeting of the society for academic emergency medicine in San Francisco, California* (Vol. 14). Available online at: http://citeseerx.ist.psu.edu/viewdoc/download?doi=10.1.1.95.4103andrep=rep1andtype=pdf

Lieder, F., Griffiths, T. L., Huys, Q. J., and Goodman, N. D. (2018). The anchoring bias reflects rational use of cognitive resources. *Psychonomic Bulletin and Review*, 25(1), 322–349.

Lindley, D. V. (1985). *Making decisions (2nd edition)*. New York: John Wiley and Sons.

Lindley, D. V. (2006). *Understanding uncertainty*. New York: John Wiley and Sons.

Locke, J. (1664). *Questions concerning the law of nature* (definitive Latin text). Translated by R. Horwitz, et al. (1990). Ithaca, NY: Cornell University Press.

Luisi, P. L., and Thomas, R. M. (1990). The pictographic molecular paradigm. Pictorial communication in the chemical and biological sciences. *Die Naturwissenschaften*, 77(2), 67–74.

Lundberg, G. A. (1926). Case work and the statistical method. *Social Forces*, 5, 61–65.

Lyon, B. K., and Popov, G. (2019). Risk treatment strategies: Harmonizing the hierarchy of controls and inherently safer design concepts. *Professional Safety*, 64(05), 34–43.

Mailloux, D. L., Abracen, J., Serin, R., Cousineau, C., Malcolm, B., and Looman, J. (2003). Dosage of treatment to sexual offenders: Are we overprescribing?. *International Journal of Offender Therapy and Comparative Criminology*, 47(2), 171–184.

Markowitz, H. M. (1990). Normative portfolio analysis: Past, present, and future. *Journal of Economics and Business*, 42(2), 99–103.

Martin, T. G., Burgman, M. A., Fidler, F., Kuhnert, P. M., Low-Choy, S., McBride, M., and Mengersen, K. (2012). Eliciting expert knowledge in conservation science. *Conservation Biology*, 26(1), 29–38.

Marx, V. (2013). The big challenges of big data. *Nature*, 498(7453), 255–260.

Maxwell, J. C. (1873). *A treatise on electricity and magnetism* (Vol. 1). Oxford: Clarendon press.

Mays, J. B. (1968). Crime and the urban pattern. *The Sociological Review*, 16(2), 241–253.

McKinney, S. M., Sieniek, M., Godbole, V., et al. (2020). International evaluation of an AI system for breast cancer screening. *Nature*, 577, 89–94.

Meehl, P. E. (1954). *Clinical versus statistical prediction: A theoretical analysis and a review of the evidence*. Minneapolis, MN: University of Minnesota Press.

Meehl, P. E. (1956). Symposium on clinical and statistical prediction: The tie that binds. *Journal of Counselling Psychology*, 3(3), 163–164.

Meehl, P. E. (1978). Theoretical risks and tabular asterisks: Sir Karl, Sir Ronald, and the slow progress of soft psychology. *Journal of Consulting and Clinical Psychology*, 46(4), 806–834.

Meehl, P. E. (1996). *Clinical versus statistical prediction: A theoretical analysis and a review of the evidence*. Northvale, NJ: Jason Aronson. Original published 1954.

Merz, J. F., Fischoff, B., Mazur, D. J., and Fishbeck, P. S. (1993). A decision-analytic approach to developing standards of disclosure for medical informed consent. *Journal of Products and Toxics Liabilities*, *15*, 191–215.

Meynell, L. (2018). Picturing Feynman diagrams and the epistemology of understanding. *Perspectives on Science*, *26*(4), 459–481.

Mill, J. S. (1863). *Utilitarianism (1st edition)*. London: Parker, Son and Bourn.

Monahan, J. (1981). *The clinical prediction of violence*. Rockville, MD: National Institute of Mental Health.

Monahan, J. (2017a). Risk assessment in sentencing. *Academy for Justice, a Report on Scholarship and Criminal Justice Reform (Erik Luna ed., 2017, Forthcoming), Virginia Public Law and Legal Theory Research Paper*, (2017–2044).

Monahan, J. (2017b). The individual risk assessment of terrorism: Recent developments. In *The handbook of the criminology of terrorism* (pp. 520–534). Chichester, UK: John Wiley.

Monahan, J. and Skeem, J. L., (2013). Risk Redux: The Resurgence of Risk Assessment in Criminal Sanctioning. *Virginia Public Law and Legal Theory Research Paper*, 2013-36. Available at SSRN: https://ssrn.com/abstract=2332165

Monahan, J., and Skeem, J. L. (2016). Risk assessment in criminal sentencing. *Annual Review of Clinical Psychology*, *12*, 489–513.

Monahan, J., Steadman, H. J., Appelbaum, P. S., Grisso, T., Mulvey, E. P., Roth, L. H., Clark Robbins, P., Banks, S., and Silver, E. (2006). The classification of violence risk. *Behavioral Sciences and the Law*, *24*(6), 721–730.

Monahan, J., Steadman, H. J., Silver, E., Appelbaum, P. S., Robbins, P. C., Mulvey, E. P., Roth, L. H., Grisso, T., and Banks, S. (2001). *Rethinking risk assessment: The MacArthur study of mental disorder and violence*. Oxford: Oxford University Press.

Moore, R. (Ed.) (2015). *A compendium of research and analysis on the Offender Assessment System (OASys) 2009–2013*. London: Ministry of Justice.

Mossman, D. (1994). Assessing predictions of violence: Being accurate about accuracy. *Journal of Consulting and Clinical Psychology*, *62*(4), 783–792.

Mousavi, S., and Gigerenzer, G. (2014). Risk, uncertainty, and heuristics. *Journal of Business Research*, *67*(8), 1671–1678.

Murphy, S. T., and Zajonc, R. B. (1993). Affect, cognition and awareness: Affective priming with optimal and suboptimal stimulus exposures. *Journal of Personality and Social Psychology*, *64*, 723–739.

Neal, T., and Grisso, T. (2014). The cognitive underpinnings of bias in forensic mental health evaluations. *Psychology, Public Policy, and Law*, *20*(2), 200–211.

Nesticò, A., He, S., De Mare, G., Benintendi, R., and Maselli, G. (2018). The ALARP principle in the Cost-Benefit analysis for the acceptability of investment risk. *Sustainability*, *10*(12), 4668–4690. https://doi.org/10.3390/su10124668

NHS and NHS Improvement. (2021). *Online library of quality, service improvement and redesign tools: Cause and effect (fishbone)*. London: National Health Service.

Nisbett, R. E., and Ross, L. (1980). *Human inference: Strategies and shortcomings of social judgment*. Englewood Cliffs, NJ: Prentice-Hall.

Nyström, L., Larsson, L. G., Wall, S., Rutqvist, L. E., Andersson, I., et al. (1996). An overview of the Swedish randomised mammography trials: Total mortality pattern and the representivity of the study cohorts. *Journal of Medical Screening*, *3*(2), 85–87.

Pachur, T., Hertwig, R., and Steinmann, F. (2012). How do people judge risks: Availability heuristic, affect heuristic, or both?. *Journal of Experimental Psychology: Applied*, *18*(3), 314–330.

Pearson, K. (1905). The problem of the random walk. *Nature*, *72*(1867), 342–342.

Peters, E., McCaul, K. D., Stefanek, M., and Nelson, W. (2006). A heuristic approach to understanding cancer risk perception: Contributions from judgement and decision-making research. *Annals of Behavioral Medicine*, 31(1), 45–52.

Petersilia, J., and Turner, S. (1987). Guideline-based justice: Prediction and racial minorities. *Crime and Justice*, 9, 151–181.

Pflug, G. C., Pichler, A., and Wozabal, D. (2012). The 1/N investment strategy is optimal under high model ambiguity. *Journal of Banking and Finance*, 36(2), 410–417.

Piaget, J. (1972). *The principles of genetic epistemology*. London: Routledge and Kegan Paul.

Plutchik, R., and Van Praag, H. M. (1994). Suicide risk: Amplifiers and attenuators. *Journal of Offender Rehabilitation*, 21(3–4), 173–186.

Plutchik, R., Van Praag, H. M., and Conte, H. R. (1989). Correlates of suicide and violence risk: III. A two-stage model of countervailing forces. *Psychiatry Research*, 28(2), 215–225.

Poisson, S. D. (1837). *Probabilité des jugements en matière criminelle et en matière civile, précédées des règles générales du calcul des probabilities*. Paris: Bachelier.

Popper, K. R. (1959). The propensity interpretation of probability. *The British journal for the philosophy of science*, 10(37), 25–42.

Port Royal Philosophers. (1861). *The port-royal logic*. Translated from the French. Edinburgh: James Gordon.

Pouls, C., and Jeandarme, I. (2014). Psychopathy in offenders with intellectual disabilities: A comparison of the PCL-R and PCL: SV. *International Journal of Forensic Mental Health*, 13(3), 207–216.

Prescott, J. J., Pyle, B., and Starr, S. B. (2019). Understanding violent-crime recidivism. *Notre Dame Law Review*, 95, 1643–1698.

Quetelet, A. (1842). *A treatise on man and the development of his faculties*. Edinburgh: William and Robert Chambers.

Quinsey, V. L., Harris, G. T., Rice, M. E., and Cormier, C. A. (2006). *Violent offenders: Appraising and managing risk*. Washington, DC: American Psychological Association.

Rajan, R. G. (2006). Has finance made the world riskier? *European Financial Management*, 12(4), 499–533.

Ramsey, F. P. (1931). In: R. B. Braithwaite (Ed.), *The foundations of mathematics, and other essays*. London: Kegan Paul, Trench and Trubner and Co.

Rath, F. (2007). Tools for developing a quality management program: Proactive tools (Process mapping, value stream mapping, fault tree analysis, and failure mode and effects analysis). *International Journal of Radiation Oncology, Biology and Physics*, 71, S187–S190.

Redding, R. E. (2009). Evidence-based sentencing: The science of sentencing policy and practice, 1 Chap. *Journal of Criminal Justice*, 1(1), 5–6.

Renn, O. (2008). White paper on risk governance: Toward an integrative framework. In O. Renn and K.D. Walker (Eds.), *Global risk governance*. Dordrecht: Springer.

Rice, M. E., and Harris, G. T. (2005). Comparing effect sizes in follow-up studies: ROC area, Cohen's d, and r. *Law and Human Behavior*, 29(5), 615–620.

Rice, M. E., Harris, G. T., and Lang, C. (2013). Validation of and revision to the VRAG and SORAG: The Violence Risk Appraisal Guide—Revised (VRAG-R). *Psychological Assessment*, 25(3), 951–965.

Richards, T., Coulter, A., and Wicks, P. (2015). Time to deliver patient centred care. *BMJ*, 350, h530. doi: 10.1136/bmj.h530

Risk Management Authority. (2016). *Standards and guidelines for risk management*. Paisley, UK: RMA.

Robinson, C., Sorbie, A., Huber, J., Teasdale, J., Scott, K., Purver, M. and Elliott, I. (2021). *Reoffending impact evaluation of the prison-based RESOLVE Offending Behaviour Programme*. London: Ministry of Justice.

Robinson, D. G. (2017). The challenges of prediction: Lessons from criminal justice. *ISJLP*, 14, 151–186.

Romero, J. J., and Williams, L. M. (1983). Group psychotherapy and intensive probation supervision with sex offenders. *Federal Probation*, 47, 36–42.

Rosa, E. A. (1998). Metatheoretical foundations for post-normal risk. *Journal of Risk Research*, 1(1), 15–44.

Rose, C. (2012). RIP the IPP: A look back at the sentence of imprisonment for public protection. *The Journal of Criminal Law*, 76(4), 303–313.

Rothman, K. J., Greenland, S., and Lash, T. L. (2008). *Modern epidemiology* (Vol. 3). Philadelphia, PA: Wolters Kluwer Health/Lippincott Williams and Wilkins.

Rowe, W. D. (1975). *An "Anatomy" of risk*. Washington, DC: Environmental Protection Agency.

Ryan, T. J. (2010). *An examination of the interrater reliability and concurrent validity of the Spousal Assault Risk Assessment Guide–Version 3 (SARA-V3)*. Unpublished Master of Arts dissertation, Simon Fraser University.

Sageman, M. (2021). The implication of terrorism's extremely low base rate. *Terrorism and Political Violence*, 33(2), 302–311.

Sagoff, M. (2004). *Price, principle and the environment*. Cambridge: Cambridge University Press.

Santayana, G. (1905). *The Life of Reason, Or, The Phases of Human Progress: Reason in society* (Vol. 2). New York: C. Scribner's sons.

Sarbin, T. R. (1944). The logic of prediction in psychology. *Psychological Review*, 51, 210–228.

Saunders, J., Hunt, P., and Hollywood, J. S. (2016). Predictions put into practice: A quasi-experimental evaluation of Chicago's predictive policing pilot. *Journal of Experimental Criminology*, 12, 347–371.

Savage, L. (1954). *The foundations of statistics*. London: Chapman and Hall.

Schneider, S. H. (2004). Abrupt non-linear climate change, irreversibility and surprise. *Global Environmental Change*, 14(3), 245–258.

Schott, G., Pachl, H., Limbach, U., Gundert-Remy, U., Ludwig, W. D., and Lieb, K. (2010). The financing of drug trials by pharmaceutical companies and its consequences: Part 1: A qualitative, systematic review of the literature on possible influences on the findings, protocols, and quality of drug trials. *Deutsches Ärzteblatt International*, 107(16), 279–285.

Scurich, N. (2016). An introduction to the assessment of violence risk. In J.P. Singh, S. Bjørkly and S. Fazel (Eds.), *International perspectives on violence risk assessment*. New York: Oxford University Press.

Scurich, N., and Monahan, J. (2016). Evidence-based sentencing: Public openness and opposition to using gender, age, and race as risk factors for recidivism. *Law and Human Behavior*, 40(1), 36–41.

Shapiro, D. (2002). Renewing the scientist-practitioner model. *The Psychologist*, 15(5), 232–235.

Siegler, R. S. (1999). Strategic development. *Trends in Cognitive Sciences*, 3(11), 430–435.

Silva, E. (2020). The HCR-20 and violence risk assessment – Will a peak of inflated expectations turn to a trough of disillusionment? *BJPsych Bulletin*, 44(6), 269–271.

Simon, H. A. (1953). Notes on the observation and measurement of political power. *The Journal of Politics*, 15(4), 500–516.

Simon, H. A. (1955). A behavioral model of rational choice. *The Quarterly Journal of Economics*, 69(1), 99–118.

Sinha, D., Chandra, P., and Biswas, M. (2018). Recent advancements in the behavioral portfolio theory: A review. *Vidyasagar University Journal of Commerce, the UGC of India Listed Journal*. Available online at: http://inet.vidyasagar.ac.in:8080/jspui/bitstream/123456789/5121/1/Paritosh%20Chandra%20Sinha.pdf

Skeem, J. L., and Monahan, J. (2011). Current directions in violence risk assessment. *Current Directions in Psychological Science, 20*(1), 38–42.

Skeem, J., and Monahan, J. (2020). Lost in translation: "Risks," "needs," and "evidence" in implementing the First Step Act. *Behavioral Sciences and the Law, 38*(3), 287–297.

Skeem, J., Monahan, J., and Lowenkamp, C. (2016). Gender, risk assessment, and sanctioning: The cost of treating women like men. *Law and Human Behavior, 40*(5), 580–627.

Slobogin, C. (2017). Principles of risk assessment: Sentencing and policing. *Ohio State Journal of Criminal Law, 15*, 583–596.

Slobogin, C. (2018). Principles of risk assessment for researchers and practitioners. *Behavioral Sciences and the Law, 36*(5), 507–516.

Slovic, P. (1987). Perception of risk. *Science, 236*, 280–285.

Slovic, P. (2002). Terrorism as hazard: A new species of trouble. *Risk Analysis, 22*(3), 425–426.

Slovic, P., Finucane, M. L., Peters, E., and MacGregor, D. G. (2007). The affect heuristic. *European Journal of Operational Research, 177*(3), 1333–1352.

Slovic, P., Monahan, J., and MacGregor, D. G. (2000). Violence risk assessment and risk communication: The effects of actual cases, providing instructions and employing probability vs. frequency formats. *Law and Human Behavior, 24*, 271–296.

Smith, A. G. (2018). *Risk factors and indicators associated with radicalization to terrorism in the United States: What research sponsored by the National Institute of Justice tells us*. Washington, DC: US Department of Justice, Office of Justice Programs, National Institute of Justice.

Smith, D., and Fischbacher, M. (2009). The changing nature of risk and risk management: The challenge of borders, uncertainty and resilience. *Risk management, 11*(1), 1–12.

Spiegelhalter, D. J., and Knill-Jones, R. P. (1984). Statistical and knowledge-based approaches to clinical decision-support systems, with an application in gastroenterology. *Journal of the Royal Statistical Society: Series A (General), 147*(1), 35–58.

Starr, S. B. (2014). Evidence-based sentencing and the scientific rationalization of discrimination. *Stanford Law Review, 66*, 803–872.

Starr, S. B., and Rehavi, M. M. (2013). Mandatory sentencing and racial disparity: Assessing the role of prosecutors and the effects of Booker. *Yale Law Journal, 123*, 2–80.

Steadman, H. J., and Cocozza, J. J. (1974). *Careers of the criminally insane: Excessive social control of deviance*. New York: Lexington.

Steadman, H. J., Monahan, J., Duffee, B., and Hartstone, E. (1984). The impact of state mental hospital deinstitutionalization on United States prison populations, 1968–1978. *Journal of Criminal Law and Criminology, 75*, 474–490.

Steadman, H. J., Silver, E., Monahan, J., Appelbaum, P., Robbins, P. C., Mulvey, E. P., and Banks, S. (2000). A classification tree approach to the development of actuarial violence risk assessment tools. *Law and Human Behavior, 24*(1), 83–100.

Storey, J. E., Kropp, P. R., Hart, S. D., Belfrage, H., and Strand, S. (2014). Assessment and management of risk for intimate partner violence by police officers using the brief spousal assault form for the evaluation of risk. *Criminal Justice and Behavior, 41*(2), 256–271.

Storey, J. E., and Strand, S. (2013). Assessing violence risk among female IPV perpetrators: An examination of the B-SAFER. *Journal of Aggression, Maltreatment and Trauma, 22*(9), 964–980.

Svalin, K. (2018). *Risk assessment of intimate partner violence in a police setting*. Unpublished Doctoral dissertation, Malmö University.

Svalin, K., Mellgren, C., Torstensson Levander, M., and Levander, S. (2018). Police employees' violence risk assessments: The predictive validity of the B-SAFER and the significance of protective actions. *International Journal of Law and Psychiatry*, 56, 71–79.

Taleb, N. N. (2015). *The Black Swan: The impact of the highly improbable*. New York: Random House.

Thaler, R. H. (2000). From homo economicus to homo sapiens. *Journal of Economic Perspectives*, 14(1), 133–141.

Thomas-Peter, B. A. (2006). The modern context of psychology in corrections: Limitations, influences and values of 'What Works'. In G.J. Towl (Ed.), *Psychological research in prisons*. Oxford: BPS Blackwell.

Thompson, K. M., and Graham, J. D. (1996). Going beyond the single number: Using probabilistic risk assessment to improve risk management. *Human and Ecological Risk Assessment: An International Journal*, 2(4), 1008–1034.

Thomson, N. D. (2021). The biopsychosocial model of psychopathy. In D.A. Crighton and G.J. Towl (Eds.), *Forensic psychology (3rd edition)*. Chichester, UK: John Wiley.

Torrey, E. F., Stanley, J., Monahan, J., and Steadman, H. J. (2008). The MacArthur Violence Risk Assessment Study revisited: Two views ten years after its initial publication. *Psychiatric Services*, 59(2), 147–152.

Towl, G, J., (2015). Risk and Resilience. In D.A. Crighton and G.J. Towl (Eds.), *Forensic psychology (2nd edition)*. Chichester, UK: John Wiley.

Towl, G. (2021). The politics of forensic psychological research, policy and practice. In D.A. Crighton and G.J. Towl (Eds.), *Forensic psychology (3rd edition)*. Chichester, UK: John Wiley.

Towl, G. J., and Crighton, D. A. (1996). *The handbook of psychology for forensic practitioners*. London: Routledge.

Towl, G. J., and Crighton, D. A. (1997). Risk assessment with offenders. *International Review of Psychiatry*, 9(2–3), 187–194.

Towl, G., and Crighton, D. (2016). The emperor's new clothes?. *Psychologist*, 29(3), 188–191.

Towl, G., and Crighton, D. (2017). *Suicide in prisons: Prisoners' lives matter*. Sherfield on Loddon, UK: Waterside Press.

Towl, G., and Podmore, J. (2019). Still in denial? The sex offender treatment industry. *The Justice Gap*, 2nd August. https://www.thejusticegap.com/still-in-denial-the-sex-offender-treatment-industry/

Towl, G. J., and Walker, T. (2019). *Tackling sexual violence at universities: An international perspective*. London: Routledge.

Tversky, A. (1981). L.J. Cohen, again. On the evaluation of inductive intuitions. *Behavioral and Brain Sciences*, 4(3), 354–356.

Tversky, A., and Kahneman, D. (1973). Availability: A heuristic for judging frequency and probability. *Cognitive Psychology*, 5, 207–232.

Tversky, A., and Kahneman, D. (1974). Judgment under uncertainty: Heuristics and biases. *Science*, 185(4157), 1124–1131.

Tversky, A., and Kahneman, D. (1983). Extensional versus intuitive reasoning: The conjunction fallacy in probability judgment. *Psychological Review*, 90, 293–315.

UK Parliament. (2016). *Question for Ministry of Justice UIN 23107, tabled on 19 January 2016*. London: UK Parliament. Available at: https://questions-statements.parliament.uk/written-questions/detail/2016-01-19/23107

Venn, J. (1866). *The logic of chance: An essay on the foundations and province of the theory of probability, with especial reference to its application to moral and social science (1st edition)*. London and Cambridge: Macmillan.

Von Hirsch, A. (1985). Review essay/lifeboat law. *Criminal Justice Ethics*, 4(2), 88–94.

Wald, A. (1947). An essentially complete class of admissible decision functions. *The Annals of Mathematical Statistics*, 549–555.

Wald, M. S. (2014). Beyond maltreatment: Developing support for children in multiproblem families. In *Handbook of child maltreatment* (pp. 251–280). Dordrecht: Springer.

Wald, M. S., and Woolverton, M. (1990). Risk assessment: The emperor's new clothes? *Child Welfare: Journal of Policy, Practice, and Program*, 69(6), 483–511.

Walker, T., and Towl, G. (2016). *Preventing self-injury and suicide in womens prisons*. Sherfield on Loddon: Waterside Press.

Washington, A. L. (2018). How to argue with an algorithm: Lessons from the COMPAS-ProPublica debate. *Colorado Technology Law Journal*, 17, 131–160.

Wason, P. (1981). The importance of cognitive illusions. *Behavioral and Brain Sciences*, 4(3), 356–356.

Wason, P. C., and Johnson-Laird, P. N. (1970). A conflict between selecting and evaluating information in an inferential task. *British Journal of Psychology*, 61(4), 509–515.

Wason, P. C., and Johnson-Laird, P. N. (1972). *Psychology of reasoning: Structure and content*. Cambridge, MA: Harvard University Press.

Watt, K. A., Hart, S. D., Wilson, C., Guy, L., and Douglas, K. S. (2006). *An evaluation of the Risk of Sexual Violence Protocol (RSVP)*. Paper presented at the meeting of the International Association of Forensic Mental Health, Vienna. Quoted in Hart, S. D., and Boer, D. P. (2014). Structured professional judgment guidelines for sexual violence risk assessment: The Sexual Violence Risk-20 (SVR-20) and Risk for Sexual Violence Protocol (RSVP). In: R. K. Otto and K. S. Douglas (Eds.), *Handbook of violence risk assessment*. New York: Routledge.

Watt, K. A., and Jackson, K. (2008). *Interrater and structural reliabilities of the Risk of Sexual Violence Protocol (RSVP)*. Paper presented at the meeting of the International Association of Forensic Mental Health, Vienna. Quoted in Hart, S. D., and Boer, D. P. (2014). Structured professional judgment guidelines for sexual violence risk assessment: The Sexual Violence Risk-20 (SVR-20) and Risk for Sexual Violence Protocol (RSVP). In: R. K. Otto and K. S. Douglas (Eds.), *Handbook of violence risk assessment*. New York: Routledge.

Wikström, P. O. H., and Treiber, K. (2009). What drives persistent offending? The neglected and unexplored role of the social environment. In J. Savage (Ed.), *The development of persistent criminality*. Oxford: Oxford University Press.

Williams, K. R., and Houghton, A. B. (2004). Assessing the risk of domestic violence reoffending: A validation study. *Law and Human Behavior*, 28(4), 437–455.

Wilson, T. D., Houston, C. E., Etling, K. M., and Brekke, N. (1996). A new look at anchoring effects: Basic anchoring and its antecedents. *Journal of Experimental Psychology: General*, 125(4), 387–402.

Wilson, D. K., Purdon, S. E., and Wallston, K. A. (1988). Compliance to health recommendations: A theoretical overview of message framing. *Health Education Research*, 3(2), 161–171.

Wundt, W. (1973). *An introduction to psychology*. Translated by R. Pinter New York: Arno. (Original work published 1912).

Yang, M., Wong, S. C., and Coid, J. (2010). The efficacy of violence prediction: A meta-analytic comparison of nine risk assessment tools. *Psychological Bulletin*, 136(5), 740–767.

Zoullouti, B., Amghar, M., and Nawal, S. (2019). Using Bayesian networks for risk assessment in healthcare system. *Bayesian Networks-Advances and Novel Applications*. https://doi.org/10.5772/intechopen.80464

Index

Note: **Bold** page numbers refer to tables and *italic* page numbers refer to figures.

absolute risk reduction (ARR) 176
accuracy: B-SAFER total score 50; clear and convincing evidence 70; in forensic practice 155; level of 68–69; people's decision-making 128; probabilistic risk assessments 54, 155; Risk Assessment Instruments 74–75, 79; signal detection technology 68; taxi colour identification 122
accurate assessments: Classification Tree Analysis 160, 161; linear regression analysis 159; mental health services 159; 'optimal' and 'clinically feasible' ICT approaches 162; triangulation analytical process 160
actuarial and algorithmic RAIs: academic and commercial organisations 32; case for 40–42; crime prevention and policing 32; decision-making rules 32; fundamental ethical requirement 41; large-scale computing applications 41; policing and crime prevention 34–35; pre-sentencing reports 33; risk treatment 37–40; sentencing and conditional release 35–37; 'static'risk factors and indicators 36
adaptive toolbox 125–128
Addington v. Texas case 70
affect bias, forensic practice: cognitive illusions research 115–118, 124–125; content-blind norms 118–123; ecological rationality 124–125; heuristics studies 112–115, 123–124; judgements 112–115
algorithm-based approaches 47
anchoring 109–111, 124
anti-social behaviour 28, 32, 133, 156, 178; changing environments 178; criminal probability 32; economic deprivation 28; emergency services 156; lacked social resources 28
anti-social behaviours 28
Arbuthnot, J. 12
Area Under the Curve (AUC) 37, 46, 67
As Low As Reasonably Possible (ALARP) 26
automated facial recognition algorithms 32
availability: affect heuristics 124; cognitive illusions 111; human judgement 109; RAIs checklist 45; as rapid and automatic process 112
Aven, T. 146

Bayesian decision theory 96
Bayesian methods 14, 15, 88, 98
Bayesian networks *145*, 145–146
Bayes theorem 121; probability estimate 103; signal detection theory 122
Beck Depression Inventory 29
Belfrage, H. 53
Bentham, J. 9
Bernoulli, D. 7, 12, 93, 94, 122
better explanatory models: analysing risks 132–134; create unnecessary barriers

134–137; risk evaluation 148–149; risk management 151–152; risk treatment 149–151; simple model *138*, 138–139; trivial intellectual problem 130–132
big data 8, 71
black-box algorithm 74, 127
black swan events 102
bloody code 10
Boer, D. P. 51

calibration: practical challenges 100; risk analysis perspectives 99–100; 'subjective' probabilities 99–100; and validation datasets 36
cargo cult science: changing environments 167–169; checklist RAIs 168; protocol-based RAIs 167
cause and effect analysis (CEA) 143
CEA *see* cause and effect analysis (CEA)
changing environments: anti-social behaviour 178; better decisions 169–176; cargo cult science 167–169; cognitive illusions 171; context-free problems 170; developmental psychology 170; ecological rationality approaches 171; hypothetical checklist assessment 165, *166*; knowledge-based probabilities 173; prophylactic mastectomy 176; simplicity 176–177
child protection 57, 76, 78, 135, 180
civil justice systems 66
civil mental health law 158
class privilege 131
cognitive illusions approach 109; fundamental problems 116; taxi problem 121
Cohen, L. J. 109, 115, 119
Coid, J. 37, 53
content-blind norms 113
Cooke, R. M. 98
Correctional Offender Management Profiling for Alternate Sanctions (COMPAS) 57
Cournot, A. A. 12
courts settings 33
COVID-19 pandemic 38, 71
Crime and Victimisation Risk Model (CVRM) 34
criminal justice system 33, 60, 66
criminal law: psychological and psychiatric models 60; public protection role 60; risk, ideas of 60; and utilitarian philosophical ideas 56

criminal offences 68
criminal/victimisation history 35
criminogenic risk factor 28
current forensic practice: criticisms of 2, 87; negative effects 81; probabilistic assessment 146; risk analysis idea 21
current practice critiques: psychological approaches 106–128; risk analysis perspectives 80–105; socio-legal perspectives 56–79
cut sets/minimal cut sets 144

dangerousness 47, 63, 70
Descartes, R. 4
Douglas, K. S. 53
Doyle, M. 53
dread risks 175

ecologically rational approaches 110
ecological rationality 110, *125*
Edens, J. F. 40
Ellis, R. L. 12
error-free system 115
ETA *see* event tree analyses (ETA)
event tree analyses (ETA) 144–145
evidence based sentencing (EBS) 73
expected value: portfolio approaches 94; treating risk 93, 95

facial recognition 32, 66, 156
fairness: fundamental question 58; further issue 66; hypothetical and idealised systems 66; ideas 59; marital status and employment status 61; positive and negative impacts 58; psychological and psychiatric models 60; retribution-based punishments 59; socio-demographic factors 64
Faraday, M. 133
Farrington, D. 28, 34, 61, 100
fast-and-frugal trees (FFT's) 173, 176
fault tree analysis (FTA) 144
fifth generation 46
de Finetti, B. 13, 120
first generation 46
Fischbacher-Smith, D. 2, 15, 21, 54, 80, 81, 84, 95, 96, 102, 147, 148, 149, 151
Fischoff, B. 148
Fisher, R. 96
Flage, R. 146
forensic practice: clarifying and expressing ideas 2; day-to-day basis 3; idiosyncratic terminology 2; pre-packaged methods 178

fourth generation 46
frontal medial cortex (FMC) 114
FTA *see* fault tree analysis (FTA)

gambling 12, 93
Garbage In Garbage Out (GIGO) 92
Gigerenzer, G. 112, 116, 173
gold standard 130
Goodman, N. 119
Gregory, R. 115
Grisso, T. 110, 123
group-based predictions 71

Halley, E. 17
Hamilton Depression Rating Scale 29
Harcourt, B. E. 63
Hart, S. D. 51
hazard and operability analysis (HAZOP) 91; examination and documentation phase 91
heat list 34
Hertwig, R. 124
Historical and Clinical Risk 20 (HCR-20) 52, 57
homo economicus 127, 128
Hopkin, P. 85
Houghton, A. B. 50
human judgements 107–108

indeterminate public protection (IPP) sentences 59
individual predictions 71
Inhelder, B. 110, 116, 170
International Organisation for Standardization (ISO) 19, 20, 86
International Risk Governance Council (IRGC) 20
Intraclass Correlation Coefficient (ICC) 38
iterative classification tree (ICT) 161

judgement and decision-making: cognitive illusion 109; ecologically rational approaches 110; weaknesses 106

Kahneman, D. 110, 111, 117, 122
Kazdin, A. 29
Keynes, J. M. 11, 12, 20, 44
Knight, F. H. 4, 5, 8, 11, 93, 96, 108
knowledge-based / subjective probabilities 13–15, **14, 15**; Bayesian ideas 97; calibration 99–100; changing environments 173; pragmatic criteria 99; problems with 16; syntactic criterion measures 99; uses 98
Kolmogorov, A. N. 133
Kraemer, H. 28, 29
Kroner, D. G. 168

language 20; formal frameworks and standards 20; identical / overlapping concepts 20; ISO 2009 assessment 19; overlapping risk factors 29; protective factors 27–30; risk assessment 22–23; risk factors 27–30; risk management 25–27; risk treatment 23–25; simple model 21, *21*; UK Government Treasury Orange Book assessment 19
legal and social policy criticisms 57
legal decision-making 58, 68
Level of Service Inventory Revised (LSI-R) 36, 57, 72
Linda problem 117
Lindley, D. V. 103
living circumstances 64
Locke, J. 16

The MacArthur risk assessment study 159–163
Markowitz, H. M. 126
mass imprisonment / incarceration 33, 63, 65, 150
Maxwell, J. C. 133
mental health services 27, 51, 159
Mills, J. F. 168
mitigate risk 23
Monahan, J. 28, 45, 47, 61, 63, 65, 68, 69, 72, 73, 77, 81, 92, 100, 101, 103, 112, 133, 135, 149, 158, 159

natural decision-making processes 169
Neal, T. 110, 123
new generations 46
North American mental health settings 69
number needed to treat (NNT) statistic 176

OASys General Predictor (OGP) 36
OASys Violence Predictor (OVP) 36
Offender Assessment System (OASys) 36
Offender Group Reconviction Scale third revision (OGRS-3) 36; factors 36–37
OGRS-3 *see* Offender Group Reconviction Scale third revision (OGRS-3)
OGRS-3 algorithm 36
one-reason decision-making 175

one- reason stopping rule 175
open decision tree method 174
optimisation under constraints models 108–109
Oxford Risk of Recidivism (OxRec) 57

Pachur, T. 124
Pearson, K. 102
Penson, B. N. 40
Piaget, J. 110, 115, 116, 170
Poisson, S. D. 17
policing: criminal/victimisation history 35; methodological issues 50; quasi-experimental evaluation 35; risk factors 47–48; SARA 3, six-step process 48; shooting/homicide 35; spousal assault 49; strategic subject list 34
Port Royal Philosophers 16
probabilistic risk assessment 22–23, 34; anti-social behaviour 156; area under the curve statistic 153; artificial intelligence analysis 154; changing forensic practice 156–158; implications 158–163; meta-analytic studies 153; risk analysis 146–148; sexual violence 154, *154*, *155*
probability: applying 16; knowledge-based probabilities 13–15, **14, 15**; measurements 9–11; relative frequency probability 12–13; role 16
proponents: actuarial and algorithmic approaches 32; checklist RAIs 54; ecological rationality stress 113
psychological approaches: adaptive toolbox 125–128; anchoring-and-adjustment heuristic 111; availability bias 111; cognitive illusions research *vs.* ecological rationality 109, 124–125; content-blind norms 118–122; ecological rationality 110; heuristic decision-making 123–124; heuristics 112–115; judgement 112–115; optimisation under constraints models 108–109; representativeness bias 110–111; unbounded rationality ideas 108; visual illusions and cognitive illusions research 115–118
psychological critiques 2
psychopathy 39, 51
psychopathy checklist revised (PCL-R) 51
psychopathy checklist screening version (PCL-SV) 51
punishments 60

Quetelet, A. 17

RAIs *see* risk assessment instruments (RAIs)
Ramsey, B. 120
Ramsey, F. P. 13
random walk 102
Reddon, J. R. 168
relative frequency probability 12–13
relative risk reduction (RRR) 176
retribution-based punishments 59
risk absorbing systems 85
risk agents 85
risk analysis methods: anti-social behaviour and violence 130; Bayesian networks 145, 145–146; cause and effect analysis 143; critiques 2; event tree analyses 144–145; fault tree analysis 144; Ishikawa diagrams 143; methods 140–146, *145*; planning 139–140; probabilistic assessment 146–148; sexual violence 130; structured what if technique 143–144
risk analysis perspectives: calibration 99–100; consensus 103–104; expected value 93–95; fundamental aspects 80, *82*; historic data 100–103; knowledge-based/subjective probabilities 97–99; measurement of 88–90; model-based methods 92; pragmatic criteria 99; primarily quantitative methods 92; probabilistic risk assessment 81; relative frequency probability 95–97; risk analysis 87–88; risk management 85–87; scientific approaches 104; simplified qualitative analysis 90; standardisation 103–104; standard qualitative analysis 90–92; standard quantitative analysis 90–92; syntactic criterion measures 99; vague non-numerical estimates 84
risk assessment: beyond reasonable doubt 11; descriptive and inferential statistics 16–17; economist addressing 7; good quality analysis and evaluation 22; human judgement 6; indifference principle 11–12; Knight's thinking appears 4; the language 22–23; probability 8–9; quantitative methodology 22; separate and overarching process 83; six-sided die 6; static *vs.* dynamic 7
risk assessment instruments (RAIs) 31, 81; actuarial and algorithmic 32; advantage 54; algorithms and checklists-based 107; array 57; basic characteristics 70;

Chicago heat list 62; civil legal questions 68; clinical judgement 75; day-to-day practice 47; fifth generation 46; first generation 46; fourth generation 46; impact of 77–78; individual checklist 43–44; new generations 46; psychometric properties 35; second generation 46; socio-demographic factors 64; structured checklist 43–44; third generation 46; usefulness of 76
risk evaluation: better explanatory models 148–149
risk factors, language 27–30
risk management: better explanatory models 151–152; cautionary principles 26–27; the language 25–27; precautionary principles 26–27; risk analysis perspectives 85–87; risk resilience 27; risk robustness 27
risk measurements: simplified qualitative analysis 90; standard qualitative analysis 90–92; standard quantitative analysis 90–92
risk of sexual violence protocol (RSVP) 51
risk treatment: better explanatory models 149–151; dose response 24–25; the language 23–25; structured clinical judgement approaches 52–54
RSVP see risk of sexual violence protocol (RSVP)
Ruchensky, J. R. 40
rules of thumb 109
Ryan, T. J. 50

Sarbin, T. R. 33
Savage, L. 96
second generation 46
sentencing and conditional release: structured clinical judgement approaches 51–52
sexual offenders 38
sexual offending 131
sexual violence 51, 82, 133
Shaw, J. 53
sickle cell anaemia 157
signal detection 68, 122
Simon, H. A. 110, 125
simplicity: psychological research 176–177
Skeem, J. 45, 61, 64, 65, 69, 72, 73, 100, 135, 158
Slobogin, C. 58
socio-legal critiques 2

socio-legal perspectives: accuracy 67–70; clinical judgement 56; fairness 58–67; impact 77–78; individual and group-based predictions 70–73; utility 73–77
spousal assault 49
The spousal assault risk assessment (SARA) 48
SSL see strategic subject list (SSL)
standardisation: risk analysis perspectives 103–104
Starr, S. B. 64, 65, 71
state space 96, 97
Static-99 38, 123
Steadman, H. 28, 47, 63, 68, 69, 81, 103, 133, 159
Steinmann, F. 124
Stice, E. 29
strategic subject list (SSL) 34
structured assessment of protective factors (SAPROF) 43
structured checklist approach 44
structured clinical judgement approaches: cost considerations 45; policing 47–51; recording information 43; risk treatment 52–54; sentencing and conditional release 51–52; structured checklist approach 44; unstructured clinical assessment 45; use in practice 47; use of checklist RAIs 54–55
structured/constrained decision-making methods 107
structured what if technique (SWIFT) 91, 143–144
subsequent adjustments 111
suicide 17, 29, 54, 101, 104, 111, 151, 165, 167
SWIFT see structured what if technique (SWIFT)
SWIFT methodology 92

Taleb, N. N. 102
terrorism 47, 95, 141, 146, 147
third generation 46
Towl, G. 27, 28, 52, 81, 84, 98, 101, 116, 130, 132, 134, 136, 141, 149, 150, 178
traditional statistical methods 102
tree analysis 161
triangulation analytical process: accurate assessments 160
true probability 6
Tversky, A. 110, 117, 122

UK Government Treasury Orange Book 19
unbounded rationality ideas 108

uncertainty: decisions made under conditions 5; pooling 8; situations 8
unstructured clinical assessment 31, 45
utility: criminal and civil justice systems 73; traditional mental health assessments 75; unstructured clinical judgements 75

Venn, J. 12
violence 38, 39, 40, 43, 45–53, 62, 64, 65, 67, 82, 87, 102, 104, 130–133, 146, 150, 154, 155, 159–163, 167, 171
The Violence Risk Appraisal Guide (VRAG) 39

Wald, M. S. 135, 180
Wason, P. C. 119
well-developed public health systems 38
white collar crimes 130
Williams, K. R. 50
Wong, S. C. 37
Woolverton, M. 135, 180
Wundt, W. 113

Yang, M. 37

zero tolerance 23

Milton Keynes UK
Ingram Content Group UK Ltd.
UKHW021108300724
446250UK00003B/6